TELEVISION WRITING
from the INSIDE OUT

OUT

Your Channel to Success

TELEVISION WRITING
from the INSIDE
OUT

Your Channel to Success

LARRY BRODY

APPLAUSE
THEATRE & CINEMA BOOKS

Television Writing from the Inside Out: Your Channel to Success
by Larry Brody

ISBN: 1-55783-501-2

Library of Congress Cataloging-in-Publication Data
Brody, Larry.
Television writing from the inside out : your channel to success
by Larry Brody.
    p. cm.
ISBN 1-55783-501-2
1. Television authorship. I. Title.

PN 1992.7.B76 2003
808.2´25 — dc21

           2003008256

British Library Cataloging-in-Publication Data
A catalog record for this book is available from the British Library.

APPLAUSE THEATRE & CINEMA BOOKS
151 West 46TH Street
New York, NY 10036
Phone: (212) 575-9265
Fax: (646) 562-5852
Email: info@applausepub.com

SALES & DISTRIBUTION:

NORTH AMERICA:

HAL LEONARD CORP.
7777 West Bluemound Road
P.O. Box 13819
Milwaukee, WI 53213
Phone: (414) 774-3630
Fax: (414) 774-3259
Email: halinfo@halleonard.com
Internet: www.halleonard.com

UNITED KINGDOM:

ROUNDHOUSE PUBLISHING LTD.
Millstone, Limers Lane
Northam, North Devon EX 39 2RG
Phone: (0) 1237-474-474
Fax: (0) 1237-474-774
Email: roundhouse.group@ukgateway.net

CONTENTS

ACKNOWLEDGEMENTS

Several terrific writers and good friends helped me in the writing of this book by supplying material from their own personal files.

Bonita Alpert, Gerry Conway, Dorothy Fontana, Stacey John Hoskin, and Ed Scharlach—many thanks. Couldn't've done it without you!

Thanks also to William Scarpetti, for helping me come up with the title, and special thanks to Gwen Lea Brody, without whom I could never have written this, and Katrina Wilson, without whom I would never have written this.

My thanks to you all.

INTRODUCTION

I love television.

I love what it's been. I love what it is. I love what it can be.

I've loved television since I was three years old and saw Uncle Miltie for the first time. I remember sitting in front of the television set when I was four and watching *Howdy Doody* and praying to God that I wouldn't grow up because I knew if I did I wouldn't love Howdy anymore. A few years later, *Spin and Marty* showed me what Summer camp would be like. A few years after that, Paladin taught me that philosophers could be men of action as well as men of thought.

As a pre-teen who refused to go to bed on time, I watched the "Golden Age" anthologies: *Playhouse 90, Studio One, Kraft Television Theater*. This was live drama, which meant that what I was seeing was in effect theater, Broadway brought to the small screen. What I was experiencing was the power of words. The dialogue sang to me, caressed me, barked at me, saddened me. Raw emotions, good and evil, were right out there, enveloping me, filling me with sensation, broadcasting feelings I had thought were meant to be pushed down inside and hidden.

The result of my exposure to Rod Serling, Paddy Chayevsky, Abby Mann, and other wordsmiths of that era can be boiled down to these words:

Another love affair.

I love writing.

I love the adrenaline rush that comes from facing the blank page, the risk inherent in teetering on the edge of creativity. Will I come up with something? Will it affect people? Will they enjoy what I write? Will it change their lives? Will it expose me personally and leave me too open and vulnerable as I live my life?

I love the adventure of creating new places, new people, new phrases and expressions. (Remember, "Whatever…"? It was popularized on the series *Mike Hammer*, thanks to a great actor and human being named Stacy Keach.)

I love the headiness of being led by my own words, of hanging onto a keyboard for dear life while they gallop away, transforming my thoughts and intentions beyond anything I could have imagined before sitting down to write.

And I love the sense of control writing gives me. Life is unpredictable. Our free will is buffeted at every turn by what the existentialists call "the objective correlative," that is, the conditions of life that our choices can't change. In life I make a wrong turn and, wham, there's the traffic cop, nailing me for rolling through the stop sign. But on the page my character can turn onto a street where no police officer is hidden, or where there's no stop sign, or where his glibness talks the officer into changing his mind and walking away.

On the page I can create a world with no cops. No cars. Flying platforms, soaring frigates, anything I want, exactly the way I want it.

Godhood! Who can ask for anything more?

When I was growing up, the in, hip, and trendy thing for anyone who wanted to be a writer to do was work on a novel. Writing "The Great American Novel" was considered a worthwhile goal. I too had my novel in the typewriter. Hell, I even sold it. But I never finished that book because I was seduced away by my first love—television.

Even as I tried to write prose or short stories in my head, I was mentally "saw" the events not in "reality," not on the page, but on TV. All the television shows I had seen and was still seeing (and am still-still seeing today) coalesced in my brain as patterns, blueprints, templates.

Everything I wrote—and, for better or worse, much of what I lived—went beyond its true form and was translated by my mind into TV. Weddings, bar mitzvahs, the walk from one class to another, meeting someone new, making love, breaking up...all this and more existed simultaneously on two levels: as reality and as scenes on my mental TV.

The instinctive language of television was so imbued in me that I knew when the activity I was engaged in should end so the next scene could begin. It was so much a part of me that I knew when the action in a novel I was writing reached the point where the swelling music should inundate everything and the commercial break should come in.

I even pondered the details of translating the "slow parts" in my novel, and my life, to TV. How would I show what my character was thinking? In the book I could read people's thoughts. In life I certainly knew what was on my mind. But on television how would I know what was going on in people's heads? Should they say everything out loud so the audience could understand? Or should they do something that showed what their thoughts were? What kinds of things should they do? What kinds of things do people really do that show what they're thinking?

Strange guy, this Brody, huh?

For a while I wondered if I was a psych case. Then I started spending time with more writers as well as actors and artists and other so-called creative types. Some were women, unfathomable in that way all women are to most men. The rest were guys. And they were guys like me, who, no matter how many times they stuck their heads under the hood of a car, would never be able to figure out how to change the oil. Guys who, no matter how many times they stood at home plate with the bat in their hands in P.E., would never be able to consistently connect with the ball.

And every one of them, men and women, was in some way or another as "nuts" as I was. One writer friend had a constant narration going in his head, mentally describing his every movement and thought just as though it was being written in a book. An actor friend didn't stop there; he had to literally announce everything that went on around him, using whatever was handy—a pencil, a telephone, his fist—as a mic. A brilliant painter I knew in college told me one day that she "saw" everything around her with all the guidelines for drawing already drawn in—the length lines, the breadth lines. When people moved, she even saw the diagrammatic way to illustrate their foreshortenings.

So I let my worry about my craziness go. The hell with it; a little weirdness was good for the soul. I realized that it wasn't merely "okay" to be different, it was good to be different. When you get down to it, alienation is the heart's blood of a writer. Feeling different, being different... this is what enables a writer to distance him or herself, to see the foibles of humanity, all there is to love and all there is to be infuriated by. Alienation is what enables a writer to see events from without as well as from within, and to record them not only for what they are but what they can be.

Other people I knew wanted to be doctors and heal people. Or ministers to bring people to God. Or teachers to help kids learn. But to me, television was the way to do all those things. I as a television writer because it allows me to give back all the wonderment, beauty, truth, and escape I have gotten from TV. Writing for television has given me my best chance to do something for others and, in so doing, feel a sense of fulfillment. A sense of success.

In the 30-plus years I've been writing TV, my life has been a roller coaster of twists and turns, ups and downs, and loop-the-loops. I've felt uplifted and joyous about what I've done, and I've felt disheartened and despairing at the way some shows have turned out. I've had big successes and big failures, made fortunes and blown fortunes, and met the great, the near-great, and the stuff you try to scrape off the bottom of your shoe. I've received mail from viewers to whom I gave hope and enlightenment, and I've seen news reports accusing me of inspiring criminals to imitate my characters' fictional crimes.

If I had it to do over again, would I?

You bet.

If I could go back and change anything, would I do that?

Absolutely. I'd write better and sell smarter. I'd use every creative trick I could find to make my work more effective. I'd learn as much as I could about the business end of television to make my career more vital.

As this book is being written, all the men and women who would have had a novel in the typewriter when I was beginning to write now have a screenplay in the computer instead. And many of them are sliding over into television as well.

To all of you thinking of becoming television writers I say, "Welcome. We need you. The viewers need you. The business needs you. Come in and create. Give yourself to the audience. Let your talent roll."

The average number of films released in the United States each year is about 350. To get this much film "product" (that's what we call it in the trade, maybe because those in charge want to separate it from art), approximately 1,000 screenplays are bought or commissioned and paid for. The average number of episodes and TV movies that appear first-run on TV is a staggering 6,000. To get this much television "product," approximately 10,000 premises, outlines, and teleplays are bought or commissioned and, yes, paid for.

Because of high production costs and the need to appeal to the most general of audiences in order to make money, most films today need to be big blockbusters, such as action movies and thrillers, with stories aimed at the young teens who rule the box office.

Because of the proliferation of cable and satellite channels and the need to appeal to niche markets, most television today needs to be about issues and problems, with relevancy aimed at the adults who control the remotes.

This situation makes right now the best time in history for talented, intelligent men and women to go into television writing, especially if you have an edge. That edge is the knowledge and experience in this book; the knowledge and experience of television writing, from the inside out.

section 1:
the basics

You've got talent. You've got desire. You've

got a fine, fighting heart. All well and good,

but not enough. You've got to master the basics.

You've got to go bring others into yourself and

put yourself into others. You've got to learn

not just how to write for you but how to

write for TV.

— Television producer Stanley Kallis to a young
writer named Larry Brody in a meeting about the
writer's dismal first draft for an episode, at
University City Studios in 1969. (I've blocked out
my response back then, but I think I wanted to
strangle him. Now I just want to say, Thanks, Stan.)

chapter 1:
working the room

"The best-kept secret in show business is that it's a business."
Paul Junger Witt—who has produced everything from the
television series *Here Come The Brides, The Rookies, Soap, The Golden
Girls, Beauty and the Beast,* and more, to feature films such as *The
Dead Poets' Society, Three Kings,* and *Insomnia*—said this one day
at lunch in Santa Fe, New Mexico, when he was there to speak to a
screenwriting class I was teaching at The College of Santa Fe.

According to *The Nation*, nine companies, in various combina-
tions, now own and operate almost 200 broadcast and cable networks
and channels. That means that today, with "vertical integration" of
"media content" along with all other aspects of company operations
topping executive To Do lists, understanding exactly how the business
works is essential for success.

Agents put it diplomatically: "Know your buyer," says Paul
Weitzman of the Shapiro-Lichtman Talent Agency. Working writers
have been known to put it more bluntly: "Know your enemy."

The word "enemy," of course, is an exaggeration. Television is a
collaborative medium in which many different disciplines and departments work together to create the final show (or "product" as it's been
called since the late 1980s). Forget the romantic image of the lonely
writer working away in a little room, closed off from the rest of the

world. The television writer is writing not only for him- or herself but also for the producer or producers, the studio, and the network executives, as well as the director, the actors, the crew, and a myriad of others. This number can rise to as high as 250 people (not counting executive spouses, significant others, or in-laws), all of whom have to work together to translate the script into television reality: the "product" as seen on videotape or film.

No wonder TV writers often feel overwhelmed. The most common complaint writers for the medium voice is, "It's like I'm answering to everyone. By the time we're done my vision is gone. It's been corrupted at every turn."

Is the final script truly corrupted? Is every change or accommodation a diminution of the writer's creative work? Or do the changes improve the piece and make it possible to be produced? That's another of those issues hotly discussed by professional writers whenever they get together, and a particular writer's point of view often changes as he or she moves up the ladder and gains new perspective into the *business* of television, and of showbiz as a whole.

To fully grasp the relationship between the television writer, his or her written work, and the rest of those involved in any production, we need to know all about the players and their positions. We need to examine the dreams, hopes, aspirations, and needs of everyone involved.

Yes, it's true. Everyone in the biz has dreams. Otherwise why would they have left their comfy nests and dragged themselves out to the land of fruits, nuts, smog, and cosmetic surgery? Everyone in the biz has felt a calling to it, not unlike a calling to the ministry. Everyone in the biz has an opinion about all aspects of the production. Everyone cares. Deeply.

That's probably the main reason why in television (and film) people say they're working "with" each other. Very seldom does anyone come out with "I'm working for Barry Diller." Instead it's, "I'm working with Barry Diller..." or Michael Eisner or Paul Junger Witt or whatever name fills in the blank. Everyone involved in a project expects to have a say. Everyone expects to contribute, based on his or her area of expertise.

While the concept of equality, of a business based on peer-to-peer relationships, "is a consummation devoutly to be wished," don't be taken in by the phraseology. Everyone contributes, all right. But there's definitely a hierarchy here, and it behooves you to know exactly where the power is and how to deal with it accordingly. That way you have a better chance of making your work, your script, all it can be—and, frankly, of doing the same for your career.

Currently, the business of television is organized into three separate but interrelated segments. On top we have what *Barney Miller* co-creator Theodore J. Flicker has called the "mega-media corporations:" News Corporation, Viacom, Disney, General Electric, AT&T/Liberty Media, AOL/Time Warner, Sony, Seagram, and Bertelsmann.

As multi-billion dollar conglomerates, these companies have a definite agenda when it comes to managing their entertainment divisions. It's the agenda all corporations have: maximize profits. "Vertical integration" is the preferred method of maximization. It means using "synergy," which in turn means having one division of the conglomerate promote the products of other divisions. So, Disney makes toys and advertises them on its own network and places them in shows produced by its own company and runs news stories on another network about the toys' creation.

Writers almost never have direct contact with the mega-media bigshots, but the lesson is clear. Projects that have to do with other corporate divisions will have a better chance of being bought or commissioned and produced and broadcast than those that do not.

Below the mega-media corporations are the networks they own. These are both broadcast networks and cable/satellite channels with a nationwide reach. Most of the networks are run by managers who have a great deal of experience in the entertainment business. The top network managers are seldom called CEOs. Usually the title of president is sufficient, and there are a variety of vice presidents in charge of various divisions, and divisions of divisions.

When writers reach a certain level and are acknowledged creators or "showrunners," they often interact with the presidents, and most writers who work on the staff of any series talk to one vice president or another everyday—VPs who have to be able to justify everything done under their aegis to the management of the mega-media corporations that own the companies that employ them. (In other words, this is one wary bunch of veeps, always conscious of the fact that every time they say "yes" they are putting their jobs on the line.)

The broadcast networks—ABC, CBS, NBC, The Fox Network, The

WB Network, and UPN—are in the business of attracting what they call a "mass audience," which is to say one that is broadly based in terms of age, interests, habits, ethnicity, and a multitude of other attributes. To be sure, within this mass is a smaller group, or "demographic," that advertisers are convinced are the premier buyers of most products, so this smaller "demo," (young adults between the ages of 18 and 35) is wooed the most intensely.

CNN, Fox Kids, ABC Family, MTV, Tech TV, the Sci-Fi Channel, ESPN, and other cable/satellite channels have set various niche audiences as their Holy Grails, but their organizational structure is similar to that of the broadcast nets. It's just more focused, a hierarchical "narrowcast."

Most broadcast networks have a senior or executive VP in charge of overall programming, development, and operations in what some nets call the entertainment division, another senior VP in charge of the news and public affairs division, and one more in charge of sports. News and public affairs shows are almost always scripted, and so are many sports broadcasts, but what we can call dramatic writing, writing that tells a story in a way designed to elicit specific audience emotions, isn't what's involved. For that reason we'll concentrate on what goes on in the entertainment division, which is *the* market for dramatic writing.

The senior VP of the entertainment division is the man or woman who puts together the schedule that premieres each Fall (and then fixes it for the Winter and Spring and re-makes it again for the Summer as well). The senior VP recommends what shows to go with at what time but doesn't make the final decision. That's done by the president of the network, with what we might call the "advice and consent" of the network's entire senior staff.

The senior staff is usually made up of more vice presidents, who in turn have their own staffs of managers, directors, and assistants, in that order. (If you're dealing with a director of development, know going in that this is the lowest person on the development totem pole who is allowed to take a meeting. A meeting at this level can sometimes be relaxing—there's very little pressure when talking to someone who has no authority to say yea or nay—but it can also be infuriating if you really want to sell your idea.)

The senior staff VP jobs are split up into the three main areas under the senior VP's purview, which logic dictates to be programming, development, and the day-to-day corporate management grind of operations. Beneath the programming VP are several VPS in charge of "current programming" (shows that are currently on the air). The current programming department is usually divided into primetime (anything on the air between eight and eleven P.M. Eastern Time), daytime (anything on the air earlier than primetime), late night (anything on the air after primetime, natch), and children's (which usually means shows aired in a block on Saturday mornings).

Each of the sub-departments has a senior VP and an array of managers, directors, and assistants, and the primetime department is often broken down further into series programming and made-for-TV-movie programming (formerly "movies of the week," but now no one's guaranteeing a new TV movie every week). During the era when mini-series (TV movies that ran over two hours and were shown in two or more parts on different nights) were popular there was also a mini-series department. Now, however, you're more likely to find mini-series sharing space with the made-for-TV-movie folks.

The development department, which is in effect the "future programming department," is also subdivided into series development and made-for-TV-movie development (including mini-series). Series development gets another set of sub-branches: drama development and comedy development, with action and suspense shows considered drama and primetime talk and variety shows considered comedy. (At least the networks understand what *The Jerry Springer Show* is all about.) The development department sub-divisions also have their own VPS, which may explain why organizational chart software is in such demand.

What happened to children's development? It stays in the children's programming department because of a belief that "children's television is very special," as Sidney Iwanter, a former vice president of both Fox Kids and the Hallmark Channel says. "Depending on how you look at it, developing and doing kids' shows right either takes great expertise or great childishness." (Obviously, this isn't a place where "outsiders" should meddle!)

Daytime development also is usually kept within the daytime programming department, and for a similar reason. The perspective behind daytime serials and game shows is very narrow and focused to a specific audience, and execs who understand this particular segment (and writers, for that matter) are few and far between.

The third level of television business is that of production entity.

Production entities are the companies that actually put together the "product," the shows we write for TV. They can be large studio operations with acres of office buildings, soundstages, and backlots for outdoor shooting, as are Paramount, Universal, Sony, and Fox, or they can be production companies operating out of limited office space such as the homes of their owners or space leased from the studios or networks, as are Dick Wolf Productions (the *Law & Order* shows), Cosgrove/Meurer Productions (*Unsolved Mysteries*), and Mozark Productions (*Designing Women, Evening Shade*), to name a few.

Most of the major studios doing business in television have been around since the early days of motion pictures and are owned by the same mega-media conglomerates that own the networks and cable/satellite channels. They're brothers under the corporate skin. Most of the production companies are newer and more independent, with many of them still being run by the same entrepreneurs who were their founders, and many of these founders are writers. (The joke among producers is that this proves that even the worst criminal can be reformed. The joke among writers is that it shows that even the best writer can go bad.)

Studios and production companies are not immune to Expanding-Organizational-Chart-itis, and their executive structure is much like that of the networks, or any other company. The head of a studio may be called either CEO or president and is usually a hard-charging salesman (possibly a former agent or personal manager) who may not know everything about production but does know everyone and how to use them to get what the studio needs. The head of a production company is more likely to be a writer or producer with enough chutzpah to enjoy going mano-a-mano with network and corporate heads, and with studio chiefs as well, and may call him or herself executive producer instead of ceo or president. The head of a studio almost always is a hired hand, while the head of a prodco (production company) usually is the primary owner. (I know of at least one exception. In the 1980s, after oilman Marvin Davis bought 20th Century-Fox Studio, the company's official stationery listed Davis' title as "owner," in order, I've always assumed, to make sure no one ever had any doubts about who was running the place.)

The rest of the titles and job descriptions at studios and prodcos more or less parallel those at the networks, differing from each other in that the studios have to staff their physical facility more completely, and smaller prodcos often have only an overall VP and staff of production and staff of development instead of breaking things down by air time or genre.

For writers, one of the most important divisions of a studio or prodco is what is usually called business affairs. Networks have business affairs departments also, as part of operations, but since networks usually don't employ writers directly we seldom interact with the lawyers and negotiators who make up the business affairs staff. Since the studios and prodcos are normally the entities for which writers work, though, there's a chance for closer contact.

The people in business affairs are the men and women who negotiate our deals, which to me makes their good will crucial. Most writers blow off the people in business affairs, but when you or your agent are in the middle of a high-ticket negotiation (or even one involving a subsistence wage), wouldn't you rather be known to the guy on the other side as a living, breathing, and very decent human being and not just a faceless prima donna trying to get more, more, more? It's tougher for the business affairs guy to say no, or quibble over relative peanuts, when it's a discussion about a job for a friend. If you ever get the chance, take a studio or prodco lawyer to lunch. You'll never regret it (and you probably won't have to pay. He or she will charge the meal to the company).

Studios and prodcos have one sub-division, networks don't. As production entities, they need to have "productions"—shows to produce. Every show on television, whether it's a series or a TV movie (or mini-series) is financed by a studio or prodco (which in turn charges the network a "license fee" for the use of the show). Every show has a staff that puts it together from start to finish, original idea to completed film or tape. Every show has a home base, which is a suite of offices and a soundstage and/or location or group of locations where most of it is shot.

It is here, in the office of a given series, that most television writers perform their creative toil. Just the way a doctor needs to be on the staff of a hospital to be a total doctor, a TV writer needs to be on the staff of a show.

chapter 2:
meet the gang

The staffs of all television shows are divided into two parts: above the line and below the line. This is a carryover from the early days of motion picture production, when the "line" in question was a literal line made with a ruler on the business ledger of each film. Listed first—above the line—were the personnel regarded as creative: the producers, directors, and actors. Listed second—below the line— were the personnel who made up what we still call the "crew": the cameramen, electricians, designers, builders, drivers, and anyone else who worked primarily in the actual physical production of the film set.

Yes, a certain job description is missing in the early above-the-line listing. In the not-so-good-old-days of silent movies, writers were looked upon as laborers and nothing more. We weren't considered creative and weren't used in a creative way. The job of the writer was to come up with the wording on the captions that were used to explain plot points that the visuals failed to put across. The plot itself came from the director. Here, in fact, lies the origin of the writer-director rivalry that continues in feature films to this day. How could a director not resent someone brought in to remedy his storytelling mistakes?

Now, of course, writers are above the line. In television, in fact, we comprise *most* of the above-the-line personnel of the average series. TV movies are staffed the same way feature films are, which means that although many writers may be used on one project they more than likely work serially, one after another, each rewriting his or her predecessor. Series television—and ongoing series are still the backbone of the TV industry—uses multiple writers simultaneously.

Daytime shows, which from the beginning of television have been either game shows or half-hour serials (with the occasional "After School Special" thrown in) have always used permanent writing staffs, as have late night shows, which are usually talk shows with a staff of three to six writers (including a head writer who does the final editing and, often, the "selling" of the material to the host/star) who come up with monologues or other "bits" (remember Johnny Carson's "Aunt Blabby?"), and who also craft many of the witty one-line "ad libs" for which many a host has become famous.

The staff of the average daytime serial, or "soap opera," usually consists of one head writer and as many as five sub-writers, plus a story editor, a director and a contingent of producers—an executive producer, a producer or line producer, various associate producers (called that, the old joke goes, because their job is to "associate with the producer").

In daytime serials, the head writer's job is to work with the producers and director so that together they develop the overall direction the major and minor stories will take. They figure out the plots and sub-plots and which characters will be involved in them, for each "cycle," which is 13 weeks. Then the head writer, armed with the working schedules of all the actors on the show, writes a "bible" that breaks the plots down episode by episode, day by day. Being aware of the actors' schedules is vital because this is where what could be called "real reality" impinges on "TV reality." You can't schedule a major argument, birth, or kidnapping featuring Susan Lucci's character on a Wednesday, or a murder or suicide for Kin Shriner on a Friday if Susan's contract says her character, Erica Kane, has Wednesdays off and Kin's says Friday is a day of rest for his alter ego, Scott Baldwin.

After the producers, director, and network approve the bible (and the stars of the show give it their unofficial okay as well) the head writer writes a five to ten page outline for each daily episode. Those outlines are then given to the sub-writers, who use them as guides for scripting each 30-page episode, and the script is then read by the head writer and edited by the story editor, who, based on the head writer's input, makes certain that the characterizations are accurate and that the dialogue conforms to what those running the show want it to be. The story editor's version of the script is then approved by the head writer, the producers, and the director. Although most viewers (and critics) don't realize it, each soap opera episode is the result of weeks of story planning, four to five days of script writing, and another day or so of script editing.

As much as daytime serial scripts are thought and rethought, worked and reworked, primetime and children's show scripts are the result of even more effort. The staffs for Saturday morning animation series, the bread-and-butter of children's programming, and prime-time network and cable channel series, parallel each other, with the difference being that the final creative voice on the staff of an animated series is usually that of an animator/director while the final authority on the staff of a primetime series is inevitably a writer-producer.

Until the mid-1970s, most primetime drama and action series and animated series were written by freelance writers hired to do the job on assignment, working with (or "for") a staff that consisted of a story editor, a producer, and an executive producer. Animated series would develop 65 episodes at a time, usually over a period of two years, and then air the episodes over a period of two and a half years, at the rate of 26 episodes per season. Primetime series would develop 13 episodes at a time over a period of six months, and then, if the series was picked up for a full season, 13 more scripts would be written in the next four or five months.

An animated series would use 20 to 30 writers to get its necessary number of episodes, while a primetime drama or action series would hire between six and nine, letting those two or three writers that delivered the best material write a second or third script if they could work quickly enough. ("Quickly" is a relative term. We're talking weeks and weeks and weeks of writing, reading, rewriting, and rereading on each script.)

The methodology of script creation in both cases involved the writer working things out in meetings with the story editor, who then acted as a liaison with the producer. In animation, the producer was the animator responsible for every element of the show, the overseer of the look, sound, feel, and story. In primetime drama and action, the producer was an individual with a background in physical production and an understanding of all it took to put a show on the air, including what would or not work in a script. He was usually male and seldom a writer, which meant that the story editor did all the rewriting, based not so much on the story editor's opinion of how the script should be as on the producer's.

At this time, most executive producers were salesmen whose sales skills had gotten the shows onto the air and were now being used to keep it there as long as possible by doing whatever it took to please the network executives. Specifically, the executive producer was in charge of making nice to the current programming VP and the specific current programming director assigned to the show. The current programming VP had two primary needs: to keep the program on the creative track that those above the VP expected and to make suggestions that could drive up the ratings. The current programming director assigned to the show also had two needs: to act as a middle-man between the VP and the producer and story editor (executive producers didn't speak to lowly directors of anything), and to keep the producer and story editor happy so they wouldn't have the CPD removed from the show. For the most part, network suggestions were general. They were also negotiable. The attitude was that the network had hired skilled professionals to run the shows and was just trying to help them do the job.

From 1975 to 1985, an evolutionary process occurred that changed the way animated and primetime drama and action shows were staffed and managed, making them more like half-hour comedies, or as we know them today, sitcoms. A large writing staff of up to a dozen people was a comedy tradition, begun in the days when Bob Hope, Jack Benny, and others of their generation had their own radio shows. Comedy writers were paid a weekly salary to come to work every day and be funny. Sometimes they all worked together in the same room under a head writer. Other times they broke up into smaller groups. Comedy writers were often given the title of story editor or story consultant, and the head writer was sometimes given the title of producer, even though he (or sometimes she) did no producer-like chores. The actual production was done by a line producer co-producer instead.

Freelancers rarely got assignments writing comedy because there usually wasn't any money left for them after paying the staff. It also made more sense to use staff writers who were familiar with every episode and every character because the stories on comedy series such as *The Dick Van Dyke Show, The Mary Tyler Moore Show,* and *Barney Miller* were primarily about the recurring characters. The best way to keep continuity and consistency, and to make the best use of the talents of the stars, was to have the shows written by writers who knew every episode that had already been written inside out, and who were as familiar with what made the stars shine as they were with their own faces.

In the late 1970s, story editors of primetime drama and action also began to be given the title of producer and many of the jobs that went with it—casting, set, costume, music approval, and film editing. This was done for various reasons. For one thing, the generation of professional producers was leaving the biz. Retirement and death took their toll. For another thing, writers were agitating for more control. Story editors wanted their opinions to matter because they felt that, as writers, they knew more about writing than the non-writing producers did. In conjunction with this, some unsung public relations genius started spreading the word that writers would make terrific producers because they were better able to see the interlocking requirements inherent in the written material than anyone else.

Having written scripts that served as floor plans for the totality of various productions, the theory went, writers were therefore whizzes at "servicing" the total production. Many network and studio executives, especially those who had never been on a stage or a set or a location and didn't understand what producers did, gobbled down this line of reasoning with gusto.

Why do I not buy into this line of reasoning? Because I was there. I went from being a young writer to a young producer without having a clue of what to do on the new job, without even knowing the vocabulary of production. And, frankly, without caring. Totality of production? Who cared? It was the script I worried about. In my mind at that time, the purpose of the production was to show the world the brilliance of the words in the script. Period. End of discussion.

A third factor also came into play in the writer-to-producer conversion of the era. In their never-ending quest for profit maximization, the networks, studios, and prodcos were looking for new ways to save money and discovered a big one. Putting a writer on a show as a producer was actually cheaper than putting one on as a story editor.

"It was loophole time," says Herbert F. Solow, former president of

Desilu Productions. "The Writers Guild of America's (WGA) Minimum Basic Agreement called for fringe benefits like health insurance and pension payments to be paid on 100 percent of a story editor's salary, but on a much smaller percentage of a producer's pay." Story editors were deemed to be doing writing work 100 percent of the time they were on the payroll. Producers were deemed to be doing writing work less than one-third of the time. So even if the writer-producer got paid a higher base salary than a story editor it came out cheaper for the employers in the long run. For that matter, it still does. The WGA's rule on the subject hasn't changed. Animation writing for children's television isn't covered by the Guild, but animation companies followed the trend, only instead of the writers the animators were bumped up.

The evolutionary process caused another big change in the early 1980s, when *Hill Street Blues* became a runaway success critically and in terms of ratings. Steven Bochco's series brought the traditional cop show to a new level with its gritty production look and multi-layered stories. *Hill Street* abandoned the practice of making each episode the tale of a guest star villain going mano-a-mano against the police and concentrated on a large cast of recurring regular stars, showing how their personal lives affected their jobs and how their jobs affected their personal lives. The personal stories continued from episode to episode, and so did the investigations, everything intertwining so closely that the show was either "as close to reality as television could possibly come," as television executive Judy Palone said to me at the time, or "just another soap opera, not so cleverly disguised," as David Gerber remarked.

The success of *Hill Street Blues* served as an inspiration to the entire primetime television industry, and since that time most series have presented more personal stories, extending and interconnecting them from week to week. This has created the situation we have now, where primetime one-hour shows have gone the way of sitcoms before them, having from as few as half a dozen and as many as 12 writers on staff because only writers who eat, drink, and sleep a series can know its needs well enough to write it as it has to be written to succeed.

Like sitcom writers, the hour drama (and action) writers bear a panoply of titles. The highest ranking writer, and usually the creator of the series, automatically gets the title executive producer. Within the business he or she is usually just referred to as the "showrunner," and it's the showrunner whose vision guides the scripts. The powers-that-be at the corporate, network, studio, and prodco levels have hired the showrunner to, in effect, write all the scripts, bringing to them the specific sensibility for which that showrunner is known.

When Dick Wolf runs a show, for example, those in charge expect terse, factual, in-the-news writing, with convoluted plots and a wicked twist at the end. When David E. Kelley of *Picket Fences, Ally McBeal, The Practice,* and other shows is the showrunner, those who are paying him expect a combination of whimsy and controversy, with a little pushing of the production envelope thrown in. Aaron Sorkin of *The West Wing* and *NewsRadio* can be called on to deliver fast dialogue, humor, and a passion for causes that are too often lost.

Some showrunners are indeed genuine "show runners," overseeing every element of a series in the way the lost generation of professional producers did. Others stick to supervising only the scripts, letting what we call line producers run the physical production (and maintaining control over those line producers so that, although removed from the immediate situation, the showrunner still has the final word within what we call the "shooting company," that is, the show itself). Others hire showrunners of their own, adding another layer to the chart, usually because they're executive producing several shows and don't have time to maintain personal quality control.

A show may have more than one executive producer. The others may be writers whose positions in the industry demand that they receive the highest possible title even though they aren't running the show, or directors brought in to direct multiple episodes and so insure a certain look, or line producers with terrific agents. You can distinguish between them and the showrunner by seeing whose name comes last. The name of the showrunner literally comes last, at the end of the show, superimposed at the final fade out. This is a place of honor—a credit placed there stays on the air longer and has more attention paid to it than one at the front of the show.

Beneath the executive producer(s) are, in descending importance, writers with the titles of co-executive producer, supervising producer, contributing producer, producer, associate producer, executive story consultant, creative consultant, story consultant, story editor, and/or staff writer. Regardless of the title, those writers in all likelihood have the same job. They write episodes.

Where sitcoms are often "gangbanged," which is to say, written by the assembled group of writers, with everyone on staff tossing out lines, dramatic show staffs usually get together to work out or "break" stories, scene by scene, and then the members go off into their offices, where each writes the episode he or she has been assigned. The story meetings where the plotting of an episode is done are usually supervised by the showrunner, and the showrunner reads every version of each script written by each staff member thereafter. On some shows all the staffers read and comment on everyone's material, but as it gets later into the season and time becomes more precious, the giving of notes is usually left almost entirely to the decision-making showrunner.

The showrunner is also the one who does all the final rewrites, which are called "polishes." All, or at least most, of the dialogue in any television show you see has probably been written by the showrunner, regardless of whose name is on the credits as the writer of the episode. This doesn't mean that the dialogue by the original writer had anything wrong with it, just that the showrunner had to add his or her touch—because that's what the showrunner has been hired to do. A smart television writer realizes that his or her job is to write scripts the way the showrunner would write them if the showrunner had the time to write every episode. In a very real sense, all staff writers are ghostwriters for the showrunner—except that in most cases they have their names on the screen.

chapter 3:
starting out

Now you know the game, and now you know the players.
How do you get on the team? How do you get on the staff of a television
show, and what happens to you when you get there?

The sports analogy I just used fails not only because it's hokey, as
all sports analogies are, but also because there is no authorized recruit-
ment system for television writing as there is in sports. No scouts sit in
box seats watching new TV writers write, gauging their performances.

The doctor analogy doesn't apply here, either. Unless you mess up
badly, medical school almost always leads to a license to practice medicine and a residency to work under distinguished mentors, and—also
unless you mess up badly—a license and a residency lead to a permanent position on a hospital staff and the ability to either open your
own practice or join an existing one. In sports, the team needs you. In
medicine, the hospital needs you. The recruiters in both fields have
you in their sights for most of your training and preliminary career.

Television also needs you. "New blood" is what creativity is all
about. Talented, fertile, disciplined people who not only know how to
tell stories but can put new twists on the telling of a story and thereby
appeal to the current generation of viewers are absolutely essential in
TV, but your success is entirely up to you, the new writer. You have to
storm the castle. You have to prove your value to the powers-that-be...

the writers, producers, showrunners, studio, prodco, network, and corporate execs.

Later in this book, I'll tell you about practical, personal strategies. But whether those strategies will succeed depends on one very important point:

When it comes to writing television scripts, you'd better be good. Damn good.

As in "great." Head and shoulders above the crowd. Awesome.

Awe inspiring.

In the words of Garry Marshall, who has written, produced, and directed everything from *Happy Days, Laverne and Shirley*, and *Barefoot in the Park* on television to *Pretty Woman, The Runaway Bride,* and *The Princess Diaries* as feature films, "We've already got people who can write good. We need people who can write better."

To put it another way, in order to start your career, you have to prove to those who can hire you that you have something to offer them, something they need. Something that will make them even richer than many of them already are. Your storytelling has to be more effective than the storytelling they are already getting. Your use of language has to be richer than the language they are already reading. Your dialogue has to be crisper, deeper, more clever. You have to be "better" than the best showrunner out there if you want to be employed at an entry level writing job.

And make no mistake about it. A job is what you want. Employment is what you're after. That's what staff writing is all about.

Television writers differ from writers who write for publication or feature films in one very important way: television writers almost never sell something they have already written. In publishing and films, it's always nice if you can make a deal upfront and sit down with start money in your pocket and write your article or your novel or your screenplay and then deliver it and collect the rest of your advance. But even if you don't make that deal, you still can go to the computer or legal pad or whatever you use and write something from start to finish and then sell it when it's done. You write, and you sell what you've written.

In television, however, you aren't selling your work. You're selling your ability to do the work. You're selling yourself. You are proving you are capable of handling that staff job. You are proving you deserve to be on the show, whether it be a daytime serial, an animated kids show, a primetime or first-run syndicated series, or just about anything other than a made-for-TV-movie, the one place in TV where scripts are read and considered for purchase (but even there the execs would rather hire you and be in on the writing process from the ground floor).

So what does a new writer do? Send out letters of recommendation from professors who loved the writer's work? Put résumés on windshields in Beverly Hills supermarket parking lots? Buy a billboard on the Sunset Strip? Hire a skywriter?

If you're already established as a feature film writer, you don't have to do anything. Odds are you've already been approached. Getting writing credit on a film that actually gets made is a ticket into TV. Even those who haven't seen your film will be impressed because the fact that it was produced means someone else believed in you and paid major bucks—more than a television budget—for your work or your services; the fact that your name is on the credits means you didn't let that someone else down.

If you're already established as a writer for publication you have a leg up. But unless you've written a bestseller or gotten the best reviews the *New York Times Book Review* can give, it's only a small leg. You've proven that other people believe in you and that you've delivered what they want, but what they want isn't necessarily what television wants. It's not even in the same format. So, both the complete newbie and the minor novelist, short story, or article writer have to prove, "I can do it! I can write TV better than anyone else you know!"

The way you prove it is by writing sample scripts. You have to hunker down and write your versions of shows that are already on the air, and, even though the writers on those shows are paid anywhere from $4,500 (the lowest price in town for a kids' half-hour animation show) to about $25,000 (the going rate for a primetime hour series), you've got to write yours for free. For "fun." (Well, some people find it fun. And on a good day that includes me.)

First, though, you have to make a decision: What kind of television shows do you want to write?

Members of sports teams are chosen by the position they play. Quarterbacks seldom get drafted to play linebacker. Members of hospital staffs are chosen by their specialties. Neurosurgeons seldom deliver babies. Similarly, TV writers are not taken seriously unless they have declared, and proven themselves, in a specialty. If you think you're funny, enjoy watching sitcoms, and can't live another minute unless you start making others laugh, then become a sitcom writer. If you find yourself fascinated by the trials and tribulations of characters on the daytime serials and can't wait to contribute to the agony, then present yourself as a soap opera writer. If *Bugs Bunny* or *The Silver Surfer* send you in search of your own personal Elmer Fudd or Shalla Bal, then animation is for you. And if conflict and action, cops and lawyers and doctors keep you from pressing your remote, and you've always wanted to choreograph a car chase or have a character jump up and yell, "Your honor, I object," then you'll probably find fulfillment as a one-hour drama or action writer.

Yes, I know. Writing is writing. A good writer can write anything. Conflict, meaning, heroism, and angst exist side by side with humor, sentiment, and beauty in life and literature, art, and music. Even on TV shows such as *M*A*S*H* or *All In The Family* or *Northern Exposure* or *The Sopranos*.

But that's *on* TV, not *in* TV. Not in the biz.

A new writer has to prove him or herself on many different levels, in many different ways, but the first thing on which the new writer is judged is *commitment*. To be taken seriously within the business you must present yourself in a way the business can understand. You have to be serious, dedicated, sincere. "If a writer tells me she writes both sitcoms and drama I feel uncertain about her," agent Paul Weitzman says. "I worry that if she's doing both she's not dedicated enough to either."

Weitzman speaks for the majority of the agents I know. The late Leonard Hanzer, founder of the Major Talent Agency and one of the most successful television agents to ever negotiate a deal once put it to me this way: "Daytime TV, children's TV, comedy, drama...they're each different businesses, with different needs, different wants, and different people in charge. Every executive believes that his genre is unique and that only someone totally devoted to it can do it justice. So that's what I sell them—writers totally devoted to their genre. I couldn't sell a man who wants a Rolls Royce a Porsche even if I believe the Porsche is the better car. And I can't sell a drama producer a comedy writer even if I know this particular comedy writer is the best one for that job."

Time for another note here, this one about agents. In days gone by, agents were often freewheeling, loose-cannon types, salesmen who loved show business and found their niche in it as purveyors of talent. Much of the time they had no background in entertainment or even in business but succeeded because of their people skills, which were often extraordinary.

The legendary Jay Bernstein, my executive producer on *The Adventures of Mike Hammer* was just such an agent—and personal manager and public relations man. Jay used to say, "Every day I get stacks of mail from actors and actresses who want me to represent them. They send me their reviews and tell me how great they are. But I don't want great clients. I want clients who stink. That way when they become stars I know it's not because of them; it's because of me. The whole business knows Jay Bernstein's responsible."

Current agents are a different breed. Many of them grew up in show business families. Many of them are MBAs trained for corporate wars. And many of them started their careers wanting to be writers, producers, or directors but found the agency avenue more open. They regard all their dealings in terms of profit and loss, investment of time and money, and return of the same.

As business people who have deliberately and knowingly chosen to represent talent instead of being talent, they are highly aware of the fact that their income depends not so much on what they do for their clients but on their credibility with the networks, studios, and production companies with whom they do their daily business. Like retailers, agents more often than not see themselves as having to please their buyers more than the clients, who are their merchandise. In fact, many agents move over to the "other side" and end up running studios, production companies, or networks, like Chris Albrecht, a former International Creative Management agent—who is now CEO of HBO.

To be highly regarded enough to make such a move, or just to succeed in general, agents must take on clients who will fulfill the expectations of the buyers. The merchandise—I mean the clients, who are in this case writers—must be as marketable as possible. That means they must fit into the right pigeonhole or there's no sale.

So your first order of business is to pick your pigeonhole, or genre. This is the area in which you'll be working for much of your professional life, so the decision can't be random, or without thought.

Good writing is passionate writing, filled with energy and feeling, so make certain you pick a genre that invokes passion in you, one that you can throw yourself into, as a human being and as a writer.

Having committed yourself, your second order of business is to write not one, not two, but three scripts for existing television series in your chosen genre. Each of these scripts has to be the single best episode ever written for each of three of the current critics' favorites. It also helps if you can subdivide the genres a bit too and stake out a claim in those subdivisions.

What do I mean by subdivide? If sitcom's your chosen area, make sure you write one episode of a highly regarded sophisticated comedy, one episode of a highly regarded "silly" comedy, and one episode of a warm family or kids comedy. By "highly regarded," I mean one that has been getting good reviews, and which has a certain "buzz" within the TV industry. Critics like it, other TV pros like it, even people who don't watch it agree that the show is "good." (You can find out the buzz by reading the in, hip, and trendy magazines that reflect current show business attitudes—*Entertainment Weekly*, *Premiere*, even *People*—and by checking out the Calendar section of the Sunday *Los Angeles Times*.)

Notice that I didn't mention "highly regarded" in the same sentence as "warm family or kids comedy." That's because critics very seldom give raves to those types of shows. That doesn't keep some of them from becoming hits, however, and it certainly doesn't keep networks from buying them and putting them on the air and hiring staffs of writers to develop plots and dialogue that often draw in the most rabid fans this side of the *Star Trek* "franchise," as Gene Roddenberry's creation (aided and abetted as he was by the largely unsung Gene L. Coon) has come to be known.

If you're a one-hour writer, the "highly regarded" rule still applies, but your job is to write one episode of a serious drama, one episode of an all-out action, science fiction, or fantasy show, and one episode of a "warm family drama," or primetime soap opera. Again, you probably won't find a family show with the critics' stamp of approval or, for that matter, a primetime soap opera either.

If kids' animation shows are your métier, be prepared for the fact that most of them are about superheroes. These can still be subdivided into serious shows about a lone hero, serious shows about a group of heroes, and wise guy parodies of the first two types. And, of course, there are the all-out comedies, the latest incarnations of classic Warner Brother animation characters, or new "funny animals" or funny kids or even star-crossed teenagers as well. This genre may well be the only time in your TV writing career that you get to demonstrate both dramatic and humorous scripts, so take advantage of it. You may also want to spec an existing live-action kids show, although at the moment that seems like a dying breed.

Looking for a daytime serial job? They too have subdivisions, although the differences are more subtle. There are "old-fashioned" soaps, written and presented the way soaps have been for the past 50 years, and there are newer, more daring soaps with innovative (for daytime) storylines and offbeat characters, and there also are soaps aimed at younger, hipper just-out-of-puberty audiences. Write one of each.

Writing these "spec scripts," as they are referred to in TV Land because they're written "on speculation" and not "on assignment," is a necessity, and it can be very enjoyable to spec a series you've watched and loved for years. But it isn't easy, not by a long shot. In fact, I believe that spec series writing is the most difficult writing you will ever have to do. That's because, as someone who has been on the staff of a number of series, I know how much info there is to absorb—and how much I, as a casual watcher, don't know about any show on which I'm not a staffer.

Case in point: Martin, Frasier's dad on *Frasier*. Although I've seen many episodes of this series over the years, and read even more episodes, I still don't have a clue how two uptight members of the intelligentsia, Frasier and Niles, came from a father whose basic behavior pattern is that of a high school coach. Was he a high school coach? Were he and his wife separated during the boys' formative years? If so, how did Martin come to be living with his adult son?

For me as a writer, my ignorance of these facts, of what we call the "backstory" (because it all happened before the "now" of the series), means I don't have as complete an understanding of the characters as I feel I need to write them properly, when the definition of writing them properly is being able to let their dialogue and behavior emerge from the essence of who they are. I could get the speech patterns right, and the general attitudes, but I would be faking anything deeper. Because

I'd be faking it I'd be uncomfortable with the writing, and I know myself well enough to know that if I become too uncomfortable I'm going to wake up one morning and find that I just can't write any further. (Presto! I've got the legendary and infamous "Writer's Block." Which is another way of saying, "Uh-oh, I'm not prepared.")

How do *you* avoid being blocked? How do you go deeper? You put yourself in a position where you feel as relaxed and knowledgeable as possible. You do your homework. Watch as many new episodes as you can. Watch as many older episodes as you can find, either in syndication or videotape or DVD collections. Look for the facts about the pasts of the characters—not just on *Frasier*, but on any series you choose to write.

On any show, look also for foreshadowing about the future of the characters. In what direction is the series heading? What character relationships are evolving? How much are they evolving? Specifically, how much of the evolution is revealed in each episode? How are the stories told? Are they complexly plotted? Are they simple? Do the stories go off on tangents and then come back to resolve themselves at the end? Are there sub-plots? How many? Are the sub-plots related to the main plot? Does the resolution of one help the resolution of the other?

Every series follows a pattern that you can discern if you watch enough episodes. An unkind viewer might refer to that pattern as a formula, but "formula" implies planning and foreknowledge, and I know from experience that in most cases television series fall into patterns because the basic premise and characters seem to automatically go in certain directions, or because the showrunner unconsciously favors a certain type of story, not because anyone has planned or diagrammed "the way each episode will be."

Fan sites on the internet and interviews with the creators and showrunners are another avenue to pursue; not instead of but in addition to. Reading what the actors have to say about their characters and their parts can't hurt either. And if a show for which you're interested in doing a spec has a "writer's guide" or "bible" (more on these later) that explains the who, what, where, why, and how of the series, by all means get hold of it. Fan websites are good places to find this material. Sometimes it's there with the sanction or blessing of the show. Sometimes it's not.

Even if you obtain most of the necessary info from watching

episodes and reading about the show you should still try to read as many actual scripts as you can. That way you see the exact format each series uses so you can duplicate it.

There are several reasons for duplicating the format. Firstly, you want to show that you are educable, that you can write in whatever manner a series wants you to write. Secondly, you want to gain experience in different teleplay forms so that you can learn their strengths and weaknesses and what is comfortable and what isn't. This knowledge will help you become a better writer. Thirdly, would it be so bad if whoever read your script thought it was a genuine episode of a given show? No one wants to deliberately misrepresent his or her work, but if a buyer somehow gets the impression that a newcomer has already been hired and paid to write for a hit show, well, is that really such a bad thing? (Older, "loose-cannon" agents used to encourage this sort of thing. Today's agents are much more circumspect. If directly queried about whether a script was written on assignment or as a spec, they're much more likely to say no instead of hemming and hawing.)

The show you want to write can itself be a great resource. Watch the credits carefully and find out the name of the showrunner and the production company that supplies it to the network. Then call Information and get the company's phone number. Use that number to talk to the showrunner's assistant, to whom you should honestly explain your situation as a new writer. Then ask the assistant to send you scripts, guides, whatever you can wheedle. It may surprise you to learn that this open, direct approach works about 25 percent of the time. The assistant will usually understand your needs and identify with your situation. That's because most assistants are themselves aspiring writers. As long as you don't push the wrong buttons and seem like a rival or a threat you have a good chance of making out just fine.

If you need to write notes to yourself, or make charts or graphs illustrating the storytelling and the characterization, by all means do so. Your objective is a greater understanding of the series, so do whatever it takes. If you can internalize what you see and read and get an instinctive feeling about the pattern of a series, and you can retain that feeling, then hold onto it. Make it a part of you. Be certain you do whatever you have to in order to make your knowledge of the series accessible while you write.

section 2:
writing the
television script

You've got a group of scenes here, but you
don't have a story. Everything is all sprawled
out and hard to envision. You've got to break
up these big pieces into little tiny ones.
Decide which scenes are more important
and which scenes are less, and make the
more important scenes longer.

—Television producer and writer William Blinn
to a young writer named Larry Brody in a meeting
about the writer's outline for an episode at Screen
Gems Television in 1970. (Bill Blinn was the
equivalent of Miss Kelly, my first grade teacher.
Miss Kelly taught me how to read books. Bill
taught me how to write TV. I always disagreed
with him and thought he was cutting out too
much of what I'd written. I was always wrong.
Thanks, Bill.)

chapter 4:
telling the story

Once upon a time an Eager Young Television Writer joined
a workshop given by the Most Distinguished and Highly Regarded TV
Producer of the Day and said breathlessly, "I love books! I love short
stories! I love poetry! I love plays and movies and TV! I can sit for
hours and hours and read and read and read! I want to be a writer! I
need to be a writer!"

The Most Distinguished and Highly Regarded TV Producer of the
Day looked the EYTVW up and down with disdain. "I've read your first
assignment," he said. "Just because you love to read doesn't mean you
should write."

The EYTVW was crushed. He dropped out of the workshop. But
he didn't give up writing. Instead, he vowed to prove that the producer
was wrong. He spent hours studying his craft. He pushed himself
to write and write and to submit his writing wherever he could. He
suffered rejection after rejection, and then, at last, he sold something.
Then he got an assignment. Another. More. A series he created won
an Emmy. A script he wrote for it won a Writers Guild Award.

The night of the WGA Awards ceremony the ETVW—he was no
longer Young but still Eager and definitely a TVM—came to the dais to
make his planned acceptance speech. He was ready to blast his early
nemesis into millions of shattered ego smithereens. But as he stood
there, flushed with victory, the writer realized he no longer cared.

Instead of attacking, the ETVW raised his plaque and smiled. "I want to thank the Most Distinguished Producer for his invaluable help when I was starting out. Without his motivation I would never have made it this far."

Simplistic? A fairy tale? Condescending fiction designed to make new writers feel good about what can be a bad business? Well, it certainly is the kind of tale every new artist in any creative field wants to hear. Victory. Validation. Celebration. But that doesn't make it false. In fact, the story above is based on not one real life experience but many. Your career *can* happen this way. Plenty of writers succeed. Plenty of writers win.

The purpose of our short morality tale, however, isn't to make you feel good, although it may do that little thing. It isn't even to hook you and make you read the rest of this book, although I won't mind if it accomplishes that bit of business, too. No, the true purpose of the story is to present writers, new and old, with the most basic aspects of all dramatic writing wrapped up in one very short package.

Especially the aspects from which everything else flows: story and character.

Telling a compelling story is the raison d'etre of all writing, which we may as well name, here now, Writing Element Number One.

Writing Element Number Two is interlocked with storytelling, simultaneously growing out of it and adding to the story's effectiveness: Populate your story with understandable and real-seeming characters.

In the TV biz we often put it another way: "The story is king." And it is. Everything else is an added value extra, like the luxury package that bumps up the price when you buy a new car. Writers must be storytellers first and foremost.

Think about it. Stylish language in a novel can make our sensibilities soar. Interesting locations can pull truckloads of viewers to a film. Amusing banter can bring the Nielsen Rating points to a series on TV. But unless these other elements serve a story that captivates and engrosses us, that keeps us guessing and gasping and wanting more, then who needs them? They may as well not exist.

Let's take *The Odyssey*, which I'll admit just might be a better story than the one I told at the beginning of this chapter. Do you suppose Homer's classic has been read for thousands of years because of its style and magnificent poetry? Hardly. Most of us don't even know

Homer's language. We read *The Odyssey* in translation. And we read it for its story: man against the gods who falls out of one trap and into another while lovers, partners in life, struggle to be reunited. Even those who haven't read *The Odyssey* know the plot because it's been retold endlessly, in a variety of ways by a variety of writers. Ditto all the fairy tales we grew up with. And all the other classics: *Faust, Moby Dick, The Adventures of Tom Sawyer*, even a new member of the club like *The Lord of the Rings*.

All of these works are first and foremost great stories. They appeal to primal elements of the human spirit. They entertain and they enlighten. And, yes, they have many characters who could be considered "great." This greatness, however, comes from the situation in which the characters find themselves. And our immersion in and enjoyment of the story are intensified by the way the characters and the situation interact.

Historians are fond of asking, "Do the times make the man, or does the man make the times?" In fiction—a.k.a. storytelling, a.k.a. dramatic writing—the greatness of the characters is always a function of the events, while the events of the story are, in turn, guided by and dependent upon the characters. The personalities of the characters are shaped by the basic premise of the story and demonstrate themselves by what the characters do in terms of participating in the action to which the basic premise leads. We know the characters and their traits by how they rise to the demands of the story. Because, after all, they exist only within the context of the piece.

In *The Lord of the Rings*, we love Frodo because of what he does, and what he does is in effect the "story." He bears the ring. He resists temptation. He risks his life to cause its final destruction. Tom Sawyer captivates us because of how he responds to his family and neighbors, his behavior vis-à-vis Injun Joe, and his heroism when he and Becky are lost in the cave. Ahab and Ishmael rivet us because of their places as motivators of and reactors to the whaling expedition and the encounter with the white whale. Dr. Faust's hubris, his insatiable desire for "more," teaches us a valuable lesson because we experience it in action with Mephisto, who's not an uncompelling character in and of himself.

Sartre said it best. "Existence precedes essence." People are what they've demonstrated themselves to be within the context that is the story of their lives.

Story and character. Character and story.

The examples here aren't teleplays, or even screenplays, but they are "dramatic writing," just as the title of this chapter says. If you think about it, dramatic writing is simply all writing that dramatizes—that is, presents—human behavior. (In other words, all writing that you would probably care to read, see, or hear.)

Dramatic writing exists in all media. That's because all media must grab and hold us and cause an emotional reaction within us in order to succeed. In order, as we say in television, to "work." Dramatic writing encompasses all genres as well. Even comedy presents human behavior; it just leavens it with humor. (So does much so-called "drama." What's the real difference? Intensity, perhaps? Or maybe the number of laughs per page? I believe it has to do with the overall sensibility of the work, how far it pushes and exaggerates for comic effect. For television writing the point is moot; we don't have "drama" and "comedy." We have "drama" and "sitcom," which are almost but not quite the same thing…and we'll get into both of them soon.)

The tale of the Eager Young Television Writer and the Most Distinguished and Highly Regarded TV Producer of the Day is far from a classic, but it contains all the other necessary elements that make a piece of dramatic writing work, as well as the "big two"—story and character. Many of those elements were first codified by Aristotle in his lecture, *Poetics*. In *Poetics*, Aristotle functions as a literary critic, telling us what worked in his time, and most of it still works today.

Other necessary elements are still being discovered—or is it recognized?—today. New books are always coming out, claiming to be able to teach people how to write. University writing classes run for semesters. Working writers spend their entire careers, which are usually the length of their adult lives, searching for the complete, foolproof, how-to-write equation. And, believe me, with the exception of a few geniuses we still haven't gotten it down.

This means that the odds are very good that I'm not going to hit one out of the park in one chapter. With any luck, though, the overview I give here will enable you to see something about your work that you haven't before, to recognize a flaw you can repair, or take pride in a value you didn't realize you had. If the ability to write well and with clarity and feeling were a stereo component, this chapter would be a sliding control moving your potential up just enough so further improvement can kick in.

Aristotle's *Poetics* is still in print. It's a must-read for anyone who wants to become a writer. (Another classic, you might say, although not "dramatic writing" per se.) Changes in social structure and technology have caused changes in the needs of both storyteller and audience, although not in human nature itself. Extrapolating from Aristotle, then, here are the remaining basic elements of dramatic writing today.

> For a story to "work" (that is, to have an emotional effect on its reading or viewing audience), it must be about some-one—Aristotle's "protagonist"—who has a need that must be fulfilled or a problem that must be solved. Failure to do so usually has dire consequences. The "story" is how he or she finds fulfillment or solves the problem...or both.

A little side note here: the above ain't Aristotle. I learned it in the late 1960s when I was fortunate enough to get an assignment to write a script for an NBC television series called *The Sixth Sense*. One of the story editors of that short-lived show was D.C. Fontana, who had previously been the story editor of the original *Star Trek*. At story meetings she would sit patiently, and then get to the heart of the plot and its problem: "What's the need here?" she would say quietly. "What's the problem? Who's in trouble here? Why is our hero getting involved?"

Our opening tale has a protagonist with whom any writer can easily identify: the Eager Young Television Writer. And our protagonist has a clearly recognizable need: to become a successful TV writer. Only by doing so will he be fulfilled. The dire consequence of failure? Well, as currently written, it's implied. We all know the bitterness that can engulf people who don't achieve their dreams. (And if you don't think that's a dire consequence, that just means you've never lived with someone trying to cope, or not trying to cope, with that terrible amalgam of anger, loss, and hopelessness.)

> For a story to work it needs a "beginning"—that point where the need or problem is presented and the hero is put into the situation of having to fulfill the need or solve the problem.

We're back to Aristotle now. Unlike Ms. Fontana, I never got to work with him, but from what I've heard Ari wasn't nearly as patient and soft-spoken as D.C. She, to my knowledge, has never had to flee for her life, not even from a furious network executive, whereas Aristotle had to hightail it out of Athens after his patron, Alexander the Great, died.

In our tale, the Eager Young Television Writer has a dream, which he confides to someone he respects. The man he respects crushes the dream, intensifying the need by creating a new need for vindication. There's no more time left to waver. The EYTVW has to get going.

> For a story to work it needs a "middle"—a series of events
> in which the protagonist tries to solve the problem and
> becomes enmeshed in escalating difficulties. An especially
> effective way of building the difficulties is to include what
> Aristotle called an "antagonist," an enemy who works
> against the protagonist.

In the years between Aristotle, D.C. Fontana, and beyond, one Acme helluva lot o'stories have been told, with the result that the current audience/readership often starts out one step ahead of the writer. The best way to overcome this is to speed things up, truncating the beginning and starting the story as close to the middle as possible with it still making sense. No, this isn't something anyone taught me. I learned the hard way: from experience, from rewriting and rewriting script after script, taking out more and more of the front end.

In our tale the Eager Young Television Writer dedicates himself to succeeding as a TV writer and works like the proverbial son of a bitch (all right, maybe not so proverbial, but you get the point— the phrase "works") to do so, overcoming all obstacles in his path, both haunted and driven by the mockery of the man he perceives as his antagonist, the Most Distinguished and Highly Regarded TV Producer of the Day. (In most stories the antagonist is more active— continuously so—in trying to prevent the success of the protagonist, but we're being psychologically "subtle" here.)

> For a story to work it needs an "end"—a seemingly
> impossible hurdle or climax, to which all of the other
> difficulties have built, a do-or-die effort in which

everything the protagonist has worked for is at stake. The
stake here should be so high that if the protagonist fails,
he or she will end up in a situation so terrible that even the
originally envisioned dire consequence is eclipsed.

Building, building, building is crucial. You've got to increase the
tension from scene to scene. Otherwise the story falls flat. The audience/
reader loses interest if things don't "get worse" for your protagonist.
This, too, I learned the hard way: from the experience of sitting and
quivering in a small chair as the then-executive producer of a string of
Columbia Pictures Television hits (and also the head of the studio),
David Gerber, screamed, "Where's the conflict? Where's the jeopardy?
We're almost at the end. It's time for the shooting to start!".

In our tale, the Eager Television Writer (time has passed and he's
no longer young, remember?) overcomes all the more or less expected
obstacles and seems to attain his dream. Then, at his moment of
triumph—the award ceremony—he discovers the deadliest obstacle of
all: the need for revenge, which has poisoned and may continue to
poison his life. If he gives in to the need, his cruelty may destroy him
as a person regardless of his professional success. Will the ETVW succumb
to the desire for vengeance? Or will he rise above it and become a
better human being?

Ah! He is "arisen!" Whew. Hooray! The end.

And you wondered why you've read so many books and seen so
many films and television shows about men or women avenging
the rape, murder, or other destruction of a loved one, going through
hell to track down the villain, and then at the very end refusing to
take the baddy's life. That's the ultimate victory in any story—rising
above yourself, beating the butt of the enemy within. And now you
know why there are even more stories about rape, murder, or other
destruction of a loved one than stories just about revenge. Nothing
creates more jeopardy than having a life at stake.

Our anecdotal example story is of course truncated. Within the
basic framework this story, like any other story, there can be an
infinite variety of twists and turns. Our tale ends happily, but no one
says a story has to be upbeat (especially not Aristotle). When you get
down to it, every story has at least four possible endings that can
deeply effect the audience:

The protagonist triumphs and is probably going to live happily ever after.

The protagonist fails and is either going to be miserable forever or is no longer on this mortal coil.

The protagonist triumphs and is miserable about it. (Hey, that happens. In real life it's usually in conjunction with the kind of bitterness we mentioned before.)

The protagonist fails and is probably going to live happily ever after anyway because of some important lesson the events in the story have taught him/her. (No bitterness here. Now we're dealing with that rare commodity called wisdom.)

Whether any particular ending is "better" dramatic writing than any other one is always open to discussion, and is one of the topics writers are prone to examine (some might say "belabor") for hours when they get together, have a few drinks, and finish talking about the subject closest to the hearts of most professional writers: their deals.

For that matter, when it comes to anything having to do with writing, even the concept of "better" is debatable, although I tend to think of "good" and "better" as "effective" and "more effective." In other words, good writing is writing that captures its audience and then moves them emotionally because of the events in the story and the protagonist's response to them. Good writing works. Better writing works better. The more a writer understands the audience, the more the writer will be able to appeal to and therefore manipulate the audience and its emotions... and the *better* the writing will be.

This is it, then, dramatic writing demystified. The basic elements of dramatic writing are:

The story
The beginning
The characters
The protagonist
The antagonist
The middle

The climax
The end

If you're going to work as a writer in television—or any other medium—you need to know these elements as well as you know yourself. You have to be as aware of how to shape a story as you are of how to brush your teeth, and you need to welcome each element the way you do a lover's touch. Without this knowledge you will never be able to write that spec script you need—or fulfill any script assignment you get.

But to work as a writer in television, you also need to know how to apply these basic elements the way they are applied in TV. You need to know what steps to take, in what order, to see your script through from its basic idea to its final, perfectly polished draft.

chapter 5:
taking it by
the numbers

When I began writing television it was a wonderful medium
for beginners because the business end—the nuts and bolts of creation
and production—was quick and informal. If I had an idea, I could call
my agent, or a producer, and say, "Hey, I've got an idea for such and
such a show," and in a few minutes I'd have a meeting scheduled where
I could discuss my idea with the story editor or producer.

The meeting would be within just a few days, and whoever I spoke
to had the authority to say yes or no, right there, on the spot. I would
walk out of the meeting knowing if I had a freelance assignment on
the series, or if I had to go back to the drawing board and come up
with another idea instead. There were no layers of authority to wade
through, no weeks to wait for the meeting and more weeks to wait for
the decision as there are now for both freelancers and staff members
alike. I didn't even have to use today's magic phrase "pitch meeting," so
the person to whom I was speaking would understand what our get
together would be about.

But although the sales procedure wasn't codified, even then the
writing procedure was. The methodology was etched in stone the way
a writer's draft never could be, and that methodology continues to this
day. Why? Because it works. Because this is an example of true synergy
between the creative and business processes. Creativity found what it

needed to create the best possible work for television (and feature films, for that matter), and business distinguished and defined the result. The bottom line is that if you want to write for television professionally you have to "take it by the numbers," as we used to have McGarrett, the lead character, say to his assistant, Danno, on *Hawaii Five-O*. And if you want to write for yourself, you will quickly find that these numbers will work for you very well. This is the way you approach both an assigned script and a spec.

In the beginning, of course, is the *idea*. This is the kernel of what you want to write, the statement of intention that probably came to you at three in the morning when you couldn't sleep, or, when you were sleeping and were shocked into wakefulness by your own creativity. Or your idea may have come to you in the shower. I've found that the feeling of running water pouring down on me coupled with the privacy of the shower stall gives me the confidence and solitude I need to come up with most of the bases for what I write.

My other great place for realizing my "genius" by thinking of something I otherwise never would is in the car, on a freeway. Usually I'm on my way to a meeting at the time and haven't a clue about what I want to tell someone about what I want to write. Like an infant lulled to sleep by the motion of the car, I relax the barriers of self-censorship in my mind and come up with some pretty good stuff. (I remember being in the car on the way to Paramount, where I was supposed to pitch an idea for an episode of *Star Trek: Voyager*. I tried to listen to the radio, but the only thing on was the infamous O.J. Simpson-LAPD slow chase, so I turned off the radio, let my mind wander, and came up with an award-winning episode called "Tattoo.")

These days the idea has been given an official designation and form. It is called the "logline," and anyone in the television business to whom you say, "I've got this idea," will respond with, "What's the log-line?" The word logline comes from that venerable TV publication *TV Guide*. The magazine has articles, yes, but its main focus is listing what shows will be on television at what time in any given geographical area. In short, *TV Guide* is a log of TV shows, and refers to its one-line descriptions of each show as…yes, you've got it, "loglines."

When someone in the biz says, "What's the logline?" that person is expecting to hear from you the shortest and catchiest possible statement of your idea. Your job at this point is to recognize that the best ideas are those that can be expressed the most succinctly and strike a chord. Find a way to boil your idea down to one or two great sentences that you can say to anyone who asks, and that you can write down to be effortlessly read. Don't let your listener or reader—or yourself—down. (Don't worry—a chapter on loglines is coming. I won't let *you* down.)

Your idea, of course, is merely a starting point. The next step is to refine it, to create a shape for the story that comes out of it. That's right, now you've got to come up with the beginning, the middle, and the end. Not the details, just the broad strokes. Who are the characters? How do they discover their problem? What do they try to do about it? How do they fare at the end?

In "officialese," this step has a name also. It's called the "leave-behind." Anyone in show business to whom you tell your idea—or "pitch your logline"—will then ask, "What happens?" and it becomes your job to tell the beginning, middle, and end just as you would tell a friend the main ingredients of a feature film you'd seen and were recommending. This "what happens" is also something best born in bed, the shower, or traffic, because for the action to "work" it should come easily and logically from the idea. Because it is basic and simple, it shouldn't take you more than five minutes to state, and if your listener agrees that this is a good potential story he or she will then ask the musical question, "Do you have a leavebehind on that?"

The correct response here is to whip out a few pages and hand them over. They should say everything you just said verbally, no more and no less, with the only addition being a catchy title. (The title has to be relevant as well. You'd be surprised how many people aren't aware of that.) The value of the leavebehind in an assignment or attempted assignment situation is obvious. It gives your listener a way of refreshing his or her memory after you're gone, and something to show to the bosses in order to obtain their approval. The leavebehind's creative value is less clear but definitely there. Sitting down and writing what are, in effect, the most vital elements of your three-act structure forces you to face your material and see if it really is as interesting as you originally thought. And then it forces you to organize it and establish a skeleton on which you can hang your next step! (Yes, a chapter on leavebehinds is in your future. Don't despair.)

The next step is an outline. Creatively speaking, the outline is, without a doubt, the most important thing you will write. It's important to those you work with, if you're working with anyone, because it tells them exactly what you're going to write in the teleplay. It gives a scene-by-scene breakdown of what is going to happen, of how the story will unfold. When you write on assignment you always have to turn in an outline and have it approved by the powers-that-be. It's the first step of this process for which you get paid, and the payment isn't small. Usually the writer receives one-third of the total fee.

The outline is even more important to the writer than to those whose jobs are to work with the writer. The outline is simultaneously the writer's floor plan and the writer's lifeline. Without a good outline you—we—stand a good chance of becoming lost while writing the script. Of floundering. Of spending hours, sometimes days, staring at the keyboard and thinking, "What happens next? What do they do? Why do they do it?" Your outline answers all those questions. It guides you along so that when you're working on the script (when you're "in teleplay" is the official phrase for that), all you have to worry about is writing great dialogue and using the most effective possible language in your descriptions.

Officially, an outline is referred to as a "story." Unofficially, we sometimes call it a "beatsheet" (as in putting down the "beats" of the story— hence the phrase "beating out the story" which you will certainly hear if you get near a staff job), or a stepsheet (as in putting down the "steps" and, yes, "stepping out the story"). Another phrase you'll hear is "breaking a story," which means the same thing as figuring out what the beats or steps—or moves, moments, or any of a dozen words—will be. "Breaking" comes from the concept of "breaking the story down to its individual scenes," which seems reasonable. However, over the years I've noticed that those who use this particular term are invariably those who are the worst at concocting a logical, believable, and interesting plot. So be warned, story breakers (and be of good cheer, because a chapter on outlining is headed your way).

After the outline comes the fun part—facing the blank page as it appears on the screen of your computer monitor and writing the "first draft." The first draft is where you put it all together, using all your skills as a writer—your insight into human behavior, your gift for descriptive language, your uncanny ear for how people talk, your knowledge of production and cinema technique. In short, this is the *real writing*, everyone, the step where you give it all you've got. If you're on assignment this is the version you send in to the show so the bosses can see what they like and what they don't like, what they want on what they often call "our air," and what they don't want. If you're writing a spec, this is the version that you save with a great sense of pride before going out and celebrating.

Just don't think for a moment that what you're celebrating is finishing the project. Because whether you're working for someone else or for yourself, the first draft is just that—first, not last. I think of it as an opening salvo. Be prepared to wait a few days, then read it, and go back and make it even better than before. Businesswise, you'll have to do that. Most deals obligate you to do at least two rewrites, officially called, a "revision" and a "polish." Creatively—well, you've probably heard the phrase "writing isn't writing, it's rewriting." Whoever first said that wasn't kidding. Most writers I know write until they drop, or run screaming from the computer.

Brannon Braga, the highly regarded writer-producer of *Star Trek: The Next Generation*, *Star Trek: Voyager*, and *Star Trek: Enterprise* once remarked to me that "Teleplays are difficult to write because you can't depend on mere inspiration. You have to sit down and slog it out." But I find writing all drafts of teleplays fascinating for just the opposite reason. The script and its characters and its situations become so real to me that they reach out and grab me at all hours of the day or night. I'll be eating dinner and suddenly hear the next line of dialogue in my mind...and have to run to the computer and get it down. Or I'll be watching one series and suddenly be struck by a better retort for a scene I've already written for another series...and I am off to the computer again.

Do I also get these divine inspirations in the car on the freeway? Of course. Thank God for all that Southern California traffic. It's made it possible for me to safely jot down some interesting turns of phrase on a legal pad while technically still driving. Think cell phones are dangerous when you're behind the wheel? Wait till you find yourself inescapably writing.

The chapter on teleplays is coming along with the others. But first...

chapter 6:
the logline

The first order of business when you're writing anything is to come up with an idea. When you're writing for television this is a little more complicated than it sounds, because you're not merely trying to please yourself; you're also trying to come up with an idea that will please the audience.

This isn't as self-evident as it sounds. If you write for publication, you're writing something that is complete when your work as a writer is finished. It's made to be read, by you, your friends, your family, editors, publishers, and fans. Publishing has become such a niche business these days that odds are good that if you write something that pleases you, and do it in a solid and professional manner, it'll also please your intended audience. And, in a worst-case scenario, even if it doesn't please them and never gets published you can read the work with some self-enjoyment.

If you write for TV, though, you're writing something that by its very nature can never exist in and of itself. A television script, like that for a feature film, isn't intended to be the final product. It's only the first phase of the product—the television episode or pilot or movie. If a TV script gets no further than its written form, it hasn't achieved its objective. Aristotle once said that the "final cause" of an acorn is an oak tree. Well, the final cause of a script is a production.

A well-written script allows for this creatively by leaving space for the contribution of the directors, actors, and other specialists above and below the line. You wouldn't describe every inch of the hero's office on a medical show, for example (as you would in a novel), because no matter what your description says, the audience will only see the "reality" of a stage set (or location) that real human beings are moving through and sitting in. The viewer at home will only see a set that uses your description as a starting point for the creativity of a set designer, filled with the prop master's props, populated by actors and extras chosen by the producers, director, and casting director, lighted and shot by the director of photography and his gang, and so on and so on.

It would be a waste of time, an exercise in futility, and an insult to your co-workers to say too much in your script, just as it would be an insult to write in such a way that the actors are forced to say their lines as you, the writer, believe they should be said, and not as they, the actors, feel would be appropriate. It would be more than a waste of time, because the wonderful thing about working with good actors is that they can come up with readings, and facial expressions ("character shadings," we call them) that no writer—or director or anyone else—would ever think of.

Similarly, at the very onset of the creative process in TV, when you come up with an idea, you have to view it in terms of its purpose—as a catalyst not only for you but also for others. Your idea has to be so good that it fills you with the desire to write it out. It has to be so inspiring that it'll see you through outline after outline, draft after draft, and, if you're working professionally, meeting after meeting. Your idea must be so powerful that it can sustain you for weeks at least and, more likely, for months.

In conjunction with this, your idea has to be so exciting that it has the same effect on all those with whom you work, or with whom you hope to work, that it has on you. It has to grab them. It has to hook them. Whether you're writing a sitcom episode, a drama episode, a TV movie, an animation episode, a soap opera bible, or—especially—the premise for a new series, your idea has to take the listener or reader by the throat and not let go. Not for a second. Your idea has to be so compelling that its appeal to the larger, mass television audience is immediately apparent to anyone and everyone the minute you present it. In other words, it has to be *commercial*.

Foolproof.

Risk free.

Because the ultimate authority, the person who is going to give you an assignment to either write this script or write another script based on what you've already done with this one, the script on which you and I are working together right now, is a corporate executive who can take no risks, who has to justify everything he or she does or lose his or her job.

Think about it. As a television writer the thing you need most is access to the television audience. This audience gets the show based on your teleplay pretty much for free (keeping in mind what we might call "carrying charges" if the audience is watching via cable or satellite). That means that if you think of yourself as a salesman—and you should because, let's face it, that's what we all are—then your buyer as a television writer is the medium itself. The medium that gets you to the audience.

At the very beginning of any television project, you're writing for the showrunner, the production company, the network or cable or satellite channel, and their parent organizations. You're writing for all the executives in charge—the "suits" we all know and, because of our nature as writers, all dread. These are the men and women who run things. They control our access. They control our pay. They control our careers.

And although they don't control it in so many words, they greatly affect our creativity. The suits are the gatekeepers. "Access...no access..." It's up to them.

The keys to getting the attention of the suits and gaining support for you and your projects both present and future are your abilities as a writer as demonstrated in your previous work and on your expression of the idea you present to them. Your *logline*.

"He wrote a great script based on a great idea! So how could we go wrong in giving him another project?"

"She has a wonderful idea, a can't-miss. We've got to bring her onboard!"

These are the two things you want said about you. These are the two things you need to have said about you all through your career. The minute one of them vanishes, you're in trouble. If they both do... welcome back to your day job, partner.

So how do you do it? How do you hook that hip, trendy, yet oh-so-conservative executive and reel him or her in? What kind of logline do the suits want? What kind of logline do you want?

Try this hip, trendy, yet in its way also oh-so-conservative phrase: "high concept."

You've probably heard the term before, but few people understand what high concept is. Common explanations that I've gotten from both new writers and seasoned pros include:

"An idea that's bright, fresh, original, and commercial."

"An idea that's dull, stale, and old phrased in a bright, fresh, and original manner."

"A concise idea that grabs everyone's attention."

"An idea that can be expressed in one or two sentences so even a 22-year-old executive can understand it."

"An idea that can be told in 30 seconds so even the busiest 42-year-old executive can listen to it."

"An idea you get while you're stoned, like a sitcom about the Dalai Lama."

Every one of these descriptions is right, and every one of them is wrong. All of the comments above succeed in describing high concept but none truly understands it. To truly understand high concept, you have to know how the phrase originated.

My experience shows that it originated out of fear—the fear development executives have of losing their jobs. So many things can go wrong when a project begins, or "put into work," that the suits have to cover their tushies at all times, particularly in today's corporate environment. Because they're in the development business and not the buying business—working with writers to create scripts instead of buying finished teleplays—they can't justify giving a go-ahead based on the quality of the writing of this particular piece. There's no piece, and no quality, to judge.

This means that the executive-buyer (actually more a hirer than a buyer) needs something else to justify any decision to say or recommend "go." Something that, no matter how wobbly its under-pinnings, gives the illusion of being concrete. Something that on its face cannot be denied.

I remember the first time I heard this now-common phrase. I was at a meeting with a drama development executive at ABC who must be nameless for reasons that will become clear momentarily (one of a breed called "D-Gals," as in "Development Gals," even today— although now we have "D-Guys" as well, so everyone can feel insulted). At the time, Janis Hendler, my partner for this project, was executive story consultant of the hit NBC series *Knight Rider*, and I was supervising producer of another hit called *The Fall Guy*. The young woman listened to the idea Janis and I were pitching and nodded. And then negated that nod with a sigh.

"I like that a lot," she said. "But I can't buy it."

"Let us get this straight," either I or my partner said—I can't pretend to remember. "You like it a lot but you can't buy it. Why not?"

"It's not high concept enough."

"It's not what enough?"

"High concept. You two have told me an interesting premise that I can easily visualize as a successful series. But the main reason I can see it that way is because you two would be running it and I know how you two write. I know the look, the feeling, and the characterization you'll supply."

"And that's a bad thing?" my then-partner or I said.

"Well, the people I have to sell this to don't know you. And they probably wouldn't trust you if they did. They don't trust anybody," the development executive said. "So I can only tell them high concepts— ideas that are so incredibly cool they have no excuse to turn them down."

Take a moment and think about this. It's important. Read between the lines of what the woman said so you can go right to what she meant. She meant—and all my experience ever since that fateful day backs this up—that in order to sell a series, the writers and creators must come up with a premise so exciting that it's execution-proof. A high concept is a concept so mind-boggling that no matter how badly it's written, acted, directed, or just generally produced, people will still flock to see it.

Now you know why so many feature films are the way they are— movies with neat ideas that send viewers flocking to the theaters on opening weekends to get grosses that are never matched again after word of mouth about how well, or not well, they've been done gets out.

Even in this day of niche cable and satellite channels, television shows are still designed to appeal to as many people as possible, to get all of their particular target demographics. For that reason the practical test of high concept is that after hearing the idea—logline— each and every person who's been told it says in tones shaded with envy, "Whoa! That's fantastic! I wish I'd thought of it!"

This doesn't apply only to series premises or feature films or TV movie ideas, it also applies to ideas for series episodes and even for the arcs and extended plots of soap operas. Your idea must be an immediate grabber if you want it to be, well, grabbed.

And yes, you do have to be able to tell your high concept in one or two sentences. Not because your listener or reader has a short attention span, but because the fact is that, as has been said here before, the best ideas are the simplest ones. "Best" as in most significant, most interesting, most likely to live on for future generations. We may admire Byzantine, convoluted, deeply layered notions, and we may remember them for awhile. But they don't stick in our heads like advertising jingles. High concepts like these series' premises do:

Buffy the Vampire Slayer. *By day, she's a teenage cheerleader. By night she hunts—vampires.*

Sure it's silly. But it's also different and obviously a chance to be very, very hip. Even if Buffy hadn't been a minor hit film, who could pass this series up?

Jurassic Park. *A scientist clones modern dinosaurs for an amusement park, only to have them break free and run amok.*

Again, even if this hadn't been a hit film, it's a can't miss television series. Who doesn't love dinosaurs? (So why isn't it on the air—think "Ohmigod the cost!!!")

The X-Files. *Two FBI agents, one a believer in science, the other in intuition, must deal with their conflicts with each other as well as with the paranormal occurrences they investigate.*

Other shows have tried to show the paranormal, but most of them have debunked it, and this is the first one to feature heroes whose basic natures are in conflict. Another natural.

Will & Grace. *A gay man and a hard-driving executive woman become roommates and best friends.*

A new take on several old themes: buddy stories, repressed sexual attraction stories, men and women as platonic roommates stories. The Odd Couple with a major twist.

Here are some high concept loglines for episodes:

Star Trek: Voyager—*"Tattoo." While leading an away team on a new planet, Chakotay encounters a familiar symbol—his tattoo. How did it get here? Are more of his people still in this world?*

This one immediately implies "gods from outer space" and a chance to explore the background of one of the show's most popular characters. What showrunner could ask for more?

Star Trek: The Next Generation—"InnerVisions." *When the crew of the Enterprise tries to save the inhabitants of a doomed planet, they discover that they can't even communicate with them. The population lives not in the real world but in a planet-wide shared dream.*

This one's a ringer in the sense that it was worked out specifically to appeal to Gene Roddenberry, who was still alive, well, and running the show when it was pitched. The operative word in the logline is "dream." Gene was a dreamer and loved and respected anything that had to do with dreams and dreaming.

Walker, Texas Ranger—"Rainbow Warrior." *Walker has to take on an old friend—a Cherokee Indian Rambo—whose combat skills are every bit as good as Walker's.*

Chuck Norris versus Rambo. This one was a shoo-in with the suits and the audience.

Diagnosis: Murder—"Trap Play." *After a basketball star has a fatal allergy attack, Mark discovers it was deliberately induced. Now all he has to do is Wgure out which of the obnoxious star's many enemies was the murderer.*

This high concept logline works for a whodunit series because it features not one but two inherent twists to the plot.

The Huntress—"Cadillac Dreams." *The ladies take an old Cadillac as payment for a bounty hunting job. Little do they know that the classic car is worth so much to a local gang that its members will kill for it.*

This works because gangbanger stories always get good ratings and it has the built-in twist that the reason the car is valuable has nothing to do with the fact that it's a classic. A good puzzle.

Frasier—"Daphne's Wedding." *Daphne is finally getting married—but to whom?*

The relationship between the Niles and Daphne characters dominated this series for two seasons. Every staff member, exec, and viewer had an opinion on what should happen, and this logline made everyone who read it want to see this show.

Spider-Man—"Night of the Hobgoblin." *The origin of the Hobgoblin story is told as Norman Osborn's own creation backfires and turns against him.*

This premise gave the execs what they wanted—a chance to promote a popular Marvel Comics character on a Marvel Comics show and at the same time ironically twist both the origin and the show's main villain, Norman Osborn.

The Silver Surfer—"The End of Eternity Part One." *The godlike beings Eternity and Infinity promise to bring the Surfer home to Zenn-La. All he has to do first is save the universe from total destruction by Thanos!*

A season-ending cliffhanger offering what every network wants to see in an animated series—the destruction of the universe—and what every viewer wanted to see for the Silver Surfer—his return home. The power and appeal leapt out at any reader or listener who knew the show.

And here's the high concept for a TV movie in development as of this writing: After he takes office, an idealistic young president learns that the country is really controlled by a powerful secret force. He tries to fight it, and ends up out in the world on the run from the most dangerous group of hit men alive.

I love this premise because on every serious level it's ridiculous, but as soon as you get to that "on the run" part you understand what the powers-that-be like about it. They're certain the audience will tune in en masse because the film is giving today's audience exactly what it demands.

All these loglines are for material that has either been commissioned and written or commissioned, written, and aired. But remember that they have a creative validity as well as a pragmatic one. When you come up with a logline that jumps out at any reader or listener in the catchiest manner possible, you're hooking yourself along with everyone else. You're stating your basic premise in a way that puts squarely before you the elements of your project that are the most exciting, and therefore the most important ones when you sit down to do the rest of your writing. Working out the logline and then writing with it in mind keeps the writer focused on the basic appeal of the idea and prevents you from wandering off into story territory that may sound good at the time but which has no lasting relevance or interest.

Some quick tips on loglines:

Timing is everything.

Although truly important work has a timeless theme or premise, take into the account the tenor of the times when you come up with your high concepts. In the early 1980s I was co-executive producer (with Glen A. Larson, one of the most prolific creators of television series in history) of a show called Automan. The basic premise of Automan was this: a police department computer geek brings a computer game superhero to life to help him fight crime.

The series limped through 13 episodes and then vanished into cancellation limbo, and I can't help but believe that one of the reasons was that the personal computer had not yet established the hold it has today on the American public. Hell, I wrote or re-wrote every episode, and I didn't even have a PC! I think that today, with computers being all-pervasive (three people currently live in my home—my wife, my daughter, and me—yet we have four computers constantly fired up for either work, games, or surfing online) Automan would have a much better chance of becoming a hit. Today, the premise is precisely a "Whoa! I wish I'd thought of that!" response for just about everyone.

Phrasing is everything.

You can make a not-so-exciting idea sound more exciting—and

thereby become more exciting —by wording it correctly. Use action verbs and what propagandists call "loaded words," which are words that have such strong connotative meanings that they create an immediate impact in their listeners.

Example:

Don't write: *Murders in the Rue Morgue.* Tourists are being murdered in a popular section of New Orleans. Our Hero investigates to find out why.

Do write: *Murders in the Rue Morgue.* A serial killer strikes in the heart of New Orleans' French Quarter, and the evidence quickly leads Our Hero to the apparent murderer. But can the killer really be —a gorilla?

Similarly, don't say too much, but don't say too little either. The trick is to tell your reader or listener and yourself exactly what you all know to be able to fully envision what the idea will look like on the screen—but without using one extra word.

Don't write: *Friends*—"The One with the Killer Gorilla." Laughter abounds when Ross transplants Phoebe's brain into the body of a giant gorilla and Chandler hypnotizes her into thinking she's James Bond's new partner. Meanwhile, Rachel has decided to run off to the tundra with Joey and Monica joins the New Orleans Police Department to bring closure to her latest failed romance—with the zany surgeon who tutored Ross and has his one good eye on a deal for a great apartment in Manhattan.

Also don't write: *Friends*—"The One with the Killer Gorilla." Ross performs a brain transplant on Phoebe.

Do write: *Friends*—"The One with the Killer Gorilla." Ross transplants Phoebe's brain into the body of a giant gorilla, but the joke backfires after Chandler hypnotizes her into thinking she's the latest James bond girl.

chapter 7:
the leavebehind

Now that you've finished your logline, what do you do with it?

If you're a pro and have an agent or other friends or contacts in the TV biz, now is the time to get on the phone. If your logline is for a TV movie or series, set up meetings with execs that you and your support team of those-in-the-know think will be open to that kind of pitch, and also open to you as a writer. If your logline is for a series, be it drama, sitcom, animation or just about anything else, it's time to get hold of the showrunner of the series for which your premise is intended, and set up a meeting with him or her.

There's a technique to this kind of call, as there is to just about everything in life. A trick, you might say. The idea is to use the logline as bait—it's your hook, remember? You call, you talk, and you state your logline in a conversational manner, making this potential employer want to hear more. But don't say anything more. Remember, you want a meeting to expand on your premise and work it out further—develop it with someone (a "development executive") who can make a real deal with you on a finished version of what you've got in mind—for money.

Just make certain you don't go to the meeting(s) without your preliminary expansion of the premise, a.k.a. your leavebehind, so called because you will indeed leave it behind.

If you're not yet established, then it's straight to the leavebehind. The easiest way to understand what a leavebehind is and how to write it is to think of it as an in, hip, and trendy name for a synopsis. A synopsis, though, is created after the fact, boiling existing material down to something that's shorter and easier to read, while a leavebehind is written beforehand. Like the logline, the leavebehind has two purposes. It functions as both a sales tool and a creative one.

As we've seen, out in the practical world of the biz the logline exists to get an executive's attention. In that same cold, hard world the leavebehind exists to keep that attention by showing there's real substance behind your original high concept. It's a short, three-to-five page double-spaced expansion of your logline, giving your premise a preliminary storyline with a beginning, middle, and end. Knowing where you start, what your center action or problem is, and how you're going to end gives you the basis for your conversation or presentation at a pitch meeting, and by actually writing it down you have something to leave with your favorite suit so the project can be mulled over knowledgeably even when you aren't around.

Creatively, by giving your idea this new, basic shape, you are forced to think through your premise and see where it leads. In the process, you discover if it's as viable as you thought, by learning for yourself (without embarrassment, because if things don't turn out, you don't have to show it to anyone) if the exciting logline supports a story that's just as, or even more, exciting.

You also start to know more about your characters. If your premise is for a series or a TV movie (an "original" in the trade), you should give the characters names so you can refer to them, and you should also find yourself thinking about their occupations and backgrounds as well. This isn't something you have to force. If the idea is a good one the people who populate it will float naturally to the surface of your mind. (If they don't, my suggestion is to forget this one. Drop it and go on to another idea instead.)

If your premise is for an existing series, you'll still find yourself thinking about the characters, but in terms of how they will react to the situation you've set up and what will affect their personalities as you know them from watching the show, reading scripts, and doing all your other research.

No matter what you're writing, you'll know the problems of the characters, especially the problem that's the central core of your soon-to-be story. You'll see what needs must be fulfilled and have a rough idea of what the characters will have to go through to fulfill them. Because that, after all, *is* your story.

The importance of this story business cannot be overstated. Television is more story-driven than any other medium. TV shows eat stories up and spit them out again in a never-ending binge-purge that usually ends up leaving writers and producers emotionally and creatively exhausted. What's the protagonist's need? What's the protagonist's problem? What's a new way to show the need? A new way to express the problem? What's a new way to satisfy the need? To solve the problem?

These are the issues that have to be in your mind as a writer when you move to the step we call the leavebehind. But they're not the only ones. Now, while you're still early in the creative process, is the time to think about other aspects of the situation as well. Now is when you have to come to grips with all the ramifications of your basic idea.

Your protagonist's need has to be clear-cut and understandable: "They burned his dog! They killed his wife! They destroyed his house! Now it's time for—JUSTICE!" How many variations of that ad copy have you seen? And every time you see it, you know from the top of your head to the bottoms of your feet, and particularly in the pit of your stomach, that they ain't really talking 'bout justice, boy—they're talking about a human need that, ugly as it can be, is as basic and as universal as they come. They're talking 'bout *revenge*.

Your protagonist's problem also has to be right out there because it's what keeps him or her (or them when there's a group of protagonists) from satisfying the need. The problem has to be difficult. It's got to be meaningful, and, most importantly in television, it's got to be dangerous. We're talking risk, peril, life or death. We're talking about something every human being cares about being at stake.

If the protagonist succeeds in solving the problem and satisfying the need, good things happen, and if they happen to others as well as to the protagonist so much the better. Lovers reunite before she marries the wrong man or he runs off with the wrong woman. A killer is caught before he can strike again. An asteroid's course is deflected before it hits the earth.

If the protagonist fails to solve the problem and satisfy the need, then dark days are here, boys, and I mean really, really dark. That sun ain't gonna shine. There is no tomorrow...maybe symbolically, maybe literally. A loved one dies. A patient is crippled. Civilization as we know it, or at least as we want to know it, is destroyed.

When you're comfortable with your main character and able to see the various permutations of the main problem, your next step is to design the opening of the show. If it's a TV movie or an episode of a series, start with a little opening "argument," a sentence or two of puffery about the basic appeal to an audience for your idea. Continue by writing down the opening just as you would if you were telling the story to a friend, saying a little about the leads and what they're involved in, and more—a lot more—about how they discover their need or how the problem starts. If there's a "B" story, or "sub-plot," mention that it exists, and give it one or two sentences. Since the sub-plot is minor compared to what you really want to get across, you don't want to use up valuable pitching—or thinking—time on it...yet.

This means being specific and, in effect, writing what will end up as a very useful summary of the opening scene or sequence of scenes in your project. Stretch out a bit and take up some room. Give yourself two-thirds or three-quarters of a page for this set-up. If you're writing about a mountain climbing accident in the Alps, use your skill with language to write two or three compelling paragraphs describing the accident and telling the reader what effect it has on the protagonist.

Here's an example of the beginning of a leavebehind recently sold as both a TV movie and a video game:

AFTER THE FALL

> Completely new, yet containing the elements that have made SPAWN, BUFFY THE VAMPIRE SLAYER, and 2001: A SPACE ODYSSEY so popular over the years, AFTER THE FALL is an anime style animated feature film centered on none other than Satan, the Lord of Darkness, himself.
>
> The "fall" of our title is not Satan's fall from Heaven but rather a

more recent development—the overthrow of Satan as ruler of Hell. Defeated by discontented demons, Satan has been exiled to Earth, where he unwillingly inhabits the body of JOSH FELDMAN, a sarcastic, alienated, New York City high school senior who has no idea that the Devil is imprisoned within his soul.

All Josh wants to do is get through his last year in what he calls "high school hell," but that would take much more luck than he has…because whenever Josh is tired or weakened by anger or unhappiness, Satan's attempts to escape his "prison" allow him to temporarily take over the young man's body, and Josh becomes the devil incarnate, with all of Satan's powers. These run the gamut from individual beguilement to mass destruction, with appropriate results. Messing with Josh in P.E. class, for instance, is an open invitation to getting your guts spread out all over the hardwood gym floor.

Here's the beginning of a leavebehind left behind with the late Leonard Katzman when he was executive producer of *Walker, Texas Ranger*. This too turned into a deal:

SURVIVAL ZONE

It's WALKER versus the elements when the private plane carrying Alex and Walker crashes in the wilderness, killing the private and injuring the lady D.A.

The backstory is simple: The two of

> them are going to testify in an ongoing
> federal investigation of a Ft. Worth
> gangster, and he has had his men sabo-
> tage the plane in order to stop them.

Not exactly three-quarters or even two-thirds of a page long, is it? That's because everyone who had to read this already knew the series and the characters and had a good idea of what would work for *Walker, Texas Ranger* and what wouldn't. And, in this case, there was no need to "argue" about whether the notion would have appeal, because the leave-behind was a follow-up to a telephone meeting where the logline (which for all practical purposes is the first paragraph of this leavebehind) was welcomed by five words from the showrunner: "I want to do that."

After you've pinpointed the beginning, move on to the middle of the story by giving some linking material (a phrase like, "as things develop" sounds too simple, but believe it or not that kind of thing is all you need) and then telling the major crisis that's the centerpiece of your idea. This can involve an unforeseen danger to the protagonist which may or may not be caused by the antagonist's escalation of his or her evil plan, or the protagonist's moral dilemma, or a newly developing but dire trouble for someone else the protagonist cares about... or for the whole world. This crisis should be something stemming logically from the problem or need, but it should still be unexpected. Not only is it better storytelling to surprise your reader or listener, but a good, shocking surprise will also keep the exec or showrunner from stopping either the meeting or reading of the leave-behind and answering the next phone call. (You want to make who-ever's reading read straight through, and whoever's listening listen straight through, because that shows that you and your work are making the best possible impression.) The surprise factor's biggest importance is in relation to the finished production—the most important job of any TV writer in our digital age is, after all, to keep the audience from pressing the button on its remote.

Here's the middle of *After the Fall:*

> By the time Josh figures out what is going
> on—that he has been possessed by the

> most powerful of demons—it seems too
> late for him to do anything about it…
> because Satan has now taken complete
> control of Josh's body, and Josh is
> literally lost within his own soul.
> While Satan causes chaos on Earth,
> creating an army of demonic humans to
> help him take over Hell again, Josh fights
> his personal evil impulses, trying to
> expose Satan and cast him out completely.

Could the writer have said more about the middle? Certainly. Did he have to? No. Because the surprise and the escalation are there right before us, and adding any further details could just distract the reader or listener or, worse, give him or her something to object to. And you never—never!—want to give a suit or showrunner any excuse in the world for not loving your idea or story.

The middle of *Survival Zone* goes like this:

> Now, while TRIVETTE leads the search
> party trying to find them, Walker has to
> struggle against the perils of the
> wild—treacherous rocks, raging rivers,
> hungry wolves—and find the way back to
> civilization in time to save Alex's
> life. During this man versus nature
> trek, he and Alex learn more about what
> makes each other tick, but just when we
> think they're out of the woods, Walker
> also has to deal with another kind of
> peril: more thugs, sent by the gang-
> ster to make sure he and Alex are dead.

In this case the transition from beginning to middle is made by the word "now," and the complications are sketched in, just enough to pique the reader or listener's interest and act as a further hook for making the deal.

Speaking of "now," now it's time to get your characters to the end. This means creating a new situation of heightened conflict and jeopardy that will serve as the climax of your story. In a big action script (perhaps for a TV movie, perhaps for Saturday morning animation—the possibilities could be endless), the climax can be something like this:

> The clock is ticking. The world is going
> to blow up in 30 seconds, courtesy of a
> neutron bomb atop Mt. Everest. The Hero,
> who's the only man in the universe
> who can deactivate the bomb, is bent,
> stapled, and mutilated seemingly beyond
> all redemption, locked in a trunk at
> the bottom of the Atlantic Ocean. Can he
> rise to the occasion?

In a one-hour episodic drama you'll likely find yourself creating a climax like this:

> The Young Doctor is exhausted from her
> efforts to kick her heroin habit. She's
> weak, trembling. But the Chief of
> Surgery needs her now, to assist in an
> experimental procedure that can, if
> successful, not only make him a legend
> in his profession but assure the Young
> Doctor of a staff position at the hospi-
> tal and even save the life of the sweet
> young First Grader whose father beat him
> comatose when he learned he wasn't real-
> ly the First Grader's genetic father at
> all. Only the Young Doctor knows what to
> do. Can she rise to the occasion?

In a half-hour sitcom this could be where you are at the climax:

> The Silly Star is torn. On the one hand
> his wife expects him to be at the

> Little League game where his not-very-
> athletic son is pitching for the first
> time because all the really good
> players on the team have the flu. On the
> other hand, his ad agency's biggest
> client is threatening to take her
> account elsewhere unless he gives her
> a private presentation in her pent-
> house—a presentation that may have
> nothing to do with advertising at all.
> Can he—ahem—rise to the occasion?

Detect a little similarity there, do you? The truth is that whether you're writing a drama, an action piece, or a comedy, the climax in general terms is almost always the same. The pressure is piled on. The protagonist has to either come through or psychologically (and maybe physically) explode. Your job in the leavebehind is to use another one of those easy transition phrases ("ultimately" is a common one; so is "at last") to get us to this set-up.

Then, if this is a TV movie, you're done. You've baited the hook, shown you can create an outstandingly tense situation, and if anyone wants to know the resolution, it's time to make a deal. If this is an episode of an existing series, you're *almost* done. You have to go one degree further and tell how the hero solves the problem.

Why the difference? Creatively, at this point there isn't one. You should in fact know as much as you can about how the story is going to end because when you outline and script it you're going to have to push things in the proper direction. But pragmatically something else is going on here. On the practical level, when you write a leavebehind for a TV movie, you're trying to get enough interest from the powers-that-be to pay you for more of what you've given them for free so far. What better way to get an assignment than to have your audience salivating for the finale? Or, at the very least, what better way to get another meeting? Besides, what if they don't like your Big Finish? You might lose everything as a result. (If they make a deal with you and then don't like the conclusion, they're not going to kick you out the door; they're going to sit down and work with you to make it "better.")

When you write a leavebehind for an episode, you include the solution because its brilliance is one of the most important reasons a showrunner will need you. Writing staffs quickly become exhausted from coming up with new premises. (No one likes to admit it, but I've been there and know it's true. The only thing more tiring than thinking up premises for a series where you're a member of the staff is working for a living at any real job.) Members of the writing staff of a series also burn out on great stratagems. A writer who can come up with a new and clever way for the hero or heroine of a current series to solve the big problem is worth his or her weight in contracts.

Here's the ending of *After the Fall* as portrayed in its leavebehind:

> As Satan and his new horde prepare to
> invade Hell, our setting changes from
> Manhattan to the vast, surrealistic
> Underworld. The demons who have been
> ruling in Satan's place are no worse
> than Satan but neither are they
> any better, and Josh realizes that
> he must use Satan's own power against
> both sides in order to stop the
> invasion…because the power unleashed
> in the hellish battle will destroy
> the Earth! Moody, ironic, and larger-
> than-life, AFTER THE FALL is edgy and
> different, challenging, frightening,
> and entertaining to the viewer all
> at the same time.

There it is, the big finish, communicated in language that makes the ending anything and everything the reader or listener can imagine, giving 'em what they want even though they don't know what that is. And with another sales pitch to top it off.

Survival Zone's ending goes like this:

> In the end, Walker vanquishes the thugs
> by creating a Native American trap he

> was taught by his father when he was a
> child. He reaches Trivette and the
> searchers just in time to save Alex's
> life by getting her injuries the
> treatment they need. Then they'll be
> off again to testify, with even more
> evidence stacked against their foe.

And again, the ending is right out there, no subtlety and no guess-work. It completes the shape of the episode, giving the showrunner exactly what he needed to know to choose this project with this writer for his show.

Want to create your own series? Then you need to write a leave-behind that will help you sort out what the series will be, as well as elicit interest from the development suits. Here's a few tips:

1) The basic idea for a TV series is referred to as a "series concept" or a "series premise." The document that states that concept is called a "series presentation" or "series proposal."

2) The series proposal is like a mini-business plan, where your series is the business. Instead of telling one individual story you are creating the overall context in which all stories will be set. If in the future you have the chance to write a plot for your series (a first episode that will show the suits what each succeeding episode will be like and allow them to gauge—or attempt to gauge—the performance and popularity your series will have) you'll sit down with a group of development executives and work out the story for it together.

3) The series proposal should begin with a statement of the general nature of your show. This should be a preliminary, half-page elaboration of the logline, telling the genre, theme, and general idea.

4) After that it's time to name and describe the main recurring characters and the general tone of their relationships with one another, as well as the kinds of situations in which they'll be involved. Explain as clearly as possible the kind of thing you envision happening every week and what the effect of those happenings will be on the characters.

Is your lead a single father struggling to raise his 87 kids? How did he get those kids? What kind of person is he? What does he do for a living? What kind of people are the kids? How do they spend their time? Do they love each other? Is the father the Sultan of Zambowi, with 87 children all trying to kill each other so they can inherit the throne? (Call me crazy, but I think that could be pretty funny.) While they're working on their assassination attempts, what other kinds of things happen to them?

In other words, what are the general problems? What are the conflicts? And, most importantly in a series, why will the audience care about these folks? The word "formula" is usually condemned by writers, but all TV series depend on a formula. This is your opportunity to develop yours, and, again, it will serve two purposes. The execs will see what's what so they can make a decision, and you'll know the basis from which you'll be working in the future if the series goes ahead.

5) The last section of your series presentation should consist of loglines for possible episodes. This shows the execs that the series has "legs," that is, staying power, and a variety of possible stories within its basic parameters. It also shows you the same thing. If you as the creator can't easily come up with half a dozen or so potential story-lines, then the odds are you don't really have a series here. If your interesting characters and location don't automatically generate interesting needs and problems and the conflicts that go with them, I'm afraid it's time to think of something else.

Here's a sample leavebehind for a television series. It's an award-winning sitcom premise that was optioned by a cable and satellite channel called VegaUniverse. Sadly, VegaUniverse didn't make it. The average start-up cost for a new cable or satellite channel at the time of this writing is $100 million. That's $50 million for infrastructure and start-up programming and another $50 million for what's called "carriage" by the cable and satellite companies. Carriage refers to "being carried by." That's right; whether or not the viewer is paying to see what the cable and satellite carriers are putting on the air, the companies that own the channels are paying to put it there. There's something very significant here, but that's probably another book.

And now for the sitcom series leavebehind:

GORD & STAN
by Stacey John Hoskin

Gord and Stan are both clerks at
'VICTIMS OF VIDEO,' an independent
video rental store located in a strip
mall in a suburb of Los Angeles. They
are both 20 years old, high school
graduates (barely), and as far as
they're concerned, as long as they keep
getting free rentals from their job,
they are set for life.

Post-slacker, post-doom generation,
these two guys are classic suburban
zombies, with no ambitions or moral
barometer to guide their lives. They
have been best friends since the age
of six, and have lived together in
a small apartment near their job since
graduating from high school. They
like to party and watch TV, and their
lives at home aren't a whole lot
different from what they do at work.

There is, however, one small thing
that sets these two apart, not just from
each other, but from the rest of the
world. Gord ("God" with an "r" thrown in)
is the Second Coming of Christ, and Stan
("Satan" minus an "a") is The Beast, the
Anti-Christ. Unlike films like "Damien:
Omen II," where the child of Satan is an
overachieving brainiac bent on world
domination, Stan just wants to know
where he can score his next dime-bag of
weed. And, unlike any religious film
you've ever seen where Jesus or the

Second Coming is a selfless martyr, Gord too just wants to know where he can score his next dime-bag of weed.

How has this come to be? Well, to combat their failures in these modern times to incarnate two people worthy of the titles bestowed upon them, God and the Devil have changed the rules of the game. The definitions of 'Good' and 'Evil' have been altered to accommodate the lifestyles of their star players, but their small activities all have literally cosmic consequences.

Now, when Gord does something "good," like let a late charge slide for a customer who had an accident on the way to return the movie, a tornado will narrowly miss a trailer park somewhere. When Stan does something "bad" like fail to inform a parent that a Japanese animated video rented by their child contains graphic sex, an emerging nation is invaded. Because Gord and Stan are friends and have the same lifestyle, most of the time their actions will cancel each other out, with the people of the world never knowing how close to damnation or salvation they really are.

Possible episodes include:

"Self-Improvement." Stan takes a computer class so he can reprogram the store's computer to automatically over-charge every customer. If he succeeds, a tsunami will wipe out Brooklyn. What can the unwitting Gord do that's good enough to counteract the "Stan Effect?"

"First Contact." Gord starts a video

giveaway program for local children,
which in turn causes an intergalactic
race of very good guys to head toward
Earth. If the kids are made happy
enough the aliens will arrive and bring
the world utopia. But that's a mighty
big "if…"

"That Long Lonesome Highway." God and
Satan (yep, they're regular characters,
too) have a little side bet going over
whether Stan can go 24 hours without
committing any evil, no matter how
small. If Stan is good, God will cause
the miracle of loaves into fishes at
lunchtime worldwide. If Stan doesn't
make it, Satan will cause New York City
to be on the route of nuclear waste
trucks.

"The Orange Blossom Special." Gord
falls in love with MARY, a girl Stan
doesn't think is good enough for him,
so while Gord tries to woo her, Stan
works on the alienation thing. If Stan
succeeds the polar ice caps will melt.
If Gord succeeds the show'll have a new
regular.

"Future Shock." At Mary's prompting,
Gord vows to stop wasting time and money
smoking weed so he'll have a better
future. If he succeeds, the U.S.
national debt will be erased. Meanwhile, Stan has just scored the best
shit he's ever had and wants to share
it with his friend. Which pressure on
Gord will be the strongest?

GORD & STAN is a cross between BEAVIS
AND BUTTHEAD, and OH GOD, YOU DEVIL,
with the soundtrack of DAMIEN: OMEN II,

and if that hasn't made you pull out
your checkbook yet, why not? How are you
gonna explain it to your boss when this
show is Number One on another network
next season?

This presentation is clear, concise, and complete. I particularly like the little wrap-up at the end, which summarizes the premise the way a closing argument wraps up an essay or a debate. It's also important to see how the concept is so simple and natural that it seems to invite every reader to come up with episode ideas as though that kind of thinking was a parlor game. The most effective part of the presentation, though, is its tone. Its hip, breezy good humor is perfectly in keeping with the tone the series itself should have. The language of the presentation tells both the creator and the potential buyer exactly what the scripts will be like.

Speaking of series and their underpinnings (and, come to think of it, God and Satan), now is a good time to bring up one of those concepts about which almost everyone who wants to get into the television business has heard but few understand: "bibles."

In TV, when we refer to a bible, we're not talking about either the Old or New Testaments. We're talking about a thick document, often 100 or more pages in length, containing detailed character descriptions, overall attitudes and cautions, long term character and story arcs, and breakdowns of individual episodes for a series. Invariably, new writers ask if they should write a bible for their series idea. Invariably, I say no. Invariably, the new writers are surprised. "How will I sell it without a bible?" they often ask. And, less often, "Without a bible, how will I know what the show is about?"

The answer to the first question is, "Bibles are very seldom used as sales tools, mainly because very few executives want to read anything that long. They want the condensed version, which is what your leave-behind series presentation gives them."

Now here's the answer to the second question: "In all likelihood you don't need a bible to understand your own show at this point. Bibles are created with the input of all the usual suspects—producers, directors, prodco, studio, network and corporate execs—and are used primarily by daytime serials and children's shows (both animated and otherwise) to serve as a guide for everyone working on the production of the show. That's "production" as in "scheduled" and "on the air."

Primetime series, with the exception of some science fiction and fantasy shows, which have to set out the rules of their unique settings, almost never use a bible. Why not? In part it's tradition: "We never used one of them newfangled things before." In part it's arrogance: "Bible? I don't need no stinkin' bible. I've got it all in my head." And in part it's caution: Society changes. The economy goes up or down. Network bosses come and go. New primetime series often have big stars attached to them, or small stars who become big stars by the end of the first season. All of these things can affect the direction of a show, but the most likely causes of shift in emphasis are the stars. The bigger the star or stars and the more successful the show, the bigger the star or stars' input becomes. Their ideas about what should happen next or which elements should be emphasized and which should be played down come out of the performers' visions of the characters they're playing and out of their own inner needs (and sometimes demons) as well.

As a result, what the stars want in a series is often quite different from what the creator and his phalanx of helpful executives intended. Showrunners are usually the ones who have written the bible and who believe in it most strongly. But a smart showrunner learns to adjust to the changes caused by success, meaning that the game plan has to be kept as fluid as possible.

There's little point in etching a primetime series in stone when you can almost always expect that stone to be shattered. And if the showrunner and the star or stars disagree strongly, any existing bible will be the first casualty. In any conflict between a creator/showrunner and a big star, put your money on the big star. When the dust settles, the star will have a raise in pay and the creator/showrunner will be gone.

chapter 8:
the outline — part 1

The step-by-step development of the story underlying your teleplay is crucial to its success, yet it's no exaggeration to say that for most writers, even the most experienced, plotting a TV movie, drama episode, action episode, sitcom episode, animation episode—you name it—is the most difficult part of the writing process.

I don't believe for one instant that there isn't a writer who hasn't sat down to work out a story and then thrown his or her hands up in despair, absolutely convinced that, "This isn't right! This scene doesn't belong here! Ohmygod! Ohmygod! I can't figure out what happens next!" All of us go through this at least one time or another—or another or another, but, "Damnit, Jim, we're storytellers, not doctors!" we can do this. *You* can do this.

Realistically speaking, you've got no choice.

In an assignment situation, once you've worked out the beginning, middle, and end and gotten someone to hire you based on that, you're going to come in for a meeting with the staff of the show (or the rest of the staff if you're already on the weekly payroll), or the development team if it's a TV movie or pilot. Together, everyone involved is going to dig in and "break" that story. They—you—are going to figure out every single scene you will write in the teleplay, with each scene defined as an "event," (sometimes a long one, sometimes just a moment) in the development of the situation you created in your leavebehind, moving it from the beginning to the end.

You're going to plan the teleplay like a military expedition, step by step by step. For a TV movie, that means determining in advance what happens in approximately 60 different scenes. For a one-hour episode, that means pinning down 25 to 30 scenes. For a sitcom episode, it means working out 10 or 12. For an animated episode, it means coming up with as many as 30 different moments. (I was once given an outline for an episode of the SpiderMan animated series that had 104 beats to be crammed into the half-hour script...a half-hour script that ran only 22 minutes!) After working in animation, you'll want to write a daytime serial even if you hate them; a soap episode is usually comprised of only five or six scenes.

Depending on the expertise and the experience of those involved, and on the subtlety, or lack thereof, of your idea, the meeting where all this goes on can take as little as a couple of hours or it can last for several days. It's not uncommon to spend a full week working out all the moves of a one-hour television show. And remember, this is only the "fun" part, the thinking and note-taking. After the meeting is over and everyone agrees on the order of things, it's up to you, the writer, to go home or to your office and press asdfjakl; and all those other keys and create an outline that not only serves as a blueprint for a great script, but is also intelligent, entertaining, and readable in and of itself. That's because even though everyone seemed to agree on how the story should go, the outline still has to be officially approved—by several people, including some who were nowhere near your meeting, haven't read your leavebehind, and don't know the first thing about what you and the gang have been trying to do.

During the story-breaking process, newcomers invariably are amazed by two things. Firstly, the amount of devotion and care that is put into each story. Who does what to whom and when and why and how becomes the most important thing in the universe to everyone on the creative team. Brows furrow. Tempers flare. A conciliatory voice speaks, "Calm down, everyone. We're not looking for the cure for cancer here. It's just a story." Invariably, the conciliatory voice is ignored. If the speaker were an actor in a Broadway play, that actor would be booed off the stage. I've often thought that if as much time and effort were expended looking for the cure for cancer as were in trying to figure out how to get Nurse Hathaway and Doug into their next fight, or Mary Richards from meeting with a new guy to realizing he wasn't right for her, cancer would've been cured long ago.

Secondly, they cannot believe the amount of story that gets packed into every television script. That's one of the ways TV eats up material. The medium demands that every scene carry the story forward, bring in a new twist, or cause a surprising reversal. No walking in place here, folks. No standing on the beach and gazing out at the sunset. No "meanwhiles." No "moving left," or "moving right." In TV there is only a steady and complicated march to the ending. If the basic premise of a story allows for A or B or C to happen, then the outline is the place to make it happen. Every scene—every moment—must be seen by the writer as a giant fork in the road, leading to endless possibilities, and at every fork the protagonist(s) and the antagonist(s) must make the choice and plunge into the future. Onward! Ever onward, march the 150 or so new tales that are told on television each *week*.

Why do television pros regard the outline as so important? Creatively, a strong, well-constructed outline means a strong, well-constructed episode. Practically, a strong, well-constructed outline means the executive approval that allows the writer to "go to teleplay," or write the script.

With very few exceptions, all television writing deals are "story with option." That means that you are guaranteed the chance to write an outline and be paid for it, but the prodco is only optioning your services as a teleplay writer. If the powers-that-be like the outline and believe it will work well as a teleplay, the prodco will exercise the option and you can do what you've gotten into the business to do— write a script. If the honchos don't like the outline they'll require you to revise it and make the changes they believe are necessary. If you make the changes and they work, it's teleplay time. If they don't work in the eyes of those who requested (although here the definition of "request" has been altered to mean "require") them, more changes will be demanded—I mean, asked—of you. If the execs still aren't satisfied this usually will mean the end of the assignment.

In the parlance of the biz, you'll be "cut off at story." The most positive way to regard being cut off is that the idea just wasn't as good as it sounded back in the days when it was a one-liner. The most negative way to regard being cut off is, "They hate me." As someone who has both cut off writers and been cut off by others, I can tell you with complete confidence that, human nature being what it is, you won't skate through your career without being cut off at some point, and you will *always* think, "They hate me." The truth is "they" don't hate you. They don't hate us. We don't hate you. The people who cut off writers—sometimes it's the showrunner, sometimes a prodco exec, most often a network exec—normally are too busy to make anything that personal. However, they're not very pleased with your writing, and if that situation continues it's not exactly going to help your career.

Why does television demand such complex stories? There are a number of reasons. One is that research has shown that most TV sets malfunction in some way, usually visually. Even if they don't, the images are broadcast on screens that make them small and hard to see. I know, I know. The modern world holds many marvels, including cable television that in theory comes in perfectly and big-screen television sets, but in the words of Richard Lindheim, former vice president of research at NBC, "Some cable companies have more technical glitches than broadcast TV. And projection television works only if you dim the lights and sit centered at the proper distance from your set. A viewer cooking dinner and watching can't be bothered with that." In all likelihood that viewer also can't be bothered to watch. Instead, he or she is probably listening. The more story, the more to listen to. The more to hear. The more to keep the viewer interested.

Another reason for telling complex stories is that it's a habit. In the early days of filmed television, executives saw themselves as being very much in competition with books, especially novels and films. Novels have the time and page count to tell a great deal of story. Films in the late 1940s and early 1950s were shorter and crisper than they are today, but they tried to pack as much plot as could be found in a 300 page novel into their 100 minute running time. "So it was decreed," according to Herb Solow, "that one hour television shows one-up movies by telling as much story in less time."

Paradoxically, another reason for story complexity is purely contemporary. "The current television audience has seen every story ever told," John Mantley, executive producer of the long-running CBS series *Gunsmoke* once told me. "That means we must come up with new twists to get them watching." And, I'd like to add, those new twists also help keep itchy trigger fingers from pressing the remote control in the never-ending search for novelty that television watching, in many cases, has become.

Another reason for complicated stories was offered to me by David Gerber years ago at a story meeting for a series called *Police Woman*. "We keep the scenes short," Gerber said, "because they can't stand scrutiny." He was joking, but there was an element of truth in what he said. The television production pace doesn't allow for the perfect shot. In feature films, with an average shooting schedule of 60 days, you can do 40 or 50 takes of a scene and get it just right. In TV we have three weeks (max) to shoot a TV movie, five days to shoot a sitcom episode, and seven or, at most, eight days to shoot an hour episode. That means four or five takes of each shot at best, which, in turn, means that mistakes that would be thrown away otherwise end up being printed and edited into the show. Feature films can be any length necessary to tell the story most effectively. All network television shows, and most cable and satellite shows as well, must be a specific length to fit into two-hour, one-hour, or half-hour timeslots, with several minutes (about 12 to 16) shaved off for commercials and various announcements. Make the stories too simple, and those short scenes will come back to haunt you when you don't have enough footage to fill all the available time.

Even when you're writing a spec TV episode, all the above has to be taken into consideration. In all likelihood no one but you will be reading your outline, but if things go as planned you're going to have a career in TV, where outlines are read regularly. Use this opportunity to practice writing an outline that is concise and clear and communicative, with the kind of story that those to whom you will send your teleplay expect. For your spec script to be perfect, the story's going to have to be perfect with just the right number of steps, happening in the right order. The right balance of plot and sub-plot or sub-plots, the right behavior by the characters, and the right attitude from the characters. The outline is where you make that happen. The outline is where you, working alone as a spec writer, have to do better than the brain trusts of the staff writers.

Notice, by the way, that I keep saying "outline." Not "treatment." The term "treatment" has been thrown around since the beginning of the commercial film industry. So, for that matter, has the word "scenario." After a literal lifetime in the television business, I still don't know what a "scenario" is. (No one's ever asked me to write a scenario. No one's ever shown me a scenario written by someone else. I *think* a scenario is the kind of sketchy, visual script directors used in the days of silent movies—but I admit that's just a guess.) I do, however, know what a treatment is. A treatment is a particular type of outline that in all probability you will never, ever have to write.

Specifically, a treatment is a 30-to-60-page work telling the move-by-move story of a film or TV show in the same narrative form as a short story or novelette, but written in the present tense instead of past tense. A treatment may or may not include dialogue, but it should be written so that the style of its language delivers the same impact that the film itself will have.

I've been called upon to write a treatment exactly twice. The first time was for a film that never got made—probably because my treatment was over 100-pages long. It was a kind of virtual novel that took me months to write, and it took the producers who had assigned me to write it months to read also. (I'm still amazed that Paul Junger Witt and his partner Tony Thomas still talked to me after that. Although, come to think of it, they never did hire me again.)

My treatment, like all of them, was a strange bastard, literally. Its literary elements detracted from the filmic possibilities instead of enhancing them. That's because when you write something in narrative you're not writing in scenes. You're telling the story but not showing the concrete instances that occur in the story. You're glossing over "fuzzy" parts, speeding things up or slowing them down for literary effect, instead of listing the scenes so everyone knows what the script will be like.

That's why TV uses outlines: so everyone involved can see exactly what the script will be like, especially we the writers. The standard format for a television outline has become the beatsheet or stepsheet. (Different names; same animal. Whether you call it a burro or a donkey it's still the same little equine.) There's no official format for an outline, but over the years they've evolved into a more or less standard appearance dictated by the usefulness of that appearance.

A typical outline for a one-hour show looks like this:

HEAVEN HELP US
Upstairs, Upstairs
Act One

1. EXT. LUXURY HOTEL POOL—DAY. DOUG and LEXY
   are sunning and oiling each other, leading to
   thoughts of doing something other than
   swimming. A nearby Watchman TV is tuned to a
   baseball game with Doug's former team playing,
   and the game gets his attention when the
   pitcher screws up. Doug's irate, feeling he
   should be pitching that game, that the team
   needs him. Lexy pushes for more, and he tells her
   he misses pitching. He loves Lexy, but oh for
   the roar of the crowd! Lexy's hurt by this, and
   the argument escalates until she stomps off to
   the elevator, heading up to:

2. INT. LUXURY HOTEL SUITE—DAY. Realizing what
   he's done, Doug follows, enters as Lexy
   bustles into the master bedroom for a change of
   clothes. Suddenly, the angel chimes twirl and
   tinkle, and MISTER SHEPHERD appears. In one
   hand he has a business card, in the other, a
   newspaper want ad for domestic help for a maid
   and butler. It all has to do with their next
   assignment—a man who's terrified that if his
   secret gets out, he'll lose his family's love.

3. INT. HOLBROOK ESTATE—DAY. JEANINE HOLBROOK,
   a mid-40s matron, living the wealthy life
   to which she always aspired, is up to her
   surgically lifted neck in things to do: Not
   only does she have to make sense of these plans
   for the new pool house, she also has to prepare
   the engagement party for her 20 year old

daughter, MEGHAN, and, to top it all off, lined up in the driveway of the huge home are all the applicants for the maid and butler positions that have to be filled.

4. EXT. HOLBROOK ESTATE—DAY. Pulling up are Doug and Lexy, she in a French maid's uniform that accentuates her good looks, he in a cutaway and bowler hat right out of an Arthur Treacher movie. To Lexy, this is a lark, but Doug's uncomfortable as can be. How do you keep these hats on? And the tails from blowing up all the time?

When they see how many other candidates there are for the jobs, both are dismayed—until Lexy gets an idea. Doug and Lexy become invisible, and, not so coincidentally, a tractor lawn-mower starts up. With no one at the wheel (or, at least, no one who can be seen), it picks up speed, roaring toward the wannabe members of the household staff. Résumés go flying as everyone runs for cover…

5. And, when Jeanine comes out the door to talk to the applicants, the only ones left are a slightly disheveled, grinning Doug and Lexy. Lexy's too beautiful, and Doug's too casual, but Jeanine has no choice. They're hired. Meghan tries to comfort her mother, but one thing is uppermost in Jeanine's mind: If only her husband hadn't fired the staff! Why on earth did he even think they had to save money?

6. INT. HOLBROOK ENTERPRISES—DAY. A huge place specializing in business stationery and forms. JOHN HOLBROOK, a self-made millionaire, is in his office with his attorney, CHARLIE MADIGAN,

going over recent developments. Computers are cutting deeply into Holbrook's sales, because companies can use them to make their own forms and no longer need to buy. Profits are way down.

As they talk, the phone rings. It's a major conglomerate that has been Holbrook's biggest account. John gets the bad news: As soon as this contract's up next month, the conglomerate is out. And when that happens, profits won't merely be way down, they'll be gone. FADE OUT.

Act Two

1. INT. HOLBROOK ESTATE—NIGHT. Doug and Lexy are on the job, in more appropriate attire. RITA, the cook, flips channels on her portable TV, looking for her favorite game show as she fills them in on the family: John works too hard, Jeanine is totally wrapped up in the social scene, and Meghan is a sweet, decent, down-to-earth girl. "What about these guys?" Doug points to a pair of Pomeranian dogs yapping and begging and getting underfoot. Rita shrugs, "You'll have to find out for yourself."

2. Dinner is served, with Lexy doing the best she can to cover for Doug, who just can't get the humility part of the job right and keeps inter-rupting—especially when John and his pompous future son-in-law, EVANS HILLMAN III, talk about sports. John is disturbed by the presence of the new household help. He thinks the family should try to get along without them, although he won't go into why. Evans thinks this is nonsense; what's money for, if not to spend?

3. Dinner is interrupted by the arrival of KEITH

WALKER, late 20s, affable, idealistic, and the architect for the pool house. He's right on time for a meeting everyone else has forgotten, and it's clear that he thinks Meghan is about the greatest girl he's ever seen—which Evans doesn't like at all. Both John and Jeanine like Keith very much. The only thing they have against him is that he isn't ambitious enough. He's a guy who'll probably "waste" his life smelling the flowers instead of selling them.

4. As the Holbrooks and Keith discuss the construction in the library, Lexy goes with Meghan to help her change clothes for an evening out with Evans. Impressed by Lexy's enthusiasm and taste, Meghan opens up to Lexy, and admits her worries about the marriage. It's such a strain being with Evans; she always has to act so sophisticated. Meghan really wants a man she can be herself with, who won't care if she just puts on an old lumber jacket and kicks back.

5. Downstairs, Evans is on the phone, and, as a "servant," Doug isn't invisible but might as well be. Evans is talking to his broker, putting in a "buy" order for some stock. When the Broker, who's been burned before, wants to know where the margin money will come from, Evans's reply is airy, "This is a marriage that will pay for itself." Doug wants to clobber the young man, instead "stumbles," and spills a tray of drinks on Evans's perfectly tailored suit. Doug apologizes insincerely and the fortune hunter rants, as we FADE OUT.

Act Three

1. EXT. HOLBROOK ESTATE—NIGHT. Doug is walking

the two Pomeranians, talking to them as he
would to the guys, telling one of his baseball
hero stories, acting as though the little dogs
not only are listening but answering as well.

Lexy approaches, hears Doug talking about how
much the limelight meant to him. When he sees
her, he stops short. There's a painful silence,
broken when Lexy avoids their personal problem
and instead points out that they have a lot of
work to do on their mission. Doug appeals to Mr.
Shepherd for some answers. All he gets is a cry
of "emergency!" and then he and Lexy see what
Mr. Shepherd means: the dogs have done what
Doug took them out to do—all over the tennis
court.

2. EXT. AIRPORT/INT. JOHN'S LIMO—DAY. Doug opens
the door to usher in John and the just-arrived
DAVID BARBER, president of a bank John's been
talking to about a new line of credit for
Holbrook Enterprises. They pull away from the
airport, Doug discreetly lowering the divider
between his passengers and himself enough
to hear the conversation. Barber's here to
personally check out John's company, and
both men know that without the bank's help
Holbrook will, quite literally, go under.

3. EXT. RODEO DRIVE/INT. EXPENSIVE SHOP—DAY.
Jeanine is shopping for centerpieces and such,
Lexy's there to hold packages and take notes.
As they enter the shop, Jeanine spies MARY, an
old friend she hasn't seen in years. The two of
them giggle like schoolgirls, truly delighted,
and for the first time Jeanine shows her human
side. She invites Mary to lunch—right now,
let's go—but Mary unhappily says she can't.

Jeanine pushes, and finally Mary tells her why: She has to stay in the shop because she works there. Jeanine is more embarrassed than shocked, but her icy, patrician veneer slams down, and she and Lexy head outside.

4. INT. HOLBROOK ENTERPRISES—DAY. John takes Barber on a tour of the printing plant, Doug staying off to the side, fascinated by the beautiful woodwork on the furniture in the cafeteria. The banker seems pleased with what he sees, with a "Yes" answer as good as given...

Abruptly, we hear a cry. A WORKMAN's arm is trapped in the roller of one of the big presses, and he's about to lose it! Doug races to the Workman and jams the press. The machine is ruined, but the worker is saved. Barber tightens. Instead of agreeing to the loan, all he can say is a wary, "I'll think about it." FADE OUT.

Act Four

1. EXT. HOLBROOK ESTATE—DAY. Keith is here with a disagreeable CONTRACTOR, showing him the grounds, while Meghan swims laps nearby. Bringing out some drinks, Lexy sees the way Keith's gaze keeps going to the young woman, and, seeing her chance, Lexy brushes against the architect. Into the water he goes, just as Meghan swims by. The two young people end up in a wet, embarrassed collision that dissolves into laughter and new friendship while the Contractor frowns and Lexy beams.

2. INT. HOLBROOK ENTERPRISES—DAY. Doug is having a cup of coffee in the cafeteria when John

comes in with Charlie, the lawyer. The two of them huddle together, and Doug overhears the bad news: Barber has turned John down. Charlie leaves to try and figure out a game plan, and John sits alone, his hand idly rubbing the finish on his chair.

Doug joins his boss, tells him he knows the problem. John hesitates, then says Doug doesn't really know anything. He indicates the furniture around them. It's in pretty bad shape now, but he made it, years ago. He loved every minute of the work, but the future was in the forms business—and now look what's happened. Maybe being a master craftsman would've been a better life, after all.

3. INT. HOLBROOK ESTATE—KITCHEN—NIGHT. Doug, Lexy, and Rita the cook are preparing dinner, Doug switching Rita's TV—"just for a second, I swear!"—from her game show to the news. In Major League highlights he sees his team in trouble until the pitcher who screwed up in the earlier game gets them out of the jam. The crowd roars, and Doug's first response is to be thrilled. Then he grows resentful. He should've been the hot guy out there! Lexy hides her pained reaction from Doug—but it's definitely there.

4. Doug and Lexy bring in the dinner, finding themselves in the middle of a Holbrook family meeting, in which John is struggling to explain the economic truths of life to his wife and daughter. The only person he's doing business with, he says, who is charging a fair price, is Keith Walker, whose final bill is less than his estimate. He feels like everyone else is picking his pocket!

Jeanine ignores him. Important decisions
have to be made about next week's party. She
appeals to Meghan, who now seems uncomfortable
with the topic in general, and with Evans in
particular, but even she doesn't understand
her father's desire to cut back. It's the
perfect time for John to tell his family what's
really going on, but although he tries, he
can't bring himself to do it. The truth seems
to just fly away. FADE OUT.

Act Five

1. INT. HOLBROOK ESTATE—DAY. Lexy dusts in the
   library, where Jeanine and Meghan are hard at
   work on the party. Meghan's more interested in
   talking about the new pool house—and its
   architect—than anything else, including a
   phone call from Evans, and Jeanine's getting
   irritated. There are times when she wishes
   John had never gotten rich. They've lost all
   their old friends—like Mary—and virtually the
   whole guest list for the engagement party is
   business associates. Instead of solving
   problems, having money seems to have created
   them. Maybe she should leave her husband, just
   so she can be a real person again. Then Jeanine
   realizes what she's saying, and stops short.
   But this time it isn't so easy to go back to the
   façade…

2. INT. HOLBROOK ESTATE – NIGHT. Doug and Lexy
   are in bed, things still awkward and
   uncomfortable between them. He wants to
   make love, but she wants to talk about the
   Holbrooks' problems. Through the window,
   they see a light go on in the guest house

across the way. Doug goes out to investigate, and Lexy tells him to be careful. He starts to agree, then catches himself. What if it is a bad guy? What can he do to a ghost?

3. INT. HOLBROOK GUEST HOUSE – NIGHT. The door is ajar, and, making himself invisible, Doug enters, sees John with a bottle of Jack Daniels. Hunting trophies and guns hang on the walls, and John takes down one of the guns. Behind Doug, Lexy enters invisibly. They look up toward the (they hope) watching Mister Shepherd, and he responds: It's definitely time for some ghostly intervention.

4. Doug and Lexy intervene, pulling out all the stops. Doug yanks the gun from John's hands, Lexy finds an old chain and padlock and rattles them like mad. Stuffed deer heads seem to moan and groan, and this is only for starters! In his half-crocked state John is sure he's getting a taste of hell. But, he cries out, like Scrooge to Marley's ghost, what can he do? Telling his wife and daughter the truth terrifies him. He's never known if they loved him for himself or his money, and, he admits, he's afraid to find out.
Doug works hard to make his voice sound spectral. Life is to be lived, not thrown away. There are risks a man has to take. And isn't the truth always better than living a lie? John doesn't know. But he's sober now, maybe more sober than ever before in his life. FADE OUT.

Act Six

1. INT. HOLBROOK ESTATE—BALLROOM – NIGHT.
A society band plays in one corner of the huge

room, while guests dance. Working with the
caterers are Doug and Lexy, in the same outfits
they wore when they applied for their jobs.
They're both good at what they do by now, but
they're still very worried.

2. Not so much worried as, simply, uptight, are s
   Evans and his PARENTS, the three of them busy
   making special demands for drinks and food.
   Also here, and not very happy, is Keith.
   Meghan finds herself searching him out, adding
   to Evans' irritation. Then it's time for a
   nervous John to go to the bandstand and make
   a toast.

3. Doug pours for him, and John raises his
   glass, starts the typical prepared father
   of the bride speech—then stops it, gathers
   his courage, and announces to the whole
   assemblage that he's broke. The first
   reaction is disbelief, but then Evans and
   his family realize it's true. They panic,
   but before Evans can tell Meghan the
   engagement is over, she says it to him
   instead. The groom and his family leave in
   a huff, and Evans, who has been smart enough
   to avoid Doug all night, finds a whole tray
   of sticky hors d'oeuvres dumped onto him by
   Lexy on the way out. At her husband's side,
   a grateful Jeanine sees it, and at last
   lets herself break out in a raucous laugh.
   My God, does she feel relieved!

4. EXT. HOLBROOK ESTATE—DAY. Doug, Lexy, and
   the Holbrooks are at the pool with Keith, who
   tears up their deal, complaining that he
   couldn't work with that jerk of a contractor
   anymore anyway. A couple of the pieces from the

cafeteria are here, and Jeanine proudly
points out that not only is John a hell of
a carpenter, he's already proved he knows
about ramrodding a business. The two men
regard each other: "Partner?" "Partner."

5. Meghan and Keith stroll off, and Jeanine
apologizes to Doug and Lexy for having to
let them go. They assure her they understand,
but what about Rita? "Oh, we've got to keep her
on. Real life is real life, but it would be
impossible without her, wouldn't it, John?"
John's answer is a grunt. He's hard at work
with his sander, fixing what the years have
destroyed. And just wait'll they see the new
stuff he plans…FADE OUT.

Tag

1. EXT. BASEBALL STADIUM – NIGHT. Deserted, dark
but for one light over the infield. Doug, in
uniform, is on the pitcher's mound, winding
up, throwing fastball after fastball, keeping
up his own running Harry Carey-like commentary
of an imaginary game. He strikes out the last
"batter," and from the dugout comes Lexy's
applause. She runs to him, and they embrace.
Doug worked hard to be a star when he was
alive, but he knows now is the time to work
hard to be a star in, well, the "after-life."
All John Holbrook wanted was for those he loved
to love him for himself, and that's all Doug
needs too.

2. From above them comes Mister Shepherd's voice,
and then the sound of thunderous applause, as
though the stadium was full. For an instant we
see it that way, as though packed with cheering

baseball fans, both Doug and Lexy taking off
their caps and waving as we FADE OUT.
             The End

Heaven Help Us was a short-lived syndicated series produced
by Aaron Spelling Productions. Because it was syndicated it was
divided into six acts and a "tag." Each of those divisions leaves room
for commercials and other announcements. Each of those divisions
demands its own beginning, middle, and end, as though it were its own
entity. Except that is, a tag, which is simply a wrap-up scene designed to
clear up any loose ends, close off the sub-plots, and leave the audience
feeling good enough to want more. (Unfortunately, this series didn't
make its audience feel good enough, and it lasted only half a season.)

Other syndicated one-hour series have four or five acts, and most
have what is called a "teaser" as well as a tag. A teaser is a short
sequence of one or two scenes that shows an action that immediately
attracts the attention of the audience, "teasing" the viewer into
wanting to see more. Primetime one-hour shows almost always have
a teaser. Even shows that don't have the teaser and tag as official
divisions in the production usually have scenes that serve the same
purposes. Primetime one-hours shown on broadcast networks and
most cable and satellite shows have four acts. One-hour dramas on
HBO and Showtime are usually written straight through, without any
act breaks, because they're not interrupted by commercials.

The *Heaven Help Us* outline lists 30 scenes, restarting the number at
each break so that the writer and reader can easily see how many scenes
there are in each act. Most hour shows are front-heavy. That is, they
have more scenes in Act One than any other. That's because the first act
is where everything that needs to be established is established. That's
where we get whatever backstory is necessary and where the need
and/or problem are laid out. Each act builds to a climax, and the
climaxes themselves escalate with more at stake each time. When the
four-act structure, which is still the most pervasive, is used, the first act,
including the teaser, is usually about eight or nine scenes long, with the
second and third acts about seven scenes each, and the fourth act the
shortest, with about five scenes, followed by a tag of one or two scenes.

Some one-hour shows favor cliffhangers as act endings. Others
play out the entire tense situation before the acts end. This is a matter

of showrunner preference. As credited ghosts for the showrunner, staff writers and writers on assignment do what the showrunner would. As new writers aspiring to staff jobs, spec script writers should try to do the same.

The *Heaven Help Us* outline is single-spaced and runs about six pages. This is a little longer than I normally write, but that's because normally I'm the showrunner and don't have to explain everything in as much detail when I'm the primary reader and the suits have already proven they've accepted my judgment and way of doing things by giving me the job. As a freelancer on assignment for *Heaven Help Us*, I couldn't assume that anyone reading the story felt that positive, and that the reader would be familiar with any aspect of the story other than the regular characters and their relationship and overall needs as shown weekly on the series.

Although it's not shown here, this outline has a title page because it's an official submission to the company that hired me. When it comes to title pages on outlines, most writers with whom I work do the same thing I do: We make it identical to the title page for a teleplay (except that instead of identifying it as whatever draft of the script it is, we say "outline"). You'll see an example of a teleplay title page in the following chapter. For teleplays, what font you use makes a difference. You'll see that later too. However, no one cares what font you use for your outline. The writers I know are equally divided between writing outlines in Courier New, Times New Roman, and Arial, usually using whichever font their computer has as the default.

Sitcom outlines look the same as one-hours, but are, of course, shorter. Usually sitcoms have teasers and tags. Some sitcoms forego the teasers and begin with what they call a "cold open," which means just that; the outline or teleplay is opening cold, without a teaser to warm up the audience. Sometimes they call the teaser the cold open instead. And sometimes the name cold open gets changed to "cold opening." It's all up to the showrunner. Sitcom outlines usually have two acts of approximately the same length, five or six scenes per act.

Here's a typical sitcom outline, for the WB show *Girlfriends*:

GIRLFRIENDS

"Mom's the Word"

Written by Bonita Alford

1. COLD OPENING—INT. AME JAPANESE RESTAURANT—
   DAY—(DAY 1) Joan is having lunch alone. Lynn,
   who's working a shift, is surprised to see her.
   Lynn: "What are you doing here?" Joan: "I'm eating lunch. What's it look like?" Lynn: "Did you
   forget we're going to Chuck E. Cheese later on
   for Jabari's birthday party?" Joan replies that
   she'll be there, she just needed some grown-up
   food beforehand. Lynn nods, understanding. Lynn:
   "Save some for me." Lynn goes back to work.

   On her way to the bathroom, Joan accidentally
   bumps into Eric Hastings, a famous basketball
   player, as he's leaving. Joan doesn't recognize him at first, but when she does, she
   starts to gush. "Oh my God. You're Eric
   Hastings." Eric: "Yes, I am. Have been since
   birth." They exchange pleasantries. Eric:
   "This is one of my favorite spots." The food
   is good, Joan agrees. Eric: "I also like the
   sophisticated people who dine here." Joan
   takes this as a compliment. Eric: "We should
   get together for drinks." Joan (nervous,
   excited): "Oh yeah. I drink. (trying to flirt)
   I do a lot of things." They exchange business
   cards. Eric: "I'm gonna be on a road trip for
   a few days, but we should definitely get
   together. Here's my private number. Call me
   anytime, but don't pass it around." After he
   leaves, Joan can barely contain her glee. "I
   have Eric Hastings's private number," she
   squeals loudly. Lynn gives her a funny look.
   "Well, I do," she replies, as she makes a
   sheepish exit for the bathroom.

   Act One

   SCENE A—CHUCK E. CHEESE—AFTERNOON (DAY 1)

Jabari's eighth birthday party is in full swing.
Sheer bedlam. The girls and William are there as
chaperones. Lynn: "It's the curse of single
people with friends who have kids." They all sit
at a table, completely frazzled from trying
to keep up with the kids, who are running
around, all hyped up on pizza, cake, and soda—
a deadly combination. The kids in Jabari's party
have on fluorescent green wrist bands. A kid
wearing a pink wristband reaches for a slice of
pizza. Maya gently slaps his hand away. "Sorry,
Mr. Pink Wristband. No pizza for you." The kid
sticks his tongue out at her and runs away.
Maya: "You better run. Like I'm gonna buy pizza
for the whole damn world on my salary."

That's the only reason Toni's there—for the free
pizza. Toni: "How did I get roped into this? I'm
horrible with kids. Why can't their parents be
chaperones?" Maya: "'Cause they need their rest.
It's an unwritten rule. When your kid gets
invited to a party, you can drop him off and get
some sleep. Hell, I wouldn't be here if I didn't
have to be."

Joan talks about running into Eric. "I can't
believe I have his private line. People would
kill for this." Joan retrieves his number from
her Palm Pilot. "My first celebrity entry," she
sighs. She asks how long she should wait before
calling. Toni: "You want to call him now, don't
you?" Joan: "Yes." She decides to wait. A beat.
"Okay, now." She calls with her cell phone.
"Hi Eric. It's Joan. It was great bumping into
you. I'm available for drinks next week. My
schedule's kinda tight, but I can do Thursday,
Friday or Saturday." Toni gives her a look.
Could she be any more pathetic? Joan quickly

covers: "I mean Friday's tricky, but I can rearrange. I know this great place for drinks. Call me when you can." She hangs up. Joan: "Oh my God. His voice sounds so good. You guys want to hear it?" Joan calls back so everyone can hear the message. Joan asks where Darnell is. She wants to play Eric's message for him. Jabari tells them: "Daddy's asleep in one of the tunnels." Maya: "See what I mean? Kids wear you out."

Joan wonders what Toni has against kids. Toni says they're too much trouble. Toni complains that they're self-centered, ??, and ??. Joan says it sounds like she's describing herself. Lynn wants to know if Toni wants kids of her own one day. Toni says, "Well, yeah, but I'll be married, rich, and have a nanny to help me." She talks about having a surrogate have the kids for her. One of the kids steps on Toni's shoes. Toni: "Hey, boo, you better get off my designer shoes before I forget I'm born again." The kid laughs. "You're funny."

Maya's exasperated. "Can you at least help a sister out and clear off the table? Is that too much to ask?" Toni agrees to that, but warns Maya against asking her to be 'Mama's little helper' in the future. This prompts Maya to ask the rest of the gang to start pitching in, too. Lynn says she'll do anything except clearing off the table. Since she does that for a living, it's the last thing she wants to do on her free time. William agrees to help, on one condition: he wants Maya to give him more tokens for the games. Maya tells him the tokens are for the kids, not him. William: "But I only need 200 more tickets to get the glow-in-the-dark paint. Yvonne and I are gonna have some fun with that later." Maya's tells him he's here to watch the kids, not act like one. William: "All right. You've left me no choice." He grabs a slice of pizza. "I bet that chubby kid will trade his tickets for this." William exits.

SCENE B—INT. CHUCK E. CHEESE—A SHORT WHILE LATER (DAY 2)Joan keeps calling and listening to Eric's machine. She grabs the closest kid and makes him listen. The kid: "Uh huh. Can you get a Power Ranger on the phone?" As the kid scampers off, Toni notices a little girl whose hair is messed up big time. Toni goes over to her.

Toni: "Hi honey. Who did your hair?" Girl: "My daddy." Toni: "Is your daddy Stevie Wonder?" The little girl smiles. "My name is Courtney." Toni introduces herself and offers to fix Courtney's hair. While doing this, they start to bond. Toni finds out Courtney lives alone with her dad. Courtney tells Toni she's pretty. Toni says, "Yeah, I know. And when you grow up, you'll be pretty too." Girl: "Really?!" Toni: "Yeah. Just don't let your daddy do your hair." Courtney: "Are your boobs real?" Toni good-naturedly smacks her with her comb.

Courtney's father, Randall, arrives to pick her up. Courtney rushes over to see him. He notices how beautiful her hair looks, and asks who did it. Courtney introduces him to Toni. Courtney then runs off to say goodbye to Jabari. Randall thanks Toni for what she did. It was no problem, Toni tells him. Randall asks her out for coffee. She says she'll think about it. Courtney comes back, tells Toni it was nice meeting her. Toni: "It was nice meeting you too." Randall and Courtney leave.

Toni discusses it with the girls. She has a strict rule against dating a man with a child because it gets too messy. Joan asks, "What gets too messy, the situation or the child?" Toni: "Both." They tell her that's the old Toni talking. She's been saved now. Joan: "Toni, you've been through a lot lately. You should go out. Have some fun. You could use it." Lynn chimes in: "You don't have to marry him, or even sleep with him…wait, I can't believe I just said that." Maya: "Go on the date. At least you'll get a free meal out of it. We're tired of paying for your broke ass." Toni decides to give it a try.

Joan continues calling to listen to Eric's message. Every time she hears his outgoing message, she gets giddy. Joan (sing song): "I'm going to marry him!" Chuck E. Cheese himself walks by (a guy in a rat costume). Joan snags him and forces him to listen to Eric's machine. After he hears the message, he says that's great, but who the hell is Eric Hastings? Joan says he's a famous basketball player. Chuck E. Cheese says, "Sorry, I'm a hockey man."

SCENE C—INT. TONI'S LIVING ROOM—EVENING (DAY 2) Randall arrives for the date, all frazzled. He was going to come alone, but the babysitter flaked at the last minute. He decided to keep the date and bring Courtney, instead of canceling. He plans to keep trying to find a babysitter so he and Toni can keep their date. Courtney suggests that Randall can go out and

get some food and videos and bring it back
instead. He leaves, so Toni and Courtney can
continue to bond. He comes back because he's not
familiar with Toni's neighborhood. Courtney
blurts out, "I really like Toni. You should
marry her and make her my mommy!" Randall has the
embarrassed look of a parent whose child just
said something inappropriate. Toni has the look
of a deer caught in headlights. She grabs a glass
of water and quickly downs it.

ACT BREAK
Act Two

SCENE D—INT. JOAN'S GREAT ROOM—EVENING (DAY
2) The girls are there. Joan can't get them to
listen to Eric's message anymore. Joan: "Who
can I play it for? I know. I'll call my mom and
put it on three way." Lynn perks up at the
mention of a three way, but she realizes it was
a false alarm. Lynn: "When are you and Eric
going out?" Joan: "I haven't heard from him
yet. I'm sure it'll be soon. My boo is busy."

Toni talks about what happened on her date with
Randall. Toni: "It felt like I was auditioning
to become a mom, and I think I got the part."
Joan: "So Toni, what are you gonna do?" Toni
doesn't know. "See, this is messy," Toni says.
"I didn't want it to get messy. That's why I
didn't want to go out with him." They suggest
that the best thing to do is break up with
Randall before Courtney becomes too attached.
Toni reluctantly agrees, though she doesn't
want to break Courtney's heart.

SCENE E—INT. TONI CHILDS LIVING ROOM—AFTER-
NOON (DAY 3) Toni has agreed to babysit

Courtney while Randall runs an errand. When he arrives, Toni pulls him aside and tells Courtney to go play in the other room. Toni tells Randall that she can't do this. "I signed up for coffee. I didn't sign up to be a mother." Randall understands. He was just trying to find a female influence for Courtney. Randall: "I'm not trying to marry you. I just want to have a woman in her life to help her be ladylike. And you're really good at that." Toni: "Wait a minute. You don't want to marry me?" Randall says not right now. It would be different if they fell in love, but he's only looking for someone to hang out with who could also help with Courtney from time to time. Toni: "Well, shoot. I can handle that. We can see each other. We can do this. But if my career gets back on track, or I find someone else, it's over." Randall's happy with the arrangement, and leaves.

Toni hears a crash from the other room. She calls Courtney into the living room. "Courtney, get in here and stop breaking my stuff." Alone with Courtney, Toni suddenly panics. She calls Joan for advice. "I don't know what to do. What do kids like? What do I do?" Joan suggests showing her a video. "Good idea." Toni hangs up. She points out her video collection to Courtney. "Go pick out a video for us to watch." Courtney goes over and looks. "What are Kegel exercises?" Embarrassed, Toni realizes that she doesn't have anything appropriate for a child to watch. Toni: "Let's find something else to do."

Courtney starts to bounce up and down on the sofa. Toni makes her stop. Toni: "I know that couch has a seen a lot of action, but you can't jump on it." Courtney announces that she's hungry. Toni goes through all her kitchen cabinets. They're completely bare. Courtney: "I thought Old Mother Hubbard was just a story." Toni opens the refrigerator. "Found something," she calls out. She grabs a plate from the fridge and puts it in front of Courtney. Courtney takes a sniff and screws up her face. "Eww. What is this?" Toni: "It's sushi. It's from that restaurant we went to with your dad." "What's sushi?" Toni: "It's raw fish." Courtney: "Yuck. I'm not eating that. What else you got?" Toni says she's not sure. What do kids eat? Courtney: "Peanut butter and jelly?" Toni shakes her head. "Mac and cheese?" Again, Toni shakes her head. Toni: "Is there a place that delivers?"

Courtney gets an attitude. "You've got a lot to learn if you're gonna be my mom." Toni: "Listen. I'm not marrying your dad." Courtney: "Oh, yes you are. My daddy likes you, and I like you. It's two to one. We win." Toni is firm and tells her it's not going to happen. Courtney starts to cry. Toni tries to console her. "I'm sorry I can't be your mommy, sweetie." "It's not that," Courtney says. Toni: "Well, then what is it?" Courtney: "Why doesn't anyone want to be with my daddy? Is it me?"

Toni: "No, no sweetheart, it's not you. If anything, it's your daddy." Courtney: "What's wrong with him?" Toni is taken aback by the question at first, but she decides to level with Courtney. Toni: "Look, honey, I don't know. Your father's a good man. A little boring, but a good man. I'm sure there's someone out there for him. It's just not me." Toni goes on to add that she knows how much Courtney likes her. "I know I'm stunning and hard to beat." Courtney interrupts: "Hey, don't get me wrong. I think you're nice and all, but you're not all that. You don't have any food, and I can't jump on the sofa. I just don't want my dad to be alone. He needs somebody." Toni agrees. "So do you," she adds. They make a deal. Toni will continue dating Randall on a casual basis, but her real goal is to find a woman who's perfect for both Randall and Courtney. They shake hands on it. Then Courtney asks Toni to take her to McDonald's because she's starving.

SCENE H—INT. AME JAPANESE RESTAURANT—EVENING (DAY 3). Joan is having dinner by herself. Lynn is there, working. Lynn teases: "Dining alone again?" "Shut up," is Joan's reply. Joan sees Eric sitting at another table with a woman who's not Joan. She tries to play it cool, but it's obviously bugging her. She decides to go over to say hello. "Hey Eric. You never called me back. Did you get my message?" Eric: "Yes, I did. All 40 of them." Joan: "What? I only called you one time and left a message."

Eric: "I have caller ID. Your number was on it 40 times. You can stop calling now, because I don't get involved with stalkers." Joan: "Stalker? I'm not a stalker." Eric's date chimes in: "Oh snap. This is the crazy stalker lady you were talking about." Joan tries to convince them both that she's not a stalker. Eric counters: "Yes, you are. Trust me, I've been through this before. Let me make this clear. Stay the hell away from me." Joan tries to stammer out an explanation but it's no use.

The more she tries to defend herself, the crazier she sounds. The other restaurant patrons begin to stare. Joan turns to address them. "I'm not a stalker! I just wanted to hear his voice." They start to shake their heads, and tsk. Joan turns back to Eric. Eric: "Do me a favor and forget my number. You need help. I'm never going out with you. And I guess I'll have to stop coming here. Too bad." He turns to his date and tells her it's time to go. They leave.

Humiliated, Joan skulks back to her table. She says loudly for the benefit of the others, "I'm not a stalker. I'm an attorney. A damn good one. Passed my bar on the first try. He's actually stalking me. He's not that cute anyway. I don't even need him. I'm married. With three kids. And a dog. A Pekinese. His name is Poopsie. Yeah, that's right. Poopsie the Pekinese. Life is good." Lynn stops by Joan's table. "Joan, could you keep it down? You're scaring the rest of our customers. In fact, you're scaring me. And that's saying a lot."

SCENE J—EXT. PARKING LOT—MOMENTS LATER (DAY 3) Joan gets into her car. She takes a moment to collect herself. We hear her thoughts in voice-over. Forget about it. It's over, it's done. His loss. She starts the car and has another thought: note to self—get his number out of my Palm Pilot. Or better yet, publish it on the Internet. She smiles and puts the car into reverse. As she backs out, she hears a commotion. Someone is shouting, "Eric Hastings! Eric Hastings!" She tries to put on the brakes but hits the gas instead. We hear a loud thump, followed by a man screaming in agony.

Joan stops the car, and gets out. She runs back to see Eric lying on the ground. Joan: "Oh, my God." Eric: "Get away from me." Joan: "Lie still. Don't move!" He replies: "Don't worry, I can't. I think my leg is broken." The guy who was shouting Eric's name comes over, but instead of offering to help, he asks for Eric's autograph. Joan: "It was an accident. I'm sorry. Let me help you." Eric: "No. You've done enough. Just leave me alone." Joan: "I feel awful. I can't leave you like this." Eric: "That's what I'm afraid of. Look, just go. I won't press charges. Just be careful not to run over my good leg when you leave." Joan gets back in her car.

End of Act Two

TAG—INT. PRESS CONFERENCE—DAY (DAY 4)
Eric Hastings is in a wheelchair. Joan approaches. She wants him to know she's sorry and she's not crazy. Eric calls for security and tries to wheel away. Joan: "Look. Just hear me out, and I promise I'll never bother you again." Joan once again tries to explain that she's not a stalker. Eric: "What do you want me to say?" Joan: "You know what. I've already said all of this to you. If you don't believe me, you don't believe me. But I wish you did believe me. I don't know why I'm acting like this. It doesn't matter what you think. I know I'm not a stalker, and that should be good enough." She turns to the two guards on either side of her. Joan: "Right?" The guards nod. "Whatever you say, lady," as they haul her away.

End of Show

This too is a very complete outline, written on assignment by Bonita Alford as a freelance writer wanting to be sure no one associated with the series could misinterpret anything.

There are proportionately fewer scenes in this outline because sitcom scenes are longer than one-hour scenes. That's because sitcoms have a more limited number of sets and outdoor locations (as in, most of the time, zero locations and only one to three sets), so there's no place to cut to. More importantly, because they're intended to be funny, sitcoms allow dialogue to run longer. Sitcom humor tends to be almost totally verbal. The last sitcom that relied on visual humor was also the first sitcom that did—*I Love Lucy*. With humor coming out of set-ups, punchlines, and banter, sitcom scenes just plain need more words.

Speaking of humor, notice that although there is dialogue in this outline, the writer, Bonita Alford, doesn't try to make it funny. Humor in outlines almost never works because the way outlines are written forces the rhythm of the speech to be off. Instead, she skillfully uses the dialogue to indicate the mood, tone, and meaning of her piece.

Animation outlines are the same as the others but tend to be longer than sitcom outlines, even though the finished episodes are also classified as half-hours. Scripts for animated series don't have the same deadlines as do those for live-action shows. Live-action shows are on, more or less, a weekly schedule with no breaks, because shutting down production for even a day or two and resuming with the same cast and crew means paying the cast and crew members for days they didn't work. This could cause a major budget disaster. Animated shows, however, aren't "shot"—that is, aren't sent out for voice recording and animation—until a block of scripts is ready. This gives everyone involved the illusion of having more time to tweak and tune the written material, usually by putting more and more details into the outlines so they'll be "just right."

Another reason is that animated kids' shows—and live-action ones as well—are in many ways infomercials for products associated with the shows. *Spider-Man* sells Marvel comics, toys, clothing, and other paraphernalia, and *Batman* does the same for D.C. Comics. Because of their vested interest in the success of these shows, and in how the various gadgets and doohickeys that will be for sale are presented, merchandisers often have a voice in the development of each episode. Material is constantly being added to please the merchandisers by showing them that their wares will be demonstrated in action and be integral to the story. It's good to keep this aspect in mind even if you're writing such an episode on spec. Getting the goodies in and putting them to good use will show that you understand the nuances, such as they are, of the genre.

Here's an example of an animation outline I wrote as a freelancer for *Superman* on the Kids WB:

"MATING DANCE"

(Beatsheet)

Written by Larry Brody

Act One

MAXIMA on her Home World, queen of a bunch of genetically screwed-up beings. She wants to improve the race, tells those who love her, who are monstrous, that they aren't good enough. Only one man in the galaxy is: SUPERMAN.

Maxima and her HANDMAIDEN teleport to earth, where Maxima sends out a "calling card" to attract Superman's attention: Using her special powers over matter, she turns an under-construction skyscraper into a giant robot that ravages Metropolis!
Superman flies in and vanquishes the foe, and Maxima sees that he's as worthy as she thought he was.

Maxima makes her proposition: "Come to my planet and rule with me as king. Together we'll have perfect descendants." Done very visually, with Maxima manipulating the very molecules of air around them to illustrate what she says. Superman turns her down.

Angrily, Maxima attacks him, this time using her physical strength. Superman overcomes the attack, stopping her without hitting her, by wrapping Maxima up in a steel girder. But then, to his surprise, she teleports away.

Act Two

CLARK KENT goes back to the "Daily Planet," and researched "relationships" on his computer so he can understand Maxima. LOIS thinks this must be part of a big story, realizes a big Pop-Psyche Guru is in town. She rushes off to interview him and, she thinks, beats Clark to the punch. PERRY turns to Clark: "What's that all about?"

Maxima has regrouped on her Home World, where her Handmaiden fearfully suggests that since Superman doesn't know much about Maxima, maybe he doesn't think she's good enough for him. Maxima is so full of herself that she never thought of that, but she's capable of learning, decides to do something that'll show him that she's the kind of woman he'll want. Her research has been complete, so she knows just what that is…

LUTHOR's in his office, holding a meeting, when, suddenly, the room melts all around him, desk and chair wrapping him up and whisking him out the window, where Maxima floats. As her "gift-wrapped" victim struggles—and threatens helplessly, Maxima flies him to:

The "Planet," where Maxima and Luthor float outside Clark's window. JIMMY rushes for his

camera, starts snapping pics, but Clark has to
duck out so he can be replaced by:

Superman, who has to reject the "gift," even
though he secretly wishes he could take it.
Maxima's totally frustrated, but if that's how
it is…She lets Luthor fall.

As Superman dives down to save his enemy, Lois
arrives at the "Planet," fresh from a very
boring meeting with the psychologist. Seeing
her, Maxima decides that the problem she has is
that there's another woman in Superman's life,
and she turns on Lois with a fury.

Act Three

As Superman deposits Luthor safely on the sidewalk, Maxima whisks Lois away, the two of them
vanishing. An instant later, Maxima reappears,
telling Superman that the only way he can free
Lois is by agreeing to be Maxima's consort.

Superman's super-senses find some residual
energy from the teleportation device Maxima
uses and, instead of agreeing, he shocks her by
grabbing her wristlet…and triggering the
device. The two of them shoot off to:

Maxima's Home World, where Superman's telescopic vision finds Lois, trapped on a volcanic
island. He flies to it as quickly as he can, and,
even though he's weakened by the noxious fumes,
he fights his way through a gauntlet of guards,
each of them former suitors of Maxima's, each
with special powers.

The third and final GUARD is the most monstrous

of the suitors—and the most obnoxious. As
Superman squares off with him, his super-
hearing enables him to hear Maxima telling her
Handmaiden that she's more impressed with him
than ever! It seems that no matter what he
does, Superman can't win: If he frees Lois
it'll just demonstrate how great he is, and
Maxima will never leave him alone. What to do?

Superman and the third Guard fight...and Superman
gets clobbered! Maxima soars in and sees it
all. The Guard is loathsome, but if he's even
more powerful than Superman, then he must be
the perfect mate after all.

Maxima leaves with her new king and, as soon as
the coast is clear, Superman gets to his feet.
Lois, who's been distraught with worry about
him, realizes that he was faking. Using the
wristlet, which he has kept, the two of them
return home, while behind them, on the Home
World, wedding bells chime...

The End

This officially proclaimed beatsheet delineates 17 scenes, is broken
up into three acts, and has no specifically labeled teaser or tag. That's
how the Kids WB does things, so that's how the showrunner, staff, and
freelancers do things as well. Most animated series have two acts, a
teaser, and a tag, but the number and placement of breaks depends on
each network's broadcast format, needs, and desires. This outline is
more stripped down than some of the other outlines shown here
because it came as the result of several meetings and intensive research,
where I was virtually inundated with *Superman* comics containing
stories about the character of Maxima, as well as forced to memorize
everything the series bible said about her and her home world.

I figured that everyone would be on the same page with this
outline, but after turning it in I learned that the Kids WB doesn't like

beatsheets. According to Stan Berkowitz, story editor of *Superman*, "the executives there find them hard to read." As a result, I rewrote the outline as—this is a confession—a treatment. Yes, it's "the exception that proves the rule" time. Animation writers for the Kids WB write treatments because the executives find outlines too no-frills. So after a meeting with Berkowitz and the rest of the *Superman* team I turned in the following:

"MAXIMA FORCE"

(Treatment)

Act One

EXT. ALIEN WORLD—DAY. A dark, mysterious plain pierced by tall, twisted, trees that create weird shadows in which two figures stalk each other.

At first we see only the shadows, both humanoid, one with four arms. Then, as the first shadow picks up the four-armed one and throws it across the plain, we WIDEN to see that the first is MAXIMA, a beautiful human-appearing woman warrior, while the second is DE'CINE, a cyborg with a metallic torso and a pair of metallic arms.

Howling with rage, De'cine flips upright, and a beam of energy blasts from his hand. Maxima dodges it, and four more energy bursts shoot simultaneously from each of his hands. Maxima leaps upward, but the last blast catches her, and she falls.

Instantly, De'cine throws himself atop the stunned woman, pinning her to the ground and shouting in guttural triumph. Maxima's body tenses, and she pushes the cyborg off her, sends him up into the air. He plummets back to the ground, lies groaning, unable to rise.

Maxima stands over him. "Too bad," she says. "And I had such high hopes. But you're like all

my other would-be husbands, weak and
unworthy."

As Maxima turns away, what looks like a HOLE
forms in the air before her. This is, in fact,
a transporter field, and through it materializes SAZU, Maxima's handmaiden, wearing a long
cloak and hood that keep her face shadowed.
"Your highness, we've found a new candidate!"
she exclaims. Maxima frowns. "This one had
better be better than the others!"

EXT. ALIEN WORLD—DAY. A fire roars through an
abandoned building, threatening to spread to
the occupied apartment houses nearby. The
flames force the last group of firemen back to
the curb, where, suddenly, their disheartened
faces take on new hope, one of them pointing
skyward. "Look!" he cries out. "If anybody can
stop this fire, it's Superman!"

We ANGLE with his look—and see SUPERMAN
soaring over them, carrying a huge water tank.
He upends the tank, and water spills down,
engulfing the flames. For a beat everything is
obscured by a cloud of steam. When the steam
clears, the fire is out. The fireman and Superman
exchange a quick thumbs up, and, as Superman
flies away, the entire scene dissolves and we
see that we're in:
MAXIMA'S PALACE, a huge structure that is
the center of government here on her home
planet of ALMERAC. It too is a place of jagged
seams, twisting planes, and foreboding
shadows, and the viewscreen on which we,
Maxima, and Sazu have been watching Superman
seems to have grown right out of the wall.

Quickly, Sazu sketches in what she and the
Council of Advisors have learned of Superman's
background. They know that he has great power,

and that although he lives on Earth he's
actually from somewhere as yet unlearned.
They know too that his headquarters is in
Metropolis.

For the first time since we've met her,
Maxima is pleased. Never mind the details.
"This Superman," she says, "is impressive
indeed." And, donning her transporter
bracelet, she opens another hole-like
transporter field. Sazu looks on thought-
fully, as, with a preemptory wave, Maxima
vanishes, heading directly for:

EXT. METROPOLIS STREET—DAY. Maxima materializes in all her glory. Pedestrians gape, but
she ignores them as she strides up the street.
Behind her, a HORN HONKS annoyingly, and
Maxima turns, sees a CRUDE GUY in a convertible
sports car pull up beside her. "Say, baby," the
Crude Guy calls out, "you look like you could
use a ride."

He swings open the passenger door. "I
know a place where looks like yours'll be
appreciated," the Crude Guy says. Reaching
over, he puts his hand on Maxima's arm. She
glares. "No one touches Maxima without leave!"
Maxima plucks the Guy from the car, and hurls
him into the air, leaving the poor jerk
trapped, clinging to a traffic light in a busy
intersection, while she moves on without a
second thought.

Reaching an ELECTRONICS STORE, Maxima
stops. In the window are a dozen TVs, all tuned
to PNB, where ANGELA CHEN is plugging her
tabloid-style news show. She runs down a list
of sensational topics—"The Secret Morgan Edge
Doesn't Want You to Know;" "Where the
President's Cat Really Spends His Nights;"

"Alien Invasions: Paranoia, or Are They Already Here?" Maxima watches, intrigued...

INT. TELEVISION STATION—DAY. The DIRECTOR yells, "Cut!" and the regular program returns. Angela rises from her stool, while the Director voices his concern that tonight's program still needs five more minutes of material.

Before Angela can reply, Maxima materializes between her and the Director, says she has deduced that, "This is a major communications center, is it not?" The Director stares, but the ever-resourceful Angela stays cool, tells Maxima she's right. "And who," Angela continues, "might you be?"

"I'm Superman's wife," Maxima announces.

Angela turns to the Director. "I think we just got our five minutes..."

INT. DAILY PLANET—LATER THAT EVENING. CLARK and LOIS are getting ready to leave for the day, Lois very pleased with herself for getting the lead story in tomorrow morning's edition. "You've got to be more aggressive, Clark," she advises. Clark shrugs it off, but then he hears something he can't ignore:

"Clark! Lois! Look at this!" The voice is JIMMY's, and he has a desktop TV tuned to Angela's show, where we see Angela and Maxima, as Maxima explains that while she and Superman aren't yet married, she is, in fact, his rightful mate, because they are the only ones in the galaxy good enough for each other.

We INTERCUT with the studio, as Maxima tells Angela that she is Queen of the planet Almerac, where she has proven herself to be the most genetically superior female. The planetary Council has decreed that she marry, but she will only marry a male who is as good as she. In all the galaxy, the only man who qualifies is Superman, so Maxima has come here to Earth to get him.

Angela finds it impossible to take Maxima seriously, starts asking mocking questions. As Clark, Lois, Jimmy, and the rest of Metropolis look on, Maxima's Imperial temper flares, and, with, "You dare question the word of a Queen?" Maxima's hand CRASHES down on the desk that's part of the set, crushing it like paper.

As Angela and the crew flee for their lives, Maxima starts destroying the place, and, in the newsroom, Lois turns to Clark with a wry remark about how Angela is making news now. But Clark is nowhere to be seen!

That's because at this very moment, Superman is flying into the studio, just as Maxima topples a backdrop. Its two-by-fours break over his body, and realizing who this is, Maxima pauses. But when Superman tells her she can't go on endangering lives and property, Maxima can't accept it. No one, but no one, has ever before told her not to do anything!

She hurls a heavy camera dolly at Superman, who catches it easily. Swiftly, Maxima pulls a section of catwalk right out of the wall, and throws it at him. The catwalk shatters on his chest.

Superman braces for the next attack, but now Maxima just smiles. "You've stood up to me as no one else ever has!" she says. "You truly are my equal!" Maxima tells Superman that together they will rule Almerac, and she holds out her hand to him. Superman shakes his head. He's flattered and says, "But I can't accept your proposal. My life is here on Earth."

Maxima stares. On Almerac, men have died for

the privilege Superman is refusing. With
uncontainable fury, she attacks him once more,
charging into him, pummeling, as we FADE OUT.

Act Two

INT. TELEVISION STATION—NIGHT—(CONTINUOUS).
Superman falls back before Maxima's
onslaught, doesn't want to hit her because
she's a woman. He ignores her insults, ducks
a blow that SMASHES all the way through the
building to the open air—and causes the roof
to collapse over them both.

When the dust clears, at first we see
nothing. Then there's a stirring in the
rubble—and Superman wearily pushes his way
out. From across what's left of the room comes
another stir—and Maxima surfaces as well,
ready to continue the battle. Desperately,
Superman looks around, uses his heat vision
to melt a sagging girder. As it falls on
Maxima, he rushes forward, winding it around
and around her until she's imprisoned with
her arms pinned to her sides.

Maxima, however, has a secret that turns
her defeat into victory. She tells Superman
that even though he has beaten her, he can't
beat her entire home planet…and unless he
agrees to marry her she will bring all of
Almerac's military might down on Earth and
destroy it!

Now Superman has no choice. Reluctantly,
he agrees. Freeing Maxima, he takes her hand,
flying off with her to:

EXT. METROPOLIS PARK—NIGHT. Superman and
Maxima walk along a grassy knoll, the lights of
the city all around them. The place is silent

and secluded, perfect for lovers, but their conversation is not lovers' intimacies. Rather, they are hammering out a bargain. Superman agrees to live with Maxima on her home planet, but she must also spend some time living with him on Earth. After all, didn't Maxima herself say they were equals? Maxima gets into the idea. "Fine," she says. "We can rule *two* planets."

"Well, I wouldn't exactly say, 'rule,'" Superman says. "You'd better see how I live."

And so, beginning the next morning, Superman sets out to show his new "mate" what his life on Earth is really like. In a series of scenes we see:

Clark Kent and his "cousin," Maxine (Maxima disguised, complete with dark wig) stuck in taxi in a Metropolis traffic jam—with Maxine not understanding why, if Clark won't fly over the traffic, he doesn't at the very least just clear it out of their way.

Clark, with Maxine looking on, being chewed out by PERRY for not getting any background on the Maxima story last night—with Maxine unable to understand why Clark lets this man, or anybody, for that matter, talk to him that way.

Clark and Maxine walking down a crowded street during the rush hour, being jostled by the crowd—with Maxine finally losing it and trying to clobber some poor guy who has brushed against her, Clark subtly blocking the blow just in time.

Clark and Maxine in the supermarket, where Clark shops carefully, sticking to his budget and doing his best to keep Maxine from simply taking everything she wants—and, of course, demanding that all those around them serve her "this minute."

As the day goes on, Maxima grows increasingly edgy, trying to get Superman to act, well, as she puts it, "Like what you are—a *superman!*" Superman constantly works at calming her down, but what he's really trying to do here is unspoil a very spoiled woman. It's his version of *The Taming of the Shrew*, as Superman attempts to show Maxima that just because a person has great power or high station, that doesn't automatically make him or her better than everyone else.

Also as the day goes on, something else is happening as well, and we INTERCUT the above with:

INT. MAXIMA'S PALACE—DAY. Sazu is watching all the activity through the viewscreen, growing more and more disturbed by what she finds there. She turns to someone we can't see, OFF-SCREEN. "Her highness has been at this all day now," she says. "This isn't like her. It isn't like her at all…"

BACK IN METROPOLIS, Maxima struggles to understand Superman's way of life, but when she sees Clark's tiny apartment that's the last straw. Once more, her temper flares. "You should be living in a palace, not some hovel! These people should acknowledge you as their master!" What she can't figure out, she says, is why Superman hasn't simply gone out and taken over the whole planet. Superman's reply is truthful: He can't figure out why she wants to rule over others when she could happily enjoy their society instead.

Maxima shows her rage, but, through a supreme effort of will, she forces herself to stay calm. Instead of ripping the apartment apart, as she wants to, she whirls and storms out.

INT. MAXIMA'S PALACE – NIGHT. Sazu's still watching, and now, she says, she's seen enough. "The timing is right!" Again, she turns to whoever it was she spoke to before, and we WIDEN to see that it's De'cine. He nods knowingly...

And so it is that, not too much later, the transporter field suddenly appears on a Midtown street. The hole in the air grows larger and larger, and De'cine appears, followed by a horde of rough-looking humanoids of all shapes and sizes, carrying dangerous-appearing alien weapons.

A pair of cops cruise by, stop at the strange sight. Drawing their guns, they get out of the car, demand to know who this is and what's going on. De'cine's response is a low growl, and when one of his minions raises his weapon, De'cine bats it down. Then, with incredible quickness, he lashes out with two of his four arms, sending both cops butt over teakettle, to lie unconscious against their own car.

The other Almerac soldier turns to his leader curiously. "Why didn't you let me blast those two?"

"For the same reason I didn't use my energy bursts," De'cine says. "We have to save our strongest weapons for a more formidable foe."

He pauses to let this sink in, then continues, "We have to save them for—*Maxima*." FADE OUT.

Act Three

EXT. METROPOLIS STREETS—NIGHT. No longer

disguised, Maxima walks through the city, deep in thought. Would it really be possible for her to live here? Her musings are interrupted by a cry, and Maxima rounds the corner to see:

Three STREET PUNKS are toying with an old HOMELESS WOMAN, skating around on her shopping cart and throwing her meager belongings into the street. Surveying the scene, Maxima doesn't quite get it, but still we get a satisfying result, as: "What kind of fight is this?" she says indignantly. "Three youths against an old woman? Where is the honor?"

The three Punks laugh mockingly, and Maxima steps into the light. One of the Punks recognizes her. "Hey," he says, "it's Mrs. Superman. Oh, man, I'm shivering in my booties now!" But his laughter stops as Maxima easily picks up the shopping cart with him on it, heaves it down an alley, the Punk crashing into a group of garbage cans.

His friends fare no better, as, off-handedly, Maxima scoops them up and deposits them, headfirst, into a dumpster. The Homeless Woman approaches Maxima gratefully. She doesn't have much, she says, but whatever Maxima wants she is welcome to take.

This is a situation Maxima's never been in before, and although she's moved by the Woman's gratitude, she doesn't know how to respond. Instead, Maxima hurries away—

And is stunned by an energy burst from behind! Maxima hits the sidewalk, and as she lies weakened she hears the gloating voice of De'cine. Standing over Maxima victoriously, De'cine tells her she has just felt the opening blow of the revolution he is going to lead on Almerac. The arrogant, trivial nobility will be wiped out, and replaced by leaders who care about the people. De'cine leans closer to her, almost whispers, "The first step in our battle plan is the death of the Queen!"

Maxima glares up at him. "Upstart!" she cries. "You'll never get away with this. Even as we speak, my loyal handmaiden is watching us. Any minute now, Sazu will dispatch the Imperial troops."

De'cine laughs. He snaps his fingers, and Sazu emerges from the shadows. She looks down at Maxima and tells her how she has always resented the way she was treated. "And now," she says, "it's time to put an end to it. A permanent end." She and De'cine exchange meaningful gazes, and the rest of the rebels start to move in on the downed ruler—

Superman, in the meantime, has taken to the skies, searching for Maxima. As he flies over the city he hears TUMULT in the distance. His telescopic vision confirms that the sound is from Maxima, not starting trouble, as he feared, but fighting for her life. Superman swoops down—

And arrives just as a laser blast from the weapon of one of the Almerac rebels CAVES in the wall of a nearby building, sending debris flying. After shielding an unlucky stray mutt and depositing him at what he hopes is a safe distance, Superman joins Maxima, and the two of them fight side by side. It's the two of them against a veritable army, with the rebels blasting away with everything they've got.

Both Superman and Maxima feel each blast, and around them the entire block is turning into wreckage. Superman knows they have to end this battle, and fast, before they weaken and are overpowered.

He gets an idea. "That bracelet you wear controls a transporter field, doesn't it?" he says to Maxima. "Can you make that field appear anywhere?"

"Anywhere I know the coordinates," she replies.

"You know their coordinates, don't you?" Superman indicates the rebels, and Maxima gets the idea. She reaches down to her wrist—

And the transformer field appears in the air over the rebels, hovers, then repositions itself directly over them. One after another, each warrior is sucked in, crying out as he vanishes. At last, only Sazu and De'cine remain. Then only De'cine. The rebel leader throws hand-blast after hand-blast at the field, but they have no effect. In a last-ditch attempt to escape, he rushes at Maxima, but Superman steps forward, and with a mighty blow sends De'cine flying into the transporter field, he and the hole in the air vanishing.

"Where did you send them?" Superman asks Maxima.

"To a prison moon orbiting my planet. They won't be able to transport out."

Superman nods. It's over. Both Metropolis and Almerac are safe. But Superman still has a problem. He turns to Maxima worriedly, and she smiles. "I knew we would make a good team," she says, and then she continues, explaining that her experiences here have taught her a lesson. Both Superman and the rebels have convinced her that the way she has always ruled has been wrong. Before Maxima does anything else with her life, she has to return home and correct the various long-standing abuses of power. She won't rest until that task is completed...nor will she

resume her search for the perfect mate
until then.

Apologizing to Superman, telling him she
knows this is hard on him, Maxima opens a
final transporter field, and, leaving the Man
of Steel with a kiss, she vanishes through
it. Superman looks on, amazed by the warrior
woman's attitude—and mightily relieved by the
reprieve!

The End

There it is. Fifteen pages single-spaced, "literary" and crystal
clear. I spent almost as much time writing that one treatment as I did
writing any three full episodes of *The Silver Surfer* when I was running
that particular animated series. (Both shows, I'm told, are now
"legends" both within the TV biz and with cults of fans, but I've got
to admit—*Superman* did stay on the air a lot longer. Because of its
treatments? Who can say?)

TV movie outlines are also similar to those for one-hour series
except that they run twice as long, with twice as many scenes.
Depending on whether the TV movie is being written for broadcast or
cable and satellite, and for which broadcast network, as a writer on
assignment you may be obliged to write the film with seven acts (with
appropriate climaxes), or with no acts at all, in which case the outline
is the same as that for any film.

Soap opera outlines are a different animal altogether. If you're a
sub-writer on a daytime serial you don't have to come up with an
outline. The head writer will send it to you. That's what head writer's
do. If you're writing one on spec there's not much to do either. Come
up with four or five emotional scenes for the show's characters that
are in keeping with the continuity as you know it. Then let 'er rip in
teleplay form.

chapter 9:
the outline — part 2

If you're writing a spec script and don't have staff and development people to join in your creative effort, it's time now for the tough part: plotting your episode or TV movie.

I still remember the first time I had to work out a story for a television episode. The series was called Here Come the Brides, which ran on NBC for, I think, three years. It was a western similar to a film from about 10 years earlier: Seven Brides for Seven Brothers. Both had to do with family of brothers who sent for a passel of mail-order brides to help populate Seattle in the days when it was a small logging town. Seven Brides for Seven Brothers was a musical. Here Come the Brides wasn't. Oh, it looked like a musical, all right. The show was shot so that the audience got the feeling that at any moment the heroes were going to break into song. But they never did it—at least not on the air. Bobby Sherman and David Soul, two of the stars, became pop stars as a result of the popularity of the series, but they never sang on the show.

See how well I recall this series? That's how it is when it's your first time. I can also vividly see in my mind's eye the way the studio gates looked as I drove up for meetings, and my body can still recreate the tingling of excitement I felt when I walked into the TV building on what was then the Screen Gems lot—and the sinking terror I felt in the North Hollywood apartment I lived in at the time, when I tried to outline all the moves of the story.

What a disaster!

It took me four weeks to come up with the various beats, and when I was finished I read my outline over and was forced to acknowledge a sad truth: nothing was happening.

The premise was that the hero, Jason Bolt, has antagonized a Big Shot Bad Guy, so the BSBG hires a gunslinger to take Jason out. But when the gunslinger gets to Seattle and meets Jason, he likes him and doesn't want to go through with the job. In those days people in television loved loglines that combined two already familiar stories into one "new" story. This episode, titled "The Manner of a Friend" (my God, I can't believe I even remember that!), was supposed to be *Shane* meets *The Quiet Man*.

After almost a month, however, all I had was *High Noon* meets *Waiting for Godot*. Jason Bolt, his brothers, the brides, and the gunslinger hung around together and joked and sawed some trees and got into a big saloon brawl and discussed the meaning of life and then, for no reason other than it was how westerns with gunslingers in them always ended, Jason and the gunslinger put on their guns and made the long walk down Main Street to see who was faster on the draw.

Knowing that I was already in big trouble for having taken so long and that I'd be even worse off if I continued gnawing on what was proving to be this indigestible bone, I got in my car, drove the outline over to the studio, and waited for the axe to fall. Instead, I got lucky. The story editor with whom I worked (really *for* whom, don't forget) was Bill Blinn, who has since gone on to write and produce *The Rookies, Roots, Eight Is Enough, Heaven Help Us* (a series with which you are now totally familiar), and a whole lotta others. He also wrote the original version of the television movie *Brian's Song*, for which he won not only an Emmy but also a Peabody Award.

So, Bill reads this outline while I'm sitting there and shakes his head. Then he looks up at me, and reads me the riot act, including the remarkable question, "Why didn't you tell me you didn't know how to plot?" And then the son of a bitch, as we storytellers also like to say, sits back and sighs and says, "Don't worry. I'll fix it."

And he did.

Overnight.

In four hours Bill Blinn wrote the story I couldn't come up with after four weeks. How? Because "the son of a bitch" knew what he was doing!

He called me over to his office at Screen Gems the next day and give me the beatsheet he had dashed off. Reading it, I didn't know whether to laugh or cry. I admired the guy for what he'd done...and I hated him. I hated him for doing something I couldn't do. Something I was afraid I'd never be able to do. And if I couldn't do it, if I couldn't plot out a story, then I could never succeed as a television writer.

I took Blinn's version of the outline home and read it again. And again. I read it not only to see what was there but to see how it got there. And then I swallowed my pride and called him and asked a few questions about what he'd done.

I figured he thought I was an idiot for failing. I figured he'd laugh when I questioned him, or puff up pompously and let me have it with both barrels of a figurative shotgun. I figured he'd lost all faith in me as a writer for this episode or this series and that I'd be cut off and never work again.

I figured wrong.

Bill Blinn was flattered that I was picking his brain. No one had ever tried to do that before. (Hey, it's hard to pick brains and nurse wounds at the same time.) He'd thought about my ignorance, youth (I was 23), and inexperience. "Of course you don't know how to plot," he said. "You're just starting out. You're so green you didn't even realize that you were already halfway there."

"Halfway there? What're you talking about? I didn't have anything!"

"Sure you did," Blinn said. "You had the opening scene [the teaser where Jason and the gunfighter meet]. You had the centerpiece [the bar fight that ended Act Two]. And you had the ending [the gunfight complete with all its preparations]. You just didn't play them out quite right—and you didn't make full use of the material just waiting to be dropped in between those moments. "You'll get there," Blinn added. "Just give yourself time."

And, sure enough, he was right. I got there. It took me seven years.

For seven years I wrote and climbed the ladder, and even became a producer, but during that time, working out a story was agony to me. Plotting was a fate worse than death. I tried everything—index cards, the Magic 8-Ball, you name it. But I was always left struggling, writing like a man trying to tramp through the desert, barely able to raise and move one leg at a time.

And then one day I got it. It was epiphany time.

After some time spent as the entire writing staff of a new series just coming out of the gate called *Baretta*, I was back at what used to be Screen Gems but since had become Columbia Pictures Television, working as executive story consultant of another new series called *Gibbsville*. *Gibbsville* was based on short stories by the brilliant John O'Hara, and every hour episode was adapted from two of them. I was slaving over an outline when it came to me: *You don't have to work so hard. You've got the short stories in front of you. Each one has one or two great moments. You've just got to drop some material in between.*

And, with that, I understood what Blinn had told me. What he'd been telling me as we continued to work together, on and off, on various shows he ran during those seven years. Plotting a television script—plotting anything—is like working a puzzle. You start with certain pieces in place, guide points, you might call them. Your job is to fill in the blanks.

Once you approach story creation as a situation in which you have A and you have maybe F and you have P and a piece we can call Z, it's a lot simpler to break your work up into the smaller tasks of simply coming up with B through E, and then G through O, and then Q through Y. It's like making a map. You have a starting point, an end point, and certain towns you're going to visit along the way. Now you have to work out the route that will take you there, and find other colorful sites to pass through as well.

Non-writers invariably are puzzled when writers tell them coming up with a story is hard work. "What can be hard?" the non-writers will say. "You've already got a great idea and some great characters. Your story should tell itself!"

"Should tell itself," yes, but too often the story doesn't do what it should—unless you as the writer know how to cajole it in the right direction. How to fill in the blanks.

The first thing you have to do—the thing Bill Blinn was trying to explain to me—is see where the blanks are...and where they are *not*. You have to understand the pattern you're creating, and what elements are necessary to complete that creation.

By being able to do that I cut down my work time considerably and amaze my friends and colleagues wherever I go. I sit in my office, a Showrunner God, because I can break an hour story from scratch in a day. Scene by scene. Moment by moment. Thirty scenes with conflict and humor and tension that keeps increasing. Thirty scenes that tell a story with action and human meaning and make the viewer want to come back next week for more (or so it is devoutly to be hoped).

Here's the trick:

Don't even try to write your outline sequentially. Taking things in order and trying to move forward by playing the mental game of, "What should happen next?" is an inefficient waste of time and effort. When a writer works that way, he or she is always in a defensive position, playing the game of wondering, "If that happens, then the result will be this. But if this happens, the result will be that…" Sitting and scratching your head and creating hypothetical situations involving human beings who exist only in your mind isn't very efficient. And we've already agreed that it's torture instead of fun, so why bother?

Instead, skip around. Write down the scenes that come quickly and easily first. Then fit the other scenes around them. To tickle my story into "telling itself" I use three separate sets of guidelines, integrating them with each other as I go along. I start by using the storytelling elements inherent in television format to design as much of the story as possible—that is, to fill in the first round of blanks. Then I start over, using what I think of as the "essential scenes" in the genre in which I'm working—or the essential or common scenes usually found in the specific series for which I'm writing—as the next set of touchstones. Then I start over again, filling in whatever gaps are left by letting the backgrounds and personalities of the main characters guide their behavior. All three of these procedures depend on the already existing triangle created by the leavebehind because I'm filling in the points between the leavebehind's three bases—the beginning, the middle, and the end.

I especially enjoy using what is, after all, the arbitrary television format for my own creative benefit. I'm turning the act breaks and artificial climax construction originated for purely economic reasons into genuine artistic assets. Instead of seeing them as constraints and bitching about them, I view them as tools and feel grateful to have them at hand. In the typical one-hour four-act structure I start out by making the beginning of my leavebehind the teaser, or, if the show I'm writing doesn't have a teaser, the first sequence of scenes in Act One. The middle I describe oh so eloquently in my leavebehind becomes the last scene or sequence of scenes in Act Two, not only because that's the middle of the episode but also because it's a heightened moment and television demands that the second act end on that kind of climactic note. That leaves me with the ending, which usually fits in perfectly as the last half of Act Four. Or, depending on the series, it may even become *all* of Act Four.

Think of it. At this point I've probably got one-fourth of the script outlined without having had to think of one new story point. And, with a little stretching I can go even further.

By "stretching" I mean that the television format demands that the tag, whether it be a separate section in the teleplay or merely the last scene, be a wrap-up scene, so again with very little brain drain I've come up with another scene. I know, generically, what the tag will be. The most important players in the regular cast—in terms of the premise as stated in the leavebehind—will get together and relax.

The TV format also demands that the scene after the teaser be some kind of reaction to whatever's happened in the teaser. For example: "The body's over here, Detective. Three bullet wounds, two to the head, one to the abdomen," or "Carter, I don't care if it's your day off! Get down here to the E.R. There's been a 38-car collision on the Kennedy Expressway and the injured are pouring in!"

Similarly, I know that the first scene in Act Three is either going to be the resolution to the immediate crisis created at the end of Act Two, or its aftermath if that crisis was resolved. And if the first scene in Act Three isn't the aftermath, then the next scene will be—because the audience needs a break from the physical action or emotional turmoil here. It needs a "slow scene" the way a CD needs slow songs periodically. Everyone has to take a breath so that we can get started building up the tension again for the *real* climax, which we've already placed in Act Four. Oh, and by knowing what happens in Act Four, I know how Act Three has to end. Act Three has to end by getting us there. In a one-hour show, Act Three usually ends with the solution to the problem known but not yet applied.

In an action series, with its melodramatic exaggeration, that means the good guys are pretty damn sure of whodunit but haven't yet caught the baddie. This, in turn, leads to the realization of terrible danger directly ahead: "Oh no, John Jacob Jingleheimer Schmidt's the one who's been offing all those hookers. And look, he's got Beale Street circled on the map, and this diary entry for today—'Tonight's the night.' Allyson's undercover as a Beale streetwalker. We've got to get there and stop him before he kills our more-gorgeous-than-any-lady-cop-has-ever-been partner!"

The drama show variant of this situation is, by definition, less melodramatic but by no means less psychologically intense. On a medical show the doctors know the patient will die unless he or she has a necessary surgery, but the surgery is yet to come. In fact, it may still have to be okayed because the victim is a Christian Scientist, or a minor whose parents can't be located to sign off. On a family show, the troubled youngest daughter has run away from home, realizes she's mixed up with a very wrong crowd, and knows she's got to get back to "Midvale," but doesn't yet know how to get away. On a legal show, new evidence against the heroes' client has just materialized, or there's a new witness who can save the client—if they can convince the witness to testify.

And we're not done yet. Because one act ending is still unaccounted for—that of Act One. Act One usually ends with a twist—the creation of a new threat, of simmering jeopardy: the bad guy planning his next crime; the defendant's lawyer getting the defendant released on a technicality; the doctor's wife leaving him when he needs to focus all his attention on the medical situation regardless of what it'll cost him as a human being. And once we know the end of Act One we know the beginning of Act Two because it's the logical outgrowth. Act Two begins with the immediate result of the danger about which we just learned: the crime or the gathering at the scene after the crime; the lawyers regrouping and strategizing; the doctor reaching for his bottle of whiskey or ampoule of smack.

There. We're finished filling in the blanks using television format as our guide, with about half of the scenes roughed in. Yes, for the most part the new material is generic. It needs to be made more specific—does the bad guy really have an entry in his diary saying he's going to kill tonight? Probably not. But somewhere in the room is a clue that'll give the cops the same information. It's just a matter of pinning it down.

I move closer to pinning down the specifics at the same time I add more generic scenes by going to my next set of touchstones, the scenes that are essential to either the genre or this particular show. For example, I know that on one of the *CSI* shows the forensics specialists will find writing imprints or hair or soil samples or something else I can come up with by doing a little research to replace the diary at the end of Act Three. I know that on *Law & Order* the assistant D.A. will either discuss a new strategy with his assistant and then be summoned into the boss's office to report, or he'll be summoned first and called to task for having failed to keep the defendant locked up and then he'll get together with his assistant and work out a plan. On *ER* I know that the tag won't necessarily be a total resolution. A problem presented as a sub-plot will still be outstanding, and the last moment of the episode may well be an unhappy realization on the part of the regular or regulars involved.

Speaking of sub-plots, this is where I start inserting them. Again, using the leavebehind as a guide, I go back through the outline and plant the necessary steps of the sub-plot at key places…the places where the specific series always plants them. Right before a crisis in the main story, or right after. Or right before or after a major move in the main story—on the doctor's way to surgery, after the married couple in the family show get out of their car, home from a miserable evening…that kind of thing. The more I know about the series, the better I can do the job of putting in the sub-plot or sub-plots. If you're writing a spec, the more research you do the better off you'll be.

For most series, the essential scenes of the genre are incorporated into the essential scenes of the show. Any show (or film or novel for that matter) in the private detective genre always has a hiring scene where someone puts the private eye on the case. This leads to two or three other scenes between the detective and the client, often showing disagreement between the two on how the case should be handled. Often the private eye becomes suspicious of the employer, and for good reason because inevitably the client is holding back some vital informa-tion that puts the detective and the client at moral and ethical odds.

Police dramas don't have hiring scenes, but they do always have the detectives arriving at the scene of the crime. They also always have two or three or more "bullpen scenes" where the detectives are at head-quarters continuing the investigation and interacting on a personal basis that involves the sub-plot. A recent addition to the essential scenes in this genre is the "grilling-the-suspect" scene. Whole episodes have been written about what goes on in "the box." Another essential scene that won't go away even though critics always complain about it is the one where the hero-detective or detectives have it out with the hard-nosed boss, the lieutenant or captain who wants them to work the case his way and not theirs.

Medical show essentials include at least one emergency procedure, a tricky surgery, conflict between the chief of staff or chief of medicine or chief of emergency or chief of surgery or chief of chiefs and the brilliant but independent younger hero. Ethical conflicts abound. Personal vendettas between staff members exist but are put aside so a patient can be saved. Someone has sex in a storage closet. Someone secretly has a fatal illness. Everyone's marriage or other relationships are in trouble.

Legal show essentials parallel those of medical shows in many ways. The senior partner of the big law firm is usually in conflict with younger, more idealistic lawyers who work there. Conflicts of interest involve every character. Staff members are at each other's throats or having secret (or not-so-secret) affairs. On most legal shows, points of law are glossed over in favor of evidentiary matters, because having the lawyers function as investigators is more visual and more interesting than having them flip pages in the law library. Every legal show has one hearing where things go wrong for the hero or heroes but usually ends with a scene where things appear to be going wrong but end up right—often because "our" lawyer has tricked a witness or the accused into saying too much and turning the jury against him or her.

It's a dog-eat-dog world out there in genre land, no doubt about it. Science fiction has its essential scenes. Fantasy has different essential scenes. Family drama has its own scenes. The superhero genre has its obligatory moments. Softer kids shows have theirs. I'd like to supply all of them but I don't have the space. It's your job as a writer to know all the pivotal points. You accumulate this knowledge by continuously reading and watching until the patterns of various types of shows and literature are ingrained in you—like that golf swing of Tiger Woods's I mentioned earlier. The best writing is writing that follows the writer's instincts. Your responsibility to yourself as an artist and to your audience is to develop your instincts to the fullest.

I realize that what I've said here can be misconstrued into, "Go for the stereotype! Write the cliché! Cling to the formula!" This would be a big misunderstanding. I view the need to include essential scenes in drama the same way I view the need for every story to have a beginning, a middle, and an end. It's not a formula, it's a way of satisfying an audience that has proven itself over time. Just as a story without an ending feels incomplete, so does a fantasy show without a quest. Certain events move an audience. That's why they're there. Certain events work and make the entire story work as well. Take those events away and the audience is confused, dissatisfied—and ultimately scarce. This isn't a matter of giving viewers what they've had before because they want it, it's a matter of giving them what they need. The essential scenes are the equivalent of the elements Joseph Campbell lays out as present in every myth. They reflect primal human hungers, and to deny those hungers is to act at your own peril. If you don't fulfill your audience you won't have one for very long.

At this point in the plotting process I usually have about three-quarters of the scenes I need. What's left most often are the linking scenes, and more specifics that have to do with the characters them-selves within existing scenes. So now is when I let the characters have their say.

In terms of television storytelling Sartre's proclamation that "existence precedes essence" means that in any specific situation a character must behave according to that character's personality as determined by his or her history and experience within the current story or backstory, or within the series as a whole. Faced with a beautiful woman from another planet, Captain Kirk wouldn't be true to himself if he didn't make love to her. Faced with a supremely logical alien creature, Spock wouldn't be true to himself if he didn't try to defeat that creature by showing how well "illogic" works for humans. Faced with an engineering crisis caused by a beautiful and logical alien woman, Dr. McCoy wouldn't be Dr. McCoy if he didn't throw up his hands and cry, "Dammit, Jim, I'm a doctor not an engineer!"

The personalities of Kirk, McCoy, and Spock seem to guide us from plot point to plot point by taking the characters and the starship Enterprise from scene to scene in terms of their relationships. I say "seem" because the needs of the story are what actually take the characters from scene to scene, but the characters' personalities make the transitions more specific. Kirk's frequent romantic interludes service the plot point of "Kirk tries to convince the alien leader to abandon her evil plan," but the method the writers choose for Kirk comes out of his characterization.

This holds true for all characters on all shows. The more you know about them—the more fully they've been developed—the more you can use them to get you where you need to go. Let's say *ER* has a sub-plot in which rebellious Dr. Doug is going to come dangerously close to being forced off the staff. Let's say further that the best way to put him in a vulnerable position is for him to not show up for work and thereby endanger the lives of several adorable little pediatric patients. Your outline may show the following sequence:

> Act X/Scene Y: The Chief of Staff is personally disappointed in Doug and wants to fire him.
> Act X/Scene Y + 1: Two schoolgirls come into the E.R. with symptoms that could be food poisoning or a rare illness found only in Malaysia, where they've just been with their father. Doug's the only doctor at the hospital who can tell the difference, but Doug's not there. No one knows where he is.
> Act X/Scene Y + 2: Nurse Hathaway was with Doug when he learned about the Malaysian flu, so she disguises herself in a George Clooney mask and saves the girls and Doug's job.

Because of the way *ER* tells its stories, digging deeply into the personalities of its regulars, there's a scene missing here: the scene that shows where Doug is instead of being at work, or that shows why he decides not to go to work. That scene should be between Act X/Scene Y and Act X/Scene Y + 1. Stemming from Doug's character, it could be a scene in which he's oversleeping because he was out on a binge last night, or it could be a scene where he wakes up beside last night's conquest and finds her beside him in bed dead from an OD (a scene that was actually on the show). This latter scene leads to further expansion of the story because it calls for a resolution of the problem it creates: a new scene in which Doug tries to revive the young woman and then races to bring her to the E.R.

Working through the outline this way finishes the basic job of plotting. My next step is to make certain that I've been as specific as possible within each beat. When you're writing on assignment, you need to do this so the showrunner can make certain that the specifics are logical and make sense, and that they're in keeping with the kinds of details used on the show. When you're writing a spec you need to plan the specifics so you don't get caught by surprise when you write the teleplay. You don't want to find yourself wondering about story details at a time when your dialogue and staging need all the creativity you can give.

After this pass through the outline, I'll go over it one more time for "literary" purposes. I'll check intelligibility and grammar and get the outline in shape to be read by the showrunner and everyone else who has to approve it. Even if you're writing a spec script, I advise you to do this. When you're using the outline as the basis for your teleplay and pounding away at INT. and EXT. and all the rest of the script necessities, you don't want anything to get in the way of your own reading or suddenly pop up and confuse you because of the way it's worded. Even the writing of an outline can be a fit of passion, and it's easy to forget what you intended after the emotional state has abated. You don't want to confuse yourself. Too many questions such as, "What did I mean by this? What did I want Amy to do here?" can alter your concentration and even keep you from finishing your script.

Example time. Here's how a first pass through a story (in this case the *Diagnosis: Murder* episode about the basketball player) looks:

TRAP PLAY

TEASER

1. Golf Course – Day. MARK with REG COOK, owner of the Mustangs pro basketball team, BORAK, the team's star, and LANIER, perennial runner-up to Borak for everything.

2. A NEWSMAN shows up, wants to know about Borak's latest affair, with actress-singer YASMIN. Borak disses both Yasmin and Lanier.

3. Everyone leaves, but Mark sees Lanier swing at Borak and get decked with a grin. "Beat ya again." Lanier looks like he's ready to kill as we FADE OUT.

ACT ONE

1. Mark at hospital with JESSIE. Jessie's thrilled because Mark's gotten him a job subbing as Mustang team physician.
2. Local gym casual practice. Interaction between Borak and others. Also here is WAYNE, the handicapped flunky. He does something that'll be a clue.
3. Jessie sees this but doesn't pay attention: Yasmin and WHEATON, her security man, barge in. Wheaton whips out a gun and demands that Borak hold a news conference retracting what he said.
4. Yasmin and Wheaton leave, and Borak demands some "medical attention" for his allergy problem. Jessie asks the usual questions and gives him a prescription for DRUG A and some samples from his bag.
5. That night, Jessie has dinner with Mark and STEVE. Jessie's troubled by Borak, hopes the star isn't going to keep zinging him like he does everyone else.
6. The next day at practice, Borak goes in for a layup, and Lanier throws a sharp elbow. Borak ducks it—and collapses. In spite of Jessie's best efforts, Borak dies as we FADE OUT.

ACT TWO

1. Hospital, shortly afterward. Aftermath scene. Jessie's with Mark, Steve, and AMANDA, feeling like a failure.
2. Cook comes in, more angry than sad, demands a complete investigation. Amanda is authorized to perform an autopsy.
3. Lab, later, Mark, Amanda, and Cook. Autopsy results show that Borak died from a bad drug inter-action—DRUG A, given by Jessie, and DRUG B, already

in Borak's system. Mark notices a future clue that doesn't mean anything now. Cook goes ballistic about autopsy results, says Borak's death is Jessie's fault, and he's going to make him pay.

4. Mark's house, that night, Mark, Steve, Jessie, and Amanda. Jessie's hospital privileges are suspended pending a hearing and he could lose his license. Amanda doesn't understand why Jessie gave Borak DRUG A if he was taking DRUG B—and Jessie says Borak swore he wasn't taking anything. Doorbell RINGS: It's a process server. Cook and the team are suing Jessie for malpractice.

5. Borak's house, the next day, for the wake. Mark and Steve here. Mark's gone through Borak's medical records and knows that he was never prescribed DRUG B. Where'd did he get it?

6. Mark snoops through medicine chest—and meets FRIEDA LONG, Borak's ex live-in and packager of health foods. Frieda gives Mark a clue about Borak's allergies and says he used only her "wellness formula" for them. Something about Frieda will be another clue as well.

7. Mark takes some of Frieda's powder from Borak's to the lab. Amanda compares it to another sample from Frieda's store. The one from Borak's house has something it's not supposed to—DRUG B. Mark realizes this was murder. FADE OUT.

ACT THREE

1. Mark's house. Mark, Steve, Amanda, and Jessie. Someone deliberately set up the drug interaction. But who?

2. Mark goes to the Mustangs office see Cook. He sees Wayne and tries to help him with his chore. Wayne insists on doing it himself.

3. Mark enters Cook's office and gets another clue. The owner wanted to sell the team but can't now because

without Borak it's worth nothing. More info: The team is broke.

4. Amanda goes to Frieda's and gets a clue about how much Borak hurt Frieda in business. He cost her a bundle—and the chance to make a fortune.

5. Steve threatens his way past Wheaton to talk to Yasmin, who says her whole relationship with Borak was a publicity stunt. She even intended to use the bad rap for more P.R. Was Wheaton in on this? Yasmin shrugs. Wheaton's in love with her. So who knows what he might do?

6. The hospital. Mark and the others compare notes. Standard putting all the clues out there scene making everyone we've met so far a suspect.

7. Jessie's Medical Board Hearing. As Mark and the others look on, Jessie tells about what it was like working on the team, gives us a clue about Wayne, who appears to be suffering from MS but actually has CONDITION X.

8. Mark suddenly gets it. He knows Condition X is usually treated with Drug B. Mark has a plan, and he and Steve hurry out. They have until the hearing is over to find the murderer and save Jessie's career.

ACT FOUR

1. Mustangs headquarters. Mark and Steve look for Wayne. He's out running errands. The SECRETARY gives them the list.

2. One of the players' luxury pad. Mark and Steve arrive and find Wayne there. He has keys to most of the players' places. He does something that plays into the clue planted the first time we saw him.

3. Mark sees something that makes him realize Wayne not only planted the drug but caused the allergy attack. Wayne at first denies involvement but then breaks down and reveals his surprise motive.

4. Steve arrests him. Mark heads back to the hospital to save the day for Jessie.

5. At the local gym, the team practices, with Jessie back on the job as their interim doc and Mark looks on. Jessie goes one on one with a CAMEO STAR as we FADE OUT for:

<u>THE END</u>

This early outline has what may seem a strange combination of specific details and sketchy points yet to be determined. Most of the specifics are there because they were agreed upon in an earlier meeting. The rest was left up to me. After two more passes that took an hour or so each I had this version of the "Trap Play" outline:

<u>TRAP PLAY</u>

<u>TEASER</u>

1. Golf Course – day. MARK with his "pal" (that is, a guy he sees around all the time but isn't really friends with at all), REG COOK, owner of the Mustangs pro basketball team, LENNY BORAK, the team's volatile Dennis Rodman/Charles Barkley-style star, and HOWIE LANIER, perennial runner-up to Borak for everything.

2. Life seems very sweet for Borak, especially at the last hole, when a NEWSMAN shows up for an impromptu interview. He wants to know about Borak's latest merchandising deal—and his relationship with YASMIN CARTER, a Madonna-like actress-singer. Borak says her sexuality is highly overrated, just like Lanier's ability to play ball.

3. Mark sees Lanier seethe, but the dissed teammate does nothing until the Newsman and his camera team are gone. Then he speaks heatedly to Borak, and in

spite of Mark's efforts at peacemaking, Lanier is
inflamed into swinging. Borak decks him, grins.
"Beat ya again." Lanier looks like he's ready to
kill him as we FADE OUT.

ACT ONE

1. Mark at hospital with JESSIE, finishing rounds and
   talking basketball with a YOUNG PATIENT. Jessie's
   thrilled because—thanks to Mark—he's subbing as
   Mustang team physician. (Of course it's only pre-
   season, but what the hell. Maybe he'll get to go one
   on one with the great Lenny Borak!) Mark looks on
   bemusedly as Jessie leaves to get to:

2. Local gym casual practice, with Borak, Lanier, and
   various CAMEO stars. See interaction between Borak
   and others, including his ruthlessness. Also here
   is WAYNE, the "towel boy," and all-round flunky—a
   handicapped man who right now is busy shooing a cat
   out of the building.

3. Jessie arrives in time to see this but not pay much
   attention: Yasmin and JIM WHEATON, her security
   man, barge in, the star screaming her about Borak's
   golf course interview. When Borak tries to blow it
   off he finds himself looking right into a gun!
   Wheaton's all icy, controlled fury as he makes his
   point: Borak holds a news conference retracting
   what he said about Yasmin...or a lawsuit will be the
   least painful option Borak's got!

4. Wheaton leaves, and Borak breaks the tension by
   clowning around, joking about how many times
   in his life he's been threatened, starting with
   his childhood in the streets. Then he makes
   straight for Jessie, demanding some "medical
   attention!" The other players join him with a

myriad of complaints: sprains, aches, allergies. In fact, Borak himself has an allergy problem. Jessie asks the usual precautionary questions and gives him both a prescription for DRUG A and some samples from his bag.

5. That night, Jessie has dinner with Mark and STEVE. Steve's envious of the fact that Jessie gets to hang out with the team. Jessie admits to being troubled by Borak's attitude. He hopes like hell that the star isn't going to keep zinging and ridiculing him like he does everyone else.

6. The next day at practice, Borak is his usual turbulent self, demanding that Dr. Jessie wrap his knee. Jessie stays cool, and Borak starts a drill. He goes in for a layup, and Lanier throws a sharp elbow. Borak ducks it—and then cries out, collapsing. All hell breaks loose as Jessie rushes to Borak, doing everything he can. But the team's star player and major tormentor is having one big mother of a heart attack, dying in spite of Jessie's best efforts as we FADE OUT.

<u>ACT TWO</u>

1. Hospital, shortly afterward. Aftermath scene. Jessie's with Mark, Steve, and AMANDA, feeling like a terrible failure for losing Borak.

2. Cook comes in, more angry than saddened by the loss. He demands a complete investigation. Amanda is authorized to perform an autopsy and find out exactly what happened—and why.

3. Lab, later, with Mark, Amanda, and Cook, who has insisted on staying at the hospital and getting every piece of info while he can. Autopsy results

show that Borak died from a bad drug interaction—
DRUG A, given by Jessie, and DRUG B, already in
Borak's system.

4. During this discussion, Mark notices a lot of cat
hair on Borak's jersey, but this discovery doesn't
mean much right now, and is overshadowed by Cook's
reaction to the autopsy result: To him, Borak's
death is Jessie's fault, and he's going to see that
this "bad doctor" pays!

5. Mark's house, that night, with Mark, Steve, Jessie,
and Amanda. Cook has always been a big contributor
to the hospital, and the shit's really hit the
fan: Jessie's hospital privileges are suspended
pending a hearing into his competence, and if
things go wrong at that hearing he could even lose
his license! Amanda doesn't understand why Jessie
gave Borak DRUG A if he was taking DRUG B—and
Jessie explains that Borak swore he wasn't taking
anything.

6. Things go from bad to worse when the doorbell RINGS:
It's a process server. Cook and the team are suing
Jessie for malpractice. If we thought Jessie was
emotionally upset before, well, he's really singing
the blues now...

7. Borak's house, the next day, where there's supposed
to be a wake—only virtually no one is there but
Lanier and some CAMEO STARS. Why go to such an
"event" for someone you don't like? Mark, however,
is present, along with Steve. He's gone through
Borak's medical records and knows that he was never
prescribed DRUG B, so where the hell did he get it?

8. Mark can't help himself; he starts snooping around
the medicine chest—and meets FRIEDA LONG, Borak's

former live-in girlfriend and packager of a line of
health foods and supplements. Frieda behaves like
someone who still thinks very highly of Borak and
tells Mark of Borak's terrible cat allergy, and
that since she introduced Borak to the wonders of
"naturopathic medicine" he never used any drugs,
just her "wellness formula." Mark finds Frieda an
amusing eccentric—and she looks familiar to him
somehow, although he just can't place her.

9. Borak's kitchen is well-stocked with Frieda's
powder. She makes a smoothie for Mark, to prove that
it both tastes good and makes you feel great. And,
after he sips it, Mark takes some of the powder away
with him—

10. But he doesn't take it home. Instead, it goes to
the lab. There, Amanda compares the sample taken
from Borak's house with another sample purchased
from Frieda's store. The one from the store contains the usual harmless and probably ineffective
natural ingredients, but the one from Borak's
kitchen contains—DRUG B. Mark realizes what's
really happened here: "This was murder!" FADE OUT.

ACT THREE

1. Mark's house, where Mark goes over his reasoning
with Steve, Amanda, and Jessie. Someone deliberately set up the drug interaction, lacing the
"wellness formula" with a drug that would cause
death when combined with allergy medicine, and
then—somehow, setting up the need for the allergy
drug. The others think it's a stretch, and Jessie's
the most adamantly against it: "You don't have to
take me off the hook. I screwed up. Let's leave it
at that." But Mark and the others know damn well
that Jessie didn't, so:

2. Mark goes to the Mustangs office, to try and talk Cook out of continuing with the impending hearing and other legal proceedings against Jessie. While he waits, he sees Wayne, the towel boy, moving around awkwardly, running an errand and taking something over to the house of one of the players. Mark tries to help him, but Wayne insists on doing it himself. It's a matter of pride.

3. Mark is ushered into Cook's office in time to hear the tail end of a phone call in which the team owner is discussing a possible sale of the team—and getting turned down because without Borak, the team is worth zilch (relatively speaking). Cook builds up the star power of Lanier, but Mark can see that he's getting nowhere. Some papers on Cook's desk tell the rest of the story: The Mustangs are broke. After seeing this, Mark isn't surprised when Cook refuses to drop his lawsuits. Hey, he needs the money!

4. Amanda stops in at Frieda's, (without telling her who she is—very sneaky) which is both a retail outlet and the manufacturing site for the wellness formula, to see what she can find. She sees that the young woman recently tried to make a major distribution push—which obviously went nowhere (leftovers, piled crates, etc. are the indication). For an instant Frieda's façade of good feeling toward Borak fades as she flashes with anger at the memory of how he has agreed to do an infomercial for her—and, after everything was all set up, changed his mind. The situation cost her a bundle— and the chance to make a fortune.

5. Steve's on the job too, having to threaten his way past Wheaton, the security man, to talk to Yasmin about her anger at Borak—and whether or not she had access to his "stash" of Frieda's powder. During

the conversation, Yasmin shows many different sides of her personality—sweet, imperious, cozy, furious—at last gets around to saying that not only was she not mad enough at Borak to kill him, she really wasn't mad at all. Dating him was a publicity stunt for them both; they never had a real relationship, or any sex. Sure, she'd been upset when he first bad-rapped her, but then she saw it as merely another chance for more P.R. Was Wheaton in on this? Did he feel the same way? Yasmin shrugs. Like every other man she's gotten close to, Wheaton's in love with her. So who knows what he might do? Steve makes his hurried exit when Yasmin starts wondering out loud what it would be like to have a relationship with a cop...

6. At the hospital, Mark and the others compare notes. Trying to figure out why Frieda seemed familiar, Mark checked hospital records and found that she was brought in by police...after having called them because Borak beat her up in a fight over the infomercial! So she actually had a couple of reasons to hate him. Steve has followed this up, learning that Frieda threatened a major lawsuit—and was paid off handsomely by Cook. That's one of the reasons the team's so in debt. Well, if she no longer had a reason to kill Borak, what about Cook? Weren't there rumors that Borak was going to leave the team? That'd ruin any sale. Of course, so would Borak's death. On the other hand, it's common practice for teams to hold big insurance policies on their stars, so killing Borak and blaming it on a medical mistake could net Cook millions. And Wheaton's a suspect too: He's an ex-FBI man who was "retired" for unethical conduct...breaking and entering and planting evidence in a suspect's home. He could've put DRUG B in the powder. As they talk,

they realize that Lanier's a suspect too: without Borak around, he's Number One!

7. None of this, though, is conclusive by any means. They don't have the specifics to find the murderer—or help Jessie defend himself. Speaking of which, it's time for:

8. Jessie's Medical Board Hearing. As Mark and the others look on, he tells about what it was like working on the team, mentions some of the players and personnel he helped. Including Wayne, who appears to be suffering from MS but actually has CONDITION X.

9. Listening, Mark suddenly gets it, turns to Steve. "Do you know what they treat Condition X with?" On Steve's look: "DRUG B." Mark starts from the room, Steve going with him. The hearing will take about an hour more. That means they've got less than that to save Jessie's reputation and career!

ACT FOUR

1. At Mustangs headquarters, Mark and Steve find that Wayne isn't around. He's running errands and had the homes of several players to go to. The SECRETARY gives them the list…

2. Mark and Steve arrive at the luxury apartment of one of the players. The player isn't home, but Wayne has a key—he has keys to most of the players' places because he does this all the time. And now he's feeding the guy's pets—a couple of cats and an obnoxious little dog.

3. Confronted by Mark, Wayne at first denies any involvement in Borak's death. But Mark is certain

they'll find DRUG B at Wayne's home, and it's clear that Wayne could get into Borak's house because he did chores for him too. Seeing the pets, Mark realizes that Wayne not only planted DRUG B, he also caused the allergy attack by rubbing cat hair on Borak's jersey.

4. Faced with all this, Wayne breaks down and confesses, telling the story (with CLOSE ANGLE POV FLASHBACKS) of how in high school both he and Borak were hot players. One night a scout came to check them out—and Borak ruthlessly and deliberately hammered Wayne so that he went flying into the wall beyond the backboard and injured his head, an injury that he's been forced to live with ever since. Wayne could've been a pro, the star that Borak became, if Borak hadn't taken his whole future away from him! Going to work for the Mustangs, Wayne wormed his way in, right under the nose of his "destroyer," with Borak never recognizing—probably never even remembering—his victim. For years, Wayne lived for the moment when he could pay Borak back...and now he has! Wayne goes along with Steve without resisting. The way he sees it, he's been imprisoned in his own body for so long that nothing could be worse!

5. At the local gym, the team practices, with Jessie back on the job as their interim doc. Mark looks on as OUR BIGGEST CAMEO star gives Jessie the thrill of a lifetime: The two of them, going one on one! Jessie pulls a quick fake, goes in for a layup as we FADE OUT for:

<u>THE END</u>

This version has all the specifics filled in—a ton of them, so that no one would have any questions about what was happening and, more importantly in a whodunit, *why*. The only information missing is the exact names of the drugs involved. Such medical info was the responsibility of a doctor on the payroll of *Diagnosis: Murder* as a medical advisor, and he didn't come through with facts that would fit the fictional need until the episode was well into teleplay. (Yes, I said "facts that would fit the fictional need." Don't be afraid to create a situation for your story and then justify it later. This happens all the time.)

This outline also has a hell of a lot of scenes. That's because *Diagnosis: Murder* is almost entirely what we call a "talk show." There's very little action, so more scenes and more dialogue are needed to fill the time. (Teleplays for this series run well over 70 pages, at least 15 pages above the norm for a one-hour show.) Also, several scenes are divided into new, numbered paragraphs so that the information they contain is more readable by both the powers-that-be and myself.

The approach to plotting used here works for more than *Diagnosis: Murder* and other one-hour series. It works for sitcoms, animated half-hours, television movies, you name it. All you have to do is modify the number of act breaks and then fit the pieces in accordingly.

OUTLINING TIPS

1) In feature film writing today, one of the "musts" is to let the audience know exactly what the film is about by page 20. No one has to know exactly where the writer is going or how the writer will get there, but they do know the problem or the need. In television writing today, one of the "musts" is to let the audience know exactly what the episode is about by page three. That's right, by the end of the teaser. When you're designing your opening sequence it not only has to pique the interest of the audience, it also has to set up the rest of your story.

   Believe it or not, there's a good reason for this. Historically, audiences will go with you just about anywhere—as long as they understand the general direction. As a viewer I'm glad to be surprised, even shocked, by the events that take place in *Macbeth*, but how could I root for the central character if I didn't know straight up that he wanted to be king?

2) In television, whatever the hero's profession, he or she is really a detective. The late actor Gig Young, winner of both an Oscar for

Best Supporting Actor and an Emmy for Best Actor, pointed this out to me when he was one of the stars of *Gibbsville*. He played a reporter, but the character spent most of his time learning things about people and using what he learned to try and solve problems. Sometimes he succeeded, but mostly he struck out. (Now you know why this series wasn't a big hit!)

This aspect of delving into mysteries is indeed the primary trait of the heroes of television shows. On cop shows and spy shows and shows featuring private eyes or superheroes it's overt: Sipowitz on *NYPD Blue* is a cop. He solves crimes. The protagonists on *Alias* are spies. They discover plots against our country and prevent them. Jim Rockford on *The Rockford Files* is a private eye. He solves crimes for clients. Spider-Man on *Spider-Man* (and several other variants including *The Adventures of Spider-Man*, *Spider-Man Unlimited*, and the film *Spider-Man*) is a superhero. He finds out what super villains are up to and stops them.

Other shows feature experts in other fields putting themselves on the line against crime. *Hack* has an ex-cop cabbie helping people in ways that cops and detectives would help. *Murder She Wrote* has a mystery writer with an unerring knack for picking the murderer out of any group of suspects. *Deadline* has a journalism teacher using his students to solve crimes. And the heroes of both *Quincy* and *Diagnosis: Murder* use their medical expertise to—you guessed it—solve murders.

Young's point goes beyond this, however. Other kinds of shows use their leads as detectives in matters other than crime. Medical shows, for example, are primarily about doctors determining what's wrong with a patient and then doing their best to cure it. The search to identify the illness and the attempt to accomplish its cure are two aspects of detective work, pure and simple. Lawyer shows are primarily about lawyers searching for the right way to prosecute or defend. That search is an investigation. It's what detectives do. Science fiction and fantasy shows are primarily about life and death dangers in strange new worlds, and their heroes also have learn all they can about their environment in order to save themselves and/or help those in need. In short, they too have to investigate. Even family dramas and sitcoms are predicated upon investigations. In *Frasier*, for example, not only does Niles invariably have a problem that must be solved by him investigating something, but the other cast members, whether they be family, co-workers, or friends, usually end up trying to root out what's bugging Niles as well.

So what's my point here? Just this: You can't go wrong if you construct your plots so they give your hero or heroes as much investigative work as possible to do.

3) In series television, always go where the money is. That means make sure that the most interesting scenes, actions, and dilemmas must involve the star or stars of the show. They're the characters for whom the audience tunes in. They have to be the ones with the decisions to make. The fatal flaw in my version of the *Here Come the Brides* outline I wrote lo those many years ago was that I gave the moral quandary to the guest star instead of the series' main man. A guy we've never seen before rides into town, and the episode's main problem becomes should he kill the hero or shouldn't he? Un-uh, folks. Who cares? Bill Blinn turned it around and made the story about Jason Bolt discovering that his new friend, by whom he has been completely charmed, is really here to kill him—so what should he, the hero, do about it in terms of both his feelings and the necessity of saving his life from a guy a lot more skilled at killing than Jason is?

4) Every scene should be about something that's happening, not something being said. Television is a visual medium, and even though the dialogue is given a great deal of weight, the actual storytelling should be in terms of what the audience sees more than what it hears. All important information has to be learned on screen. It must be seen by the hero or heroes and by the audience as well. Ideally, the audience experiences everything as it's supposed to be happening and not as "reported" later.

I know the *Diagnosis: Murder* outline included in this chapter has scenes that say the characters are in such and such a place talking about what they've learned in addition to scenes where the audience sees them learning other things. Frankly, I do not consider the former good storytelling, but those scenes are standard procedure for this particular show.

When you're working on assignment, the essential scenes for the series take precedence over "good writing" because your job, remember, is to be "ghosting" for the showrunner. When you're writing an episode on spec you can take a little latitude...but only a little. Try to stick as closely to the series' essential scenes as possible, but if one of them has elements an outside reader who doesn't know the show will absolutely detest ("What the hell?! They're just sitting in a room talking for three pages?! What kind of writer does that?!") keep the basic spirit of the essential scene but try to write it in a more "outside reader friendly" way.

5) Make every scene move the plot or sub-plot forward. TV has no time for "wasted" pages and no patience for "wasted" air time. Every scene must contain some new information or be a step forward in the satisfying of the need or the solution to the problem. In the business, the first thing a showrunner does with an outline is excise any scene that keeps the story standing still instead of hurtling forward. These days a television writer may be able to get away with having a scene in which the emotional subtext becomes primary, that is, in which characterization takes the stage and one of the series regulars moves forward in terms of his or her evolution as a "person." But notice that I said "may." You're safer as a writer if such events happen within the same scene as a plot point, so that the plot point is clearly responsible for the personal revelation and story and character move on together.

6) A corollary to the above: Never write a scene that is about more than one plot point and one character point. My experience has shown me that audiences and the executives who get us to the audiences by reading our material can only absorb one idea at a time.

If you've had experience as an employer, you'll know what I mean. Your assistant comes into the office in the morning and you greet him with, "I need you to send out that letter I dictated yesterday to Blahoot Incorporated, balance the books for last month, set up a meeting with the CEO for Thursday, do the data entry on the new orders, get me my latte from the Coffee Bean, not Starbucks this time...oh, and here's a list of calls you need to make for me before 10:30."

Your assistant nods knowingly. "Got it." You go back into your inner sanctum, and sure enough, at 10:30 in he comes with your latte in a Starbucks cup instead of the Coffee Bean—and nothing else has been done. If you've had experience as an employee (and who hasn't, except for a few lucky—and detestably enviable— freelancers in an area other than television who've managed to survive staying self-employed and working at home from day one of their careers), you know that as soon as the boss was finished talking, all you could remember was whatever point seemed the most important, or most interesting, to you. And even that you couldn't remember completely because all the other information crowded into the way and obscured the boss's point.

Don't let your point be obscured. Make it, and only it, and move on to the next scene. (The next scene, by the way, can be in the same location and even involve some of the same people, but if it's a new point it's a new scene.)

7) Drama is conflict. So, for that matter, is comedy. When you're thinking of possible scenes think of them in terms of what conflict they can have. This doesn't mean everyone has to hate everyone else, but it does mean that whenever possible your characters should disagree.

Think of all those buddy movies and buddy TV shows you've seen and will continue to see, or films and series that make use of the classic buddy relationship within a larger framework: *Butch Cassidy and the Sundance Kid, Thelma and Louise, Lethal Weapon, I Spy, Alias Smith and Jones, Starsky and Hutch, Kate and Ally, Cagney and Lacey, Miami Vice, Will & Grace, Charmed, Monk, Bram and Alice*…these are merely a few.

In every one of these productions there are two or more characters who love each other but who, because of their back- grounds, are always bickering about each individual move they make. Why do they bicker? Within the logic of each show it's because, although they agree in the end, the need to achieve their personalities dictate different means. Within the practical context of "Hey, I gotta write this stuff and keep people's attention," it's because exposition—the facts of a situation, the making of a plan, the life history or backstory of a character—is by its nature pretty dull, so having the characters argue with each other while giving the audience information keeps things lively.

This means that you as the writer must keep coming up with plot points about which the characters can be in conflict. It's the *Barefoot in the Park* syndrome. The husband is conservative, orderly, reserved. The wife is radical, sloppy, outgoing. Even though they're just starting out as a couple, he's got a good job and could probably afford any apartment the two of them like. But the playwright, Neil Simon, comes up with a logical reason to put them in a fourth floor walk-up that *she* loves and *he* can't stand, and off we go with a great comedy. The banter between them is part of the screenplay in the film version and the teleplay in the TV version, but the conflict comes from the events in the *outline*.

8) Remember what we said about plotting your story for an existing television series around the essential scenes that series uses all the time? And the earlier tip saying you can bend that a little when an essential scene would be considered just plain bad writing by someone you want to impress? Here's a corollary to both those things: When you're writing a spec episode, make sure its overall plot is constructed the way the staff would construct it. If the series for which you're writing a spec has a rigid overall formula, like *Law & Order*, where the teaser always shows people we've never seen before and probably won't see again finding a dead body, and where Act Three shifts the show's point of view from the detectives to the district attorneys, follow that formula. Don't try to "improve" on it.

In most instances, even if what you're doing really is an improvement creatively, no one in the business to whom you show your script necessarily will want to see it. Some buyers and development execs want to see you at your most creative. Others want to see if you can write to order. A showrunner usually wants to see if you can be the equivalent of a housepainter painting his or her house the color the showrunner wants. An agent wants to see the best you can do *and* also if he or she can send you out to paint other people's houses and be confident that you'll mix the colors to the exact wants of the homeowner/showrunner and not to your own taste (no matter how good it may be).

(Yes, there's a fine line of difference between this advice and that in Tip #4, but that's where intangibles such as judgment, talent, skill, and experience come in. Determining which deviations will be acceptable and which won't is something every spec writer has to do for him or herself. If you figure right, it means you probably belong in the biz. If you figure wrong, it means you probably aren't ready just yet. Just remember, young Jedi—be wary. Very wary. If you're going off the beaten path tread lightly.)

9) Keep building the tension. No matter what happens in any specific scene, the general trend of your storyline should be to continually make things harder on your hero or heroes. One step forward, two steps back. Twists and reversals. Pressure. Cal Clements Jr. puts it this way: "Our job is to bury our hero in garbage and then, just as he's clawing his way out, pile on another load." Think video games: In most video games, the reward for successfully making it through one level is to move up to a level that's even tougher, not easier, but the experience gained in the easier level helps the hero master the harder one. In good television plotting, the skill or knowledge accumulated along the way makes the difference between success or failure at the end.

chapter 10:
the teleplay— part 1

The purpose of all the work you've put in so far is, of course,
to write a teleplay. For the professional writer working on assignment,
delivery of the story means an end to meetings and outline revisions,
a check for a job well done, and, if all goes well, movement into the
first draft, delivery of which will put another 40 percent of the total
fee into the writer's pocket. For the individual writing on spec,
finishing the story means getting to what you probably thought of
as writing before you started reading this book: writing a *script*.

Once you are, as we say, "in teleplay," the first thing you need to
have under control is format. In a business in which appearances are
often more important than the reality underlying them, it is vital
to have the right format so that your teleplay looks the way a teleplay
is supposed to look. It's what separates the wannabes from the pros,
the "I-don't-get-its" from the masters. It's not just a matter of using
teleplay format properly, but, at the very least, being comfortable
enough with it so that it doesn't stifle your creativity. And for those
who thoroughly master the teleplay format there's an added bonus—
the ability to use its conventions to heighten the effect of the story
you're telling. The ability to not only make the reader mentally see
and hear what's going on, but feel all the attendant emotions as well.

Just about every book ever written on screen or television writing includes a presentation of screen or teleplay format, and modern screenwriting software has become very adept at getting the proper elements to the writer's fingertips as needed. But I've never found a source that accurately explains *why* screenplays and teleplays are set up the way they are. In my life as well as in my career, I've found that I do much better when I understand the reasons for the rules and regulations that govern so much of what I do, so as we go through the formatting process I'll try to keep the enlightenment flowing.

In television, two basic script formats are used. One-hour episodes, animation and other kids' shows, and TV movies all use variations of the feature film screenplay format that's been around since the beginning of talkies. Sitcoms and soap operas use variations of the stageplay format that's been around even longer, although some sitcoms use the same format as one-hour shows just to confuse the issue, and each series, especially sitcoms, has certain format quirks that you can only know if you get copies of their teleplays and pore over them (which, of course, you comedy writers have already done in preparation for working out your story).

Over the years, one-hour teleplay format has evolved in much the same way that screenplay format has evolved in feature films, going from complex and highly structured to more simplified and, in a way, relaxed.

What we can call Classic Teleplay Format looks something like these opening pages from a pilot I wrote for both NBC and CBS, based on a concept and story by science fiction great Harlan Ellison:

<u>THE DARK FORCES</u>
<u>THE SALAMANDER ENCHANTMENT</u>

<u>TEASER</u>

FADE IN:

EXT. U.S. MARINE AIR BASE - QUANTICO, VIRGINIA - DAY

A sprawling complex of military buildings centered around the airstrip. A speck in the sky grows larger—a military transport jet.

CLOSER ON THE BASE

Media vans and the newspeople who run them abound,
newspeople CALLING OUT, AD LIB as they jockey for
position.

>   P.A. SYSTEM (O.S.)
>   All non-military personnel, clear
>   the airfield—

No one listens, as we ANGLE WITH the descending
jet, TO:

INT. MILITARY TRANSPORT JET - DAY -
MASTER SGT. EZRA JACKSON

Haggard in his dress uniform, gazing down at
the base eagerly. Jackson is about 40 years old,
Black, a career noncom who looks like he's
returning from Hell.

>   BRANDON'S VOICE (O.S.)
>   ...Remember, Ezra, short and sweet. 'Yes,'
>   you're glad to be back. 'No,' you've
>   got no comment on the negotiations...

WIDENING, we see that seated next to Jackson is
MARTIN BRANDON, 35, dark-suited, immaculate, the
perfect State Department undersecretary.

>   JACKSON
>   Don't worry, Mr. Brandon. I'm not
>   saying anything that might hurt those
>   poor bastards still in Baghdad.

>   BRANDON
>   You're a good Marine, Sergeant.
>   Your country's proud of you.

> JACKSON
> The one I want to make proud is
> Marcie. You know, sometimes I
> felt like I was locked in a room
> full of devils.
> > (beat)
> I'm sure looking forward to
> seeing my angel again.

Brandon's face tightens. Jackson doesn't notice.
He's still gazing out the window, trying to pick
his "angel" out of the crowd.

EXT. U.S. MARINE BASE – AIRSTRIP – DAY

The jet taxis to a stop. The Newspeople surge
forward as the door opens, Jackson and Brandon
stepping out.

> FIRST NEWSMAN
> > (to cameraman)
> ...And so, after eighteen months in
> captivity, Master Sergeant Ezra
> Jackson returns to the U.S.

> SECOND NEWSMAN
> Sergeant! How's it feel to be
> back on America?

> THIRD NEWSMAN
> Were you tortured—?

Jackson looks past the Newspeople, searching
the throng.

> NEWSWOMAN
> Were you able to get news from

home, Sergeant? Did they tell
you about your wife?

CLOSER ON JACKSON

He looks at the Newswoman closely.

> JACKSON
> What about my wife?

> NEWSWOMAN
> Surely Undersecretary Brandon has
> informed you—

> JACKSON
> Of what?
> (whirling on Brandon)
> What's she talking about? What
> happened to Marcie? Why isn't
> she here?

> BRANDON
> Ezra, please—we didn't want to
> upset you—

> JACKSON
> About what? What?

Jackson grabs Brandon in an iron grip.

> BRANDON
> I'm sorry, Sergeant. She's
> dead. Murdered. Almost six
> months ago…

> JACKSON
> My God…

Slowly, Jackson's hold loosens. He collapses to the tarmac. We TIGHTEN ON Jackson's face, his breathing shallow, his eyes unfocused. His voice is a whisper:

>   JACKSON
>   No angel...only devils...

Jackson's body stiffens, and we TIGHTEN CLOSER. A shadow darkens his eyes, and within that shadow we see what looks like the FLASH OF LIGHTNING. Slithering, snakelike shapes seem to move across Jackson's pupils.

The shapes redden, and we TIGHTEN STILL CLOSER ON Jackson's eyes, seeing that the shapes have become flames.

As the flames within both his eyes FLARE UP so that the fire is all we can see, we

>   FADE OUT

>   END OF TEASER

The Contemporary Teleplay Format version of the same three plus pages would look like this:

>   THE DARK FORCES
>   THE SALAMANDER ENCHANTMENT

>   TEASER

FADE IN:

EXT. U.S. MARINE AIR BASE - QUANTICO, VIRGINIA - DAY

A sprawling complex of military buildings centered

around the airstrip. A speck in the sky grows
larger—a military transport jet.

Media vans and the newspeople who run them abound,
newspeople CALLING OUT, AD LIB as they jockey for
position.

          P.A. SYSTEM (O.S.)
     All non-military personnel, clear
     the airfield—

No one listens, as:

INT. MILITARY TRANSPORT JET - DAY

MASTER SGT EZRA JACKSON, haggard in his dress
uniform, gazes down at the base eagerly.
Jackson is about 40 years old, Black, a career
noncom who looks like he's returning from
Hell. Beside him is MARTIN BRANDON, 35, dark-
suited, immaculate, the perfect State Department
Undersecretary.

          BRANDON
     ...Remember, Ezra, short and
     sweet. 'Yes,' you're glad to be
     back. 'No,' you've got no com-
     ment on the negotiations...

          JACKSON
     Don't worry, Mr. Brandon. I'm not
     saying anything that might hurt
     those poor bastards still in
     Baghdad.

          BRANDON
     You're a good Marine, Sergeant.
     Your country's proud of you.

                    JACKSON
The one I want to make proud
is Marcie. You know, sometimes
I felt like I was locked in
a room full of devils. Now all
I want is to see my angel
again.

Brandon's face tightens. Jackson doesn't notice.
He's still gazing out the window, trying to pick
his "angel" out of the crowd.

EXT. U.S. MARINE BASE - AIRSTRIP - DAY

The jet taxis to a stop. The Newspeople surge
forward as the door opens, Jackson and Brandon
stepping out.

                    FIRST NEWSMAN
                 (to cameraman)
...And so, after eighteen months
in captivity, Master Sergeant
Ezra Jackson returns to the U.S.

                    SECOND NEWSMAN
Sergeant! How's it feel to be
back on America?

                    THIRD NEWSMAN
Were you tortured—?

Jackson looks past the Newspeople, searching the
throng.

                    NEWSWOMAN
Were you able to get news from
home, Sergeant? Did they tell
you about your wife?

                    JACKSON
What about my wife?

                    NEWSWOMAN
Surely Undersecretary Brandon has
informed you—

                    JACKSON
Of what?
          (whirling on Brandon)
What's she talking about? What
happened to Marcie? Why isn't
she here?

                    BRANDON
Ezra, please—we didn't want to
upset you—

                    JACKSON
About what? <u>What</u>?

Jackson grabs Brandon in an iron grip.

                    BRANDON
I'm sorry, Sergeant. She's dead.
Murdered. Almost six months ago...

                    JACKSON
My God...

Slowly, Jackson's hold loosens. He collapses
to the tarmac, his breathing shallow, his eyes
unfocused. His voice is a whisper:

                    JACKSON
No angel...only devils...

Jackson's body stiffens. A shadow darkens his

eyes, and within that shadow we SEE what looks
like the FLASH OF LIGHTNING. Slithering, snakelike
shapes seem to move across Jackson's pupils.

The shapes redden, and we TIGHTEN ON Jackson's
eyes, seeing that the shapes have become FLAMES.

As the flames within both his eyes FLARE UP so that
the fire is all we can SEE

FADE OUT

<u>END OF TEASER</u>

As you can see, the major difference between the Classic Format
and the Contemporary Format is that it uses fewer camera movements
within the body of the stage directions and is broken up into fewer
of what we call "shots," which are the headings in uppercase that you
see throughout the first version of the teaser as both indicators of
setting and suggested camera placement directions, but are only used
as indicators of setting in the second.

The reason for these changes is a deliberate attempt to make both
the reading and writing of the teleplay easier, an attempt instigated not
by the television (or film) business per se but by the film schools and
film departments of various universities and colleges.

Author/playwright/screenwriter Richard Krevolin, who has the
distinction of being a professor at two of the top-ranked film schools
in the nation, the University of Southern California and the University
of California at Los Angeles, comments, "I'm just guessing here, but I
think the staffs at the colleges felt that if they were going to teach
screenwriting they should teach it the way they taught other forms of
writing, as a literary endeavor. That meant getting rid of the intrusive
camera directions and concentrating on the more creative aspects of
the work."

Lenny Katzman, who not only was showrunner of *Walker, Texas
Ranger* but also created, executive produced, and wrote many, many
episodes of the popular series *Dallas*, saw it differently. As he says,

"The networks've got kids in charge who don't have a clue what a script should be. They don't know how to read them because they haven't got any experience reading them. So they keep on us to make it the scripts more like the kind of narratives they're used to seeing. So we do."

Which of these gentlemen is correct? Daring and outspoken iconoclast that I am, I'll go on record with my point of view right now: they're both right. In television writing, as in most things, there's never just one reason for anything. Nothing's black and white. (Here's another note for you: Remember this when you're fleshing out your characters, particularly their motives.)

Although Contemporary Format is in vogue now, it hasn't completely taken over, and Classic Format is still used in screenwriting as well as TV. Jeb Brody, creative executive at Magnet Entertainment, producers of the films *The Silence of the Lambs, Charade, Adaptation* and many more, has said that on an average day the pile of screenplays on his desk is evenly divided between Classic and Contemporary Formats. "New writers submitting spec screenplays seem to all use the newer, simpler, cleaner format," he told me, "while experienced writers and those writing on assignment seem to use the older version with more shots."

Which format should you use? Again, the answer is, whichever one the show for which you're writing your spec uses. (But the trend being what it is, I'm betting you can't go wrong if you go with the Contemporary Format.)

In showing the sample pages I've tried to reproduce them exactly as they were (or would be) printed out for distribution when delivered to execs, agents, actors, whoever had to see them. (I was the show-runner and already had my copy.) Regardless of whether you go Classic or Contemporary, here are the elements you've got to know and be able to duplicate, format-wise—*and* the reasons they exist as they do:

Series Title: (all uppercase, centered, and underlined)

THE DARK FORCES

The title of the series is in uppercase because, in the days of type-writers, screen and TV writers couldn't create their own italics (which is the stylistically proper way to indicate titles in literary/publishing circles), but they still wanted to make the title stand out and catch the eye. It's centered because titles are always centered. It's underlined because, within literary/publishing circles, underlining in a manuscript was a message for the printer to italicize the words. It's also underlined so that the uppercase font won't be confused with other uppercase fonts within the body of the script, which are there for a different purpose.

Some series double-space after the series title. For others single spacing is fine.

Episode Title: (all uppercase, centered, and underlined)

<u>THE SALAMANDER ENCHANTMENT</u>

The title of the episode is presented the same way the title of the series is and for the same reasons. Why do we have episode titles? To focus the writer's thoughts, for one thing, and to get the attention of the reader or audience for another. And, of course, because titles for individual volumes of connected series of books was a literary convention that early screenwriters and studios were eager to emulate.

Most series double-space after the episode title, going to the:

Act Heading: (uppercase, centered, and underlined)

<u>TEASER</u>

Yep, we're in "same old, same old" territory here, with the added fillip that act headings not only show where the commercials will be placed, but also serve the same purpose for readers that chapter headings do. They give you a convenient place to stop and put down what you're reading and eat, take phone calls, or go to the next meeting.

All series double-space after the act heading.

Opening Transition: (all uppercase and flush left)

FADE IN:

All screenplays start with FADE IN and end with FADE OUT. All acts

of teleplays start and end that way too. The term "fade in" is the closest
approximation of what you would see when looking through the lens
of one of the old cameras as it was cranked up by hand and began
shooting. "Fade out" is what happened when the cranking stopped.
The two designations are in uppercase because *all* references to what
the camera sees or does are in uppercase, even the word "CAMERA"
when it refers to the camera the director of photography is having his
camera operator aim. Historically, the reason for this is so the DP and
the director can go through the script and pay particular attention to
the visual elements the writer has deemed important enough to have
metaphorically jump out of the page and attract their attention. Why
is it positioned flush left? Because it's the first thing every viewer is
going to see, it's positioned in the first place every reader is going to
look once he or she has gotten past all those titles.

Always double-space after FADE IN. (Until the mid-1970s it was a
requirement to triple space after this transition. No one seems to
know why.)

Scene Header or Slug Line: (all uppercase, flush left; spaces, hyphens and DAY or NIGHT must be included)

```
EXT. U.S. MARINE AIR BASE - QUANTICO, VIRGINIA - DAY
```

Scene headers are in all uppercase to make sure everyone reads
them and knows where and when the scene is set. Not only is this
necessary to creatively orient execs, producers, actors, and other
personnel, it's also necessary for the unit production manager and first
assistant director. First and foremost among their duties is the creation
of the most efficient shooting schedule possible. "Efficient" in this
case means "affordable," and the most efficient and affordable way to
shoot films and one-hour television episodes is by grouping together
all the scenes taking place in a particular place at a particular time.

All day scenes set outside at Central Park, for example, ("location
shots" because they're at a location in the real world) would be shot
one after another, over a period of hours or days, depending on how
many there are. All day scenes set inside at, oh, the House of Blues,
would also be shot that way. The same with all night scenes. The UPM
and first AD try to keep the number of times the entire cast and crew

have to move from one place to another to a minimum because moving takes time and time costs money. Even when the interiors are being done on a soundstage—even the *same* soundstage—there's a delay when the setting changes. The old sets have to be wheeled into storage and the new ones wheeled out, or the cast and crew have to move from one standing (always in place and ready to shoot) set to another. The cameras have to be repositioned. The lighting has to be reset. (The card game being played by the truck drivers and extras has to get started—or come to an end.)

"EXT." of course means "exterior." "INT." means "interior." And for the production purposes already described, no matter what time the events occur the writer should never be more precise than "day" or "night." If you want a scene to be at dawn or dusk, put it in the descriptive paragraph that follows the header and not in the header itself. The UPM and first AD will then schedule that scene to be at the beginning or end of the shooting day as needed if it's an outdoor location shot. If it's an interior, the DP will make sure the lights are set up to duplicate sunrise or sunset.

Notice that the time of day comes last and is set off from the rest by a space, a hyphen, and another space. This seems to be how it's always been done, and therefore in order to look professional you've got to do it too. I admit that I'm stumped regarding the "why" of it. I don't know the reason we use a hyphen instead of a dash, and I don't know why we skip a space before and after. I tend to think it has something to do with clarity, and the fact that in the days when scripts were mimeographed instead of photocopied or otherwise printed, the ink tended to smudge —especially solid lines. (But if you know the secret, please pass it along.)

Notice also that you always double-space both before and after a scene header. However, if the header ends up taking two lines those lines are single-spaced. (Until the mid-1970s it was a requirement to triple space before scene and shot headers. Again, no one knows why.)

Action Paragraph or Line: (normal capitalization and punctuation, flush left, single-spaced)

```
A sprawling complex of military buildings centered
around the airstrip. A speck in the sky grows
larger—a military transport jet.
```

This is where you put in your various descriptions and what, in a stageplay, would be called stage directions. It's common to write the first sentence after the scene header as though it's really the next clause in the same sentence, and some shows don't capitalize the first letter of such a sentence. Notice that within the action paragraph dashes can be used when necessary instead of hyphens—but there's a space before the dash and again after it. Again, the only reason for this that I can come up with is it was meant to guard against the dreaded mimeo smudge. (Which really is a big deal when you think about it. If parts of a description or dialogue are indecipherable the production has a big problem.)

My first writing assignment was a screenplay for MGM, for a film that was never made (but which helped me in two ways—it put some money in my pocket because I got paid and it gave me a credit that caused TV producers to be interested in my work). Because of my inexperience, I was assigned a co-writer by the name of Arthur Dreifuss, a veteran writer and director who had come to Hollywood in the late 1930s, fleeing from Hitler's Nazi Germany.

Dreifuss taught me an important lesson when we wrote together, and it's time for me to pass it on: immediately following every scene header there *must* be an action line. You can't just write the header and then go into dialogue. This is because scenes are, in fact, camera shots, and in order to shoot an image the DP must know what that image is. Every scene or shot must be about something visual. Ergo, the writer has to supply a description and if characters are exchanging dialogue, the writer must also tell the reader who's there to do the speaking.

Shot Header or Slug Line: (uppercase; flush left)

CLOSER ON THE BASE

The shot header is used to tell the reader—and the director and the DP—what the writer thinks should be the visual focus of the scene. It also can be used to enhance the dramatic effect of a situation. By adding a CLOSE SHOT ON SO AND SO (someone in distress) that character's plight or emotional state is heightened for the knowing script reader, who immediately visualizes the immediacy of the "big head." This technique only works with experienced film or TV people, however. With the less experienced close-ups, and shot headers in general, usually function as affectations that get in the way. Shot headers are used in the Classic Format but not the Contemporary Format (and even then the new writer should use them sparingly, since they're so likely to be misunderstood).

Always double-space before and after shot headers if you use them.

First Mention of a Cast Member with a Speaking Part within Action Paragraph: (uppercase)

NEWSPEOPLE

This is a big one. Whenever you introduce a new character with a speaking part within the body of an action paragraph or in an action line, you must put the character's name in uppercase. Like the DP, who reads the script looking for uppercase shooting guidelines, the casting director reads looking for uppercase casting guidelines. (In fact, as you'll see, all personnel involved in the physical production who have to see the script are trained to take their cues from what's written in uppercase.)

The casting director goes through the script writing down every new character (and the short description you should be giving right after his or her name) so that they can then put out what's called a "character breakdown." The character breakdown not only tells the casting director what parts have to be filled; it's also sent to every agent in town to give them the opportunity to suggest suitable clients.

A note: In the case of "NEWSPEOPLE" we're talking about needing a more or less generic group of actors who can fire out questions like real newspeople (and who probably would be played by real news-people), so no physical or attitudinal description is required.

Postproduction Sound: (uppercase)

CALLING OUT, AD LIB

This is another example of a word or words in uppercase for production purposes. Believe it or not, most of the sounds you hear (in a teleplay that would be "SOUNDS" and "HEAR") aren't created live on the set or location. Instead, they're put in later, by the post-production sound team. In the case of CALLING OUT, AD LIB, odds are that the actors in the scene would say something that would need to be added to or otherwise enhanced or "sweetened" later, on what is called the ADR stage (additional dialogue recording).

Other sounds commonly indicated in uppercase and added later include the ringing of a telephone or doorbell, chimes, music that is supposed to be coming from a radio or recording (or, for that matter, a "live" band appearing in the scene), footsteps, tire squeals in a car chase, automobile horns, explosions, gunshots, punches, and most other THUDS, CRASHES, BOOMS, and BAMS.

Character Name (uppercase and indented)
with Dialogue: (normal, single-spaced; indented)

```
            P.A. SYSTEM (O.S.)
        All non-military personnel,
        clear the airfield -
```

Whenever dialogue is indicated, the name of the speaking character is in uppercase. This and the first appearance of the character are the *only* times uppercase is used. Otherwise, that is, within the body of an action paragraph, normal upper and lowercase fonts are used.

The position of the speaker's name for dialogue is determined by tabbing. To some people it appears to be centered on the page but, be careful: it's not. Dialogue isn't centered either. It too has a specific tab stop. I'll identify both of these soon.

Never end a page with the speaking character's name at the bottom and the dialogue itself continued to the top of the next page. In a crowded situation, skip an extra line and put the entire speech onto the next page. If the situation is slightly less crowded, put the first line of the dialogue at the bottom of the page under the character's name and then continue the speech at the top of the next page by putting the character's name at the top and then the rest of the speech beneath it.

Double-space before the name of a speaking character, but remember that the speech itself comes only one line below the name. Double-space after the speech, before either the next character name and speech or the next action paragraph or scene header or act ending.

Parenthetical Expression: (normal and single-spaced)

```
              FIRST NEWSMAN
            (to cameraman)
```

Parenthetical expressions are sometimes called "wrylies" after the fact that they're usually used to express a specific way of delivering a line, as in "happily," "sadly," "concernedly," and of course "wryly." They're also used to clarify to whom the speaker is talking when it might otherwise be confusing. Parenthetical expressions can be used within a character's dialogue to indicate an abrupt change in tone or shift in the object of the conversation. That's usually shown like this:

```
              ELVIS
          Thank you. Thank you very much.
              (quietly; to the band)
          You guys see the blonde in the
          first row?
```

A common parenthetical expression that often drives new writers crazy is "(beat)." The (beat) direction is an instruction to the actor to take a short break before saying the next line or series of lines. It should only be used in the middle of a speech, and only to emphasize to the actor that what's about to be said is very emotional and personal to the character, and therefore it's difficult for the character to get out the words. This convention could well be the most over-used parenthetical in the film and TV writer's lexicon and should be avoided whenever possible, because it takes away from the actor's creativity by not allowing the actor to interpret the dialogue as his or her talent, training, and instincts dictate (and in a perfect world all actors are hired for their talent, training, and instincts).

For that matter, most parentheticals tend to hobble actors, which is a good reason for avoiding them whenever possible. (Try not to under-line words in dialogue as well. Underlining for emphasis is a way of forcing the actor to speak the lines the way the writer hears them—and while that's often the "right" way, there are times when actors come up with perfect line readings no one writer ever could've imagined. Parentheticals also have a specific tab stop. It too is coming up soon.

Over the years I've found another reason writers use parentheticals. We stick them in to break up speeches that would otherwise appear to be big, solid blocks of dialogue on the page. Producers tend to *hate* big, solid blocks of dialogue on a page, believing—usually correctly—that when characters talk like that they sound as though they're making speeches and not conversing. Throughout my career I've often used the parenthetical trick to cover that up. In terms of my relationship with the powers-that-be, and my disinclination to rewrite the speech, the trick has worked well. But in terms of performance, almost every time I've used it I've hurt the show because—can you believe it?—the actor really does come off as someone making a pompous speech.

Parentheticals are one space below the character name or speech that precedes them and one space above the speech that comes after them. No double-spacing allowed here.

Camera Direction within Action Paragraph: (uppercase)

```
We TIGHTEN ON Jackson's face, his breathing
shallow, his eyes unfocused.
```

This is another situation where the words are uppercase in order to get the DP and the director to read them, and to guide the reader into feeling the importance of what the camera is showing. This is also another situation of the kind of thing that's pretty much done only in the Classical Format and these days should be avoided as much as possible so the folks from the film departments don't get all shook up.

Postproduction Special Effect or SFX within Action Paragraph: (uppercase)

```
A shadow darkens his eyes, and within that shadow
we see what looks like the FLASH OF LIGHTNING.
```

As special effects become more and more pervasive, indicating them becomes more and more important to the "SFX" crew that's scrutinizing the script. Using uppercase for them stems from the fact that they're always done after the film is shot and edited together. Although when I worked on *Automan*, Glen Larson, the other executive producer on the series, had a tough time imagining the effects and often had them added to "dailies," (the otherwise unedited film shown and printed the day before) so that he'd know exactly what the audience would see and better know if the scenes were going to work.

Closing Transition: (uppercase and flush right)

FADE OUT

This, of course, is the opposite of FADE IN, with the same raison d'etre. Until recently, most teleplays indicated scene-to-scene transitions in this same place, using phrases such as "CUT TO:" "DISSOLVE TO:" and others. This is no longer in style, in both Classic and Contemporary Formats. One reason is that it's up to the showrunner to decide, working on the final cut of the filmed episode with the film editor, what form the transitions will take. Another reason is that most transitions these days are simple CUT TOS and any time you change from scene to scene the film is literally being cut, so why indicate what will be there even if no one says a word? A third reason is that taking out the transitions gives the writer of a one-hour teleplay another two pages that can be used for additional story while keeping the teleplay the same length. (Or, for you cynics, it can cut two pages out of the teleplay and thereby save the production company or studio money—and a little savings here, a little there doesn't hurt.)

Act Ending: (uppercase, underlined, and centered)

END OF TEASER

And this is the opposite of TEASER and other act titles. Some shows don't underline these (or the act beginnings either). It's up to you to learn what the form is for the individual series you're writing.

An act ending is also the ending of the page for almost every series, with the next act starting on a new page no matter how much white space this may cause.

Show Ending: (not shown in example, replaces Act Ending at end of show; uppercase, underlined, and centered)

<u>THE END</u>

Not much to say about this. "The End" is the end — except that, again, this may or may not be underlined. It depends on the conventions of the show.

The phrase "THE END" replaces the "END OF ACT FOUR" or "END OF TAG" or whatever act is the last, on the simple theory that once something ends, it ends; you don't have to end twice.

Regardless of whether you're using Classic or Contemporary Format, the font face for all teleplays done in film format is Courier or Courier New, and the size of the type is 12 point. This approximates the original typeface found on typewriters and the size of the type, which was called Pica. (In the Dark Ages before computers, the only variation was a smaller type called Elite. But the look of the type was the same both ways.)

Page set-up — margins, spacings, and tabs — varies from series to series and production company to production company. Add-ons you may have seen elsewhere, such as scene and shot numbering, the words "(MORE)" at the end of a speech that continues onto the next page, and the word "(CONTINUED)" at the end of a page when the scene or shot continues onto the next page are usually added by the production staff when "pre-production" or "prep" (preparing the episode or film for production) begins. For a writer to include scene and shot numbers is in particular a DON'T DO; it's considered a sign of amateurism.

Commercial script formatting programs such as FinalDraft, ScreenWriter 2000, ScriptWare, and Sophocles automatically position each element properly and set the proper line spacing for each as well. They'll also give you the option of adding the production elements I mentioned above. Although originally created for screenplays, most of these programs have a television mode that includes act headings and endings. However, most of these programs are also expensive, with the newest of them, Sophocles, weighing in as the most affordable with a cost of just under $100 at the time of this writing.

Being the most affordable doesn't necessarily mean Sophocles is the one you should buy, though. I've tried all the programs and found that ScreenWriter 2000 is the easiest to learn and use but that FinalDraft has the most users within the TV biz. When you're writing specs and sending out hard copies that doesn't matter. But when you're working on assignment and are delivering your work as an e-mail attachment or are on the staff of a show you need to have the same program as your employer. (If you're on staff the odds are good that you'll be given a copy of the necessary software. The odds are also good that at last you'll be able to afford it. Such are the ironies of TV.)

Many writers write their teleplays in Microsoft Word and let the shows convert the files into whatever proprietary software is needed. If you're going to use Word or another word processing program for your teleplay, I recommend the following settings:

Page Set-Up: top margin 1.2"; bottom margin 1"; left margin 1.3"; right margin 1.2".

Character name above dialogue: tabbed 2.5" from the left margin. Parenthetical expression: tabbed 2.1" at the left and ending 1.8" from the right. Dialogue: tabbed 1.2" from the left margin and ending 1.3" from the right.

Various writing websites also have Word templates you can download, and most of these do the trick just fine.

The margins are where they are, by the way, so there's room for the scene and shot numbers you aren't putting in. And the reason for those numbers is so there's no confusion when the UPM and first AD make up the schedule by designating which numbered scenes are being filmed when. Using only headings could be a problem because of possible (and probable) duplication. The tabs are where they are so the actors can see their lines easily and follow the dialogue and directions without confusing one for the other.

Although "nothing is etched in stone" (another show business phrase almost as common as "This isn't brain surgery, you know," which in turn is used almost as much as the "cure for cancer" line), using this approximate set-up should enable you to create TV movies that run about 110 pages, one-hour action shows that run between 48 and 54 pages, and one-hour dramas 50 to 70 pages in length, which is the average these days.

Screenplay format is not just the basis for both one-hour and TV movie teleplays; it's also the format for animated shows. In animation we use the Classic Format—with a vengeance. Here, reproduced as closely to its original form as possible, is an example to show what I mean. This is a scene from the Fox Kids Network series *Spider-Man Unlimited* written by Gerry Conway and myself:

```
EXT. ALLEY - NIGHT (CONTINUOUS)


A SPINNING SHADOW SPREADS OVER Spidey and the Cat
as the skybus O.S. plunges toward the alley, still
outlined with the CRACKLING GLOW.


                    SPIDER-MAN
             Oh, that falling skybus.


Spidey shoots a webline straight up, and follows
it O.S. like a missile from a launching pad.


                    SPIDER-MAN
             I'll be ba-ack...


                    BLACK CAT
             Promises, promises.


CLOSER ON SPIDEY


Following the webline upward. He reaches into his
belt, and we TIGHTEN ON the spider-tracer he takes
out of it. Then:


THE SKYBUS


Whirling as it continues to fall from high above
the city, its SCREAMING passengers visible inside.
Spidey's webline shoots up from below, strikes the
nose of the bus, followed by Spidey, who lands on
the underside of the vehicle.
```

>   SPIDER-MAN (V.O.)
>   Okay, smart guy, now that you're
>   here what do you do?

His gaze finds:

SPIDEY'S POV - BLACK CAT'S ELECTRONIC PELLET

Attached to the bottom of the skybus, PULSING in
sync with the spinning.

>   SPIDER-MAN (V.O.)
>   That's *not* original equipment.

We TITLE DOWN to see the ground (which looks like
it's spinning) getting closer and closer.

>   SPIDER-MAN (V.O.)
>   Don't have much time—

BACK TO SPIDEY

He flips to the pellet, ripping it free and
crushing it with his hand.

WIDER - THE SKYBUS

The CRACKLING ENERGY vanishes, and the bus pulls
out of its dive mere yards from the street. As the
skybus soars upward, Spidey leaps off and swings
back to:

THE ALLEY

CLOSE ON the Black Cat's webbed-up boots. WIDEN TO
SEE that's all of her that's still here. Spidey
swings down, hangs from a webline upside-down,
looking at the spot.

> SPIDER-MAN (V.O.)
> Kinda figured this would happen.
> That's why I planted my trusty
> spider-tracer. All I've gotta do
> is—

He touches his eyepiece and:

SPIDEY'S POV - THE SPIDER-TRACER FIELD

Nothing happens

> SPIDER-MAN (V.O.)
> No signal?! I oughta make the
> manufacturer give me my money
> back!

BACK TO SPIDEY

He shoots a webline, swinging to the nearest
rooftop. We ANGLE PAST him to the ruined city: no
sign of the Cat...

> SPIDER-MAN (V.O.)
> Except the manufacturer is me...

> DISSOLVE TO:

In animation, it's the writer's job to include every angle and
describe every camera shot. That's because there is no real director,
so it's up to the writer to tell the storyboard artists exactly what
everything will look like so they can break it down properly. For that
reason, in animation the writer also emphasizes the most important
visuals by putting them in uppercase.

It's also the animation writer's job to tell the voice actors
what inflection to use, because often they're recording their parts
alone, without any of the interaction or stimulus that would help
them understand the words and say them with more meaning. In

animation, the writer also includes the transitions as another way of helping the storyboard artists work more effectively.

Sitcoms that don't use standard film format use a format derived from that of the stageplay because it traces its lineage to live broadcasting, particularly to the live broadcasting of stage-plays. Within the business this is referred to as "taped sitcom format" even though filmed sitcoms use it, the taped sitcom having all but disappeared. (Although it undoubtedly will make a come-back on high-definition digital tape, which may well replace film for all genres.)

The following example of taped sitcom format, written by veteran comedy writer Ed Scharlach (producer of the legendary *Happy Days* and *Mork and Mindy*), is from a series called *Nikola*. Odds are you've never heard of *Nikola* even though it's a long running hit. That's because it's on television in Germany. A superb example of the myriad opportunities that await those who take the plunge into TV writing, *Nikola* features a cast of German actors but is written entirely in English and then translated into Deutsch:

<u>NIKOLA</u>

<u>PINK & BLUE DREAMS</u>

<u>ACT ONE</u>

<u>SCENE ONE</u>

FADE IN:

INT. HOSPITAL - DAY (TEASER)

NIKOLA AND KATHI ARE OOHING AND AWWING AS THEY PAGE THROUGH A PILE OF CATALOGUES FOR BABY WEAR, TOYS, AND OTHER INFANT PARAPHERNALIA.

     KATHI
  Look at this squeaky bear.

     BOTH
 Awww...

                    NIKOLA
And the Peter Rabbit bib.

                    BOTH
Awww...

                    KATHI
And these tiny little knit
booties.

                    NIKOLA
There's probably nothing in this
catalogue that doesn't make you
say "awww."

                    KATHI
I'm having so much fun with
these. (SHUFFLING CATALOGUES)
This one's for toys, this
one's changing tables, this
one's stretchies and nappies.
Everything for the baby.

                    NIKOLA
Now all you need is the baby.

                    KATHI
We're trying...(PICKING UP MANUAL)
This booklet's on ovulation
cycles—how to get my husband
ready at the same time my body is.

NIKOLA FLIPS THROUGH THE MANUAL AND REACTS.

                    NIKOLA
(EYEBROWS RAISING) This might
keep him ready through several
cycles.

                    KATHI
          I know it's silly to collect
          these things when I'm not even
          pregnant. But we really want a
          baby so much.

                    NIKOLA
          It'll happen, Kathi. Just keep doing...
          (REFERRING TO MANUAL) page 48.

These pages are also as close to their original form as I can get
them. The elements are straightforward:

Series Title: (all uppercase, boldface, centered, and
underlined)
                    <u>NIKOLA</u>

Some series put the series title on the title page only. Others
include it on the first page of the script. Most sitcoms put it in
boldface, using a convention of the stageplay format from which
sitcom format is descended.

Double or single spacing after the series title on the first page
of a script depends on the series. This particular series single-spaces
between the series title and the episode title:

Episode Title: (all uppercase, boldface, centered, and
underlined)
             <u>PINK & BLUE DREAMS</u>

Most sitcoms put the episode title in boldface, and regardless of
whether they double-space between the series title and the episode
title they invariably double-space after the episode title. Again, this
is for visual clarity. The production staff has to see where the acts
begin and end.

Act Heading: (all uppercase, boldface, centered, and
underlined)
                  <u>ACT ONE</u>

Not much to say here except that it's been my experience that most sitcoms put the act headings in boldface, and I assume it's also an attempt to follow in the footsteps of stageplay format. (If I'm wrong and any sitcom historians want to speak up, I'm comfortable with making any corrections to this in the next edition.)

Just about every sitcom double-spaces after the act ending.

Scene Headings: (all caps, centered, and underlined):

<u>SCENE I</u>

Unlike film teleplay format, taped sitcom format uses centered scene headings as "titles" for each scene, with the scene number coming after the word "SCENE" (sometimes in Roman numerals; other times spelled out). This is another inheritance from stageplays and also is helpful to the production staff because sitcoms usually have only a few sets and often follow one scene in a given setting with another in the same setting. Without centered and highly visible scene headings, a reader or UPM could become very confused.

Most sitcoms using taped format are shot live, in sequence, before an audience, using the three-camera technique created by Desi Arnaz for I Love Lucy. ("Dad was pretty proud of the fact that shooting live with three cameras became the sitcom standard," Desi Arnaz, Jr. once told me. "But he was the kind of guy who was always excited about everything. He was probably just as proud of a new shirt. And a new grandkid was a much bigger deal than anything else.") But the UPM and the first AD still need to schedule and prep.

Every taped format sitcom script I've ever seen has double-spaced after the scene headings.

Opening Transition: (all uppercase and flush left)

FADE IN:

This is the same as in filmed screenplay format, and replaces the "CURTAIN RISES" of stageplay format. After the opening transition all series double-space to:

Scene Header: (all uppercase, underlined, flush left; spaces, hyphens and DAY or NIGHT must be included, single-spaced):

<u>INT. HOSPITAL–DAY (TEASER)</u>

This is almost identical to that in film format, with the addition of the underlining and the identification of the teaser being part of the scene header instead of the act or scene heading. Some series will use the "TEASER" heading. As already discussed, others will use the phrase "COLD OPEN" or "COLD OPENING."

The scene header is always followed by a double-space to the next element.

(Note: In some sitcoms, such as Frasier, immediately following the scene header is a "scene cast list" which is all uppercase, flush left, single-spaced, and in parentheses. It looks like this: (FRAZIER, ROZ) and is followed by a double-space to the next element as well.)

Action Paragraph or Line: (all uppercase, flush left, single-spaced)

NIKOLA AND KATHI ARE OOHING AND AWWING AS THEY PAGE THROUGH A PILE OF CATALOGUES FOR BABY WEAR, TOYS, AND OTHER INFANT PARAPHERNALIA.

The taped format teleplay action paragraph looks exactly like the stage directions in a stageplay.

The action paragraph is always preceded by and followed by a double-space.

Character Name (all uppercase) with Dialogue: (normal, double-spaced)

NIKOLA
There's probably nothing in
this catalogue that doesn't
make you say "awww."

Like stageplay dialogue, taped format dialogue is double-spaced.

There's also a double-space between the character name and the speech, and another double-space before the next character name and dialogue, action line, scene heading, or act ending. Parenthetical expressions are kept within the body of the dialogue. They get no special line, not indention, nothing but parentheses to show what you mean.

Closing Transition: (not shown in example; uppercase; flush right)

FADE OUT

This is the same as the closing transition in film format and replaces "CURTAIN FALLS" in stageplay format.

Act Ending: (not shown in example; all uppercase, underlined, centered)

END OF ACT

Same old, same old. Except that most taped format sitcoms don't start the next act on the next page. They merely double-space down and get going. (Some sitcoms space down about a quarter of a page between acts. The reason is another job for the sitcom historians.)

Show Ending: (not shown in example, comes after Act Ending at end of show; all caps, underlined, centered)

END OF SHOW

This is a strange one. Most sitcoms in taped teleplay format not only designate the end of an act but also the end of the show *after* the end of the act and not instead of it. (Possibly on the theory that even though something has ended it never hurts to mention it twice.)

This format is easier to understand and use than film teleplay format because it flows more naturally as a direct result of not taking the existence of the camera into consideration. It just tells the actors and production staff what the actors have to say and do, and where they're going to say and do it. Again the font to use is 12 point Courier or Courier New, and as with one-hour teleplays, exact page set-up, margins, spacing, and indentation vary from series to series. And add-ons such as "(MORE)" and "(CONTINUED)" are usually inserted by the production staff.

All the commercial script formatting programs have special templates for sitcoms, and most of them have them for stageplays as well. ScreenWriter 2000 and FinalDraft have specific templates for both individual one-hour series and sitcoms, although these can be more confusing than enlightening. Like their film format brothers, the sitcom format templates automatically position everything properly and set the proper line spacing and will give you the option of using the add-ons.

If you're going to use Microsoft Word, Word for Mac, or another word processing program for writing your taped format sitcom teleplay, I recommend the following settings:

Page Set-Up: top margin 1.2"; bottom margin 1"; left margin 1.3"; right margin .05".

Character name above dialogue: tabbed 2.5" from the left margin. Dialogue: tabbed 1.2" from the left margin and ending 1.3" from the right.

In taped format with this page set-up, the average television sitcom is 45 pages long. Daytime serial teleplays also use the same format, with the ever-present individual differences, but they're shorter, usually about 30 pages. Both sitcom teleplays and soap opera teleplays keep description at arm's length, using as little of it as possible—like stageplays. The exception to this rule is when a sitcom features physical comedy. Then as much of it as possible is spelled out. As Desi Jr. explains, "My mother was a genius at physical comedy, but you'd be amazed at the scripts. Every single movement and gesture and facial expression was right there. The writers knew her and what she could do, and they wrote for it. She'd follow the directions exactly, but it would still come out as a real 'Lucy' kind of schtick."

And now a few more facts about the physical script, no matter what genre and format it's in. The hard copy script is always printed out on 8.5" x 11" three-hole punched paper and held together by two 1.25" brass brads, one in the top hole and one in the bottom hole. Always use white paper—but be prepared for a literal rainbow of colored paper for each set of changes made by the staff and sent out to everyone concerned. Page numbers go in the upper right-hand corner. Most shows no longer bother with script covers, so there's no need to worry about what cover stock to put on your assigned or spec teleplay. All you need is a perfect title page instead.

Whether your teleplay is for a TV movie, a one-hour episode, animation, a sitcom, a soap opera, you name it, the title page will look something like this:

<u>SERIES NAME</u>

"Episode Title"

Written by

You

YOUR NAME (or your agent's name)   DRAFT
YOUR ADDRESS (or your agent's address)   DATE
YOUR PHONE NUMBER (or your agent's phone number)

The series name is always centered and in all uppercase and underlined. The episode name is always centered and sometimes in all uppercase and underlined and sometimes not. The same for "Written by" and your name.

It's always "Written by" and not "by." This often confuses writers who have written for publication, but the fact is that, while in the publishing industry, saying "Written by" would be redundant because the only purpose the work has is to be written and published, in film and TV "by" would refer to the entire production and not just the writing. In fact, it's becoming more common for television episodes to also list the director on the title page, giving a "Directed by" credit two or three spaces down from the "Written by." Of course, this can only be done after a director has been assigned to the project.

The practice of putting the director's name on a television script has become more popular now that more directors are being put on the staffs of shows and given producer titles. Think it's safe to say this isn't a coincidence?

The contact information for either you or your agent is always in all uppercase, flush left, and at the bottom of the page, with the last line of the info at the bottom margin. The content of the material is always in all uppercase and is tabbed as far right as it'll fit, with the date you're sending out your work in all uppercase beneath it. By content I mean that, when you're delivering an outline to a show-runner, you label it "OUTLINE," or "STORY." If you're turning in a rewritten outline, the label is "REV. OUTLINE" or "REV. STORY." Your first draft is "FIRST DRAFT." Your rewrite is "REV. DRAFT." I leave the label "REV. DRAFT" on any subsequent rewrites, but of course change the date. This is for career insurance. Why take the risk that a teleplay labeled "FOURTH DRAFT" will get into the hands of someone you want to impress? Do you really want them to know it took four tries for you to get it the way the showrunner wanted?

When you're writing a spec you can go one better. Simply put "FINAL DRAFT" on every version. If you're pouring all your talent and skill and soul into the work, then this is the FINAL DRAFT, isn't it? In your eyes, your work should always seem the best you possibly can make it before you let anyone else have a look.

chapter 11:
the teleplay—part 2

Now that we've got format, the part of television writing about which every new writer obsesses, out of the way it's time to discuss what you *should* be obsessing out:

Quality.

Admittedly, this isn't always easy in a business where, as producer/ director Norman Powell, who has also spent many years as a development executive at both CBS and Turner Broadcasting, once told an eager group of students at the College of Santa Fe, "Your goal always is to write a good script. Just remember that in TV the definition of 'good' is 'a script my boss will like.'"

What do you think? Is this cynicism?

Pragmatism?

The kind of gross exaggeration so common to showbiz?

All of the above?

I've known Powell a long time and I know he's far from a cynic. Quite the contrary. He's got an optimism that just won't quit. How else do you explain the 40-plus years he's spent in TV?

Norman Powell is, however, pragmatic. As someone who's been both a seller and a buyer he knows the sometimes harsh truth that nothing and no one gets bought unless the network or show needs it.

Did Powell exaggerate? He's certainly to that particular manor—

and manner—born. Both his parents were film stars from the 1930s through the 1950s…Dick Powell and Joan Blondell. Joan Blondell was also one of the stars of the first TV series for which I wrote, *Here Come The Brides*. (No, she didn't play one of the Bolt brothers. She was the classic great-old-gal-who-owns-the-saloon character.) So perhaps he exaggerated just a little to make an important point. A point that goes back to Paul Junger Witt's admonition that "the best kept secret in show business is that it's a business."

And because it's a business, anyone getting started in television writing has to be able to meet the real demand—not the publicized generalization, "We need new writers!" but the need for writers, new or experienced, who can give the viewing audience what the executives think it wants.

"Fine," you say. "I'm on it. What do the viewers want? And what do the suits want to give them?"

There's the problem.

No one knows.

Oh, they—the execs—have ideas about it. So do we, the writers. For the most part the execs get their notions from research. And also for the most part writers get them from their guts.

Executives at broadcast networks these days are trying to attract the audience their advertisers believe will buy their products. Executives at basic cable and satellite channels are doing the same. Executives at premium cable and satellite channels—the ones for which viewers pay extra—are trying appeal directly to the viewers' personal tastes in that "narrowcast" way of which we spoke earlier. Audience testing tries to give all three of these groups their answer. The procedure is almost identical to the focus group testing that goes on for most consumer products.

"Hi there. Here's our new car. How much do you like it? What do you like about the exterior? The interior? What don't you like about them? How much don't you like those things?"

And:

"'Lo and behold, folks. Here's our new show. How much do you like it? What do you like about the actors? The story? What don't you like about them? How much don't you like these things?"

I've been to these sessions, both for cars, as a consumer being tested, and for television series, as a showrunner praying like mad my show will get on the air. At the product testing sessions every possible aspect of design and engineering is numbered, quantified. At the television testing sessions every possible aspect of creativity gets the same treatment. Both subjects are rated, out of context and in a public setting in which the questions and their wording and the questioners and their tone of voice automatically, although not deliberately, pressure the potential buyers and viewers into giving the "right" response—one with which the other buyers and viewers as well as the questioners will agree.

At least that's how it's made me feel.

Writers—I'm speaking about the writers I know, not all writers, although I think this particular generalization would hold true—get their idea of what viewers want from other writers, critics, philosophers, and poets.

The television writers I know tend to look at the situation this way: If the writing is good enough, people will watch what comes out of it. If the production as a whole is good enough, a hell of a lot of people will watch it, because they'll enjoy what they see.

In other words, writers think less in terms of the foolproof "high concept" and more in terms of "execution." It's not, "If you build it, they will come." Rather it's "If you build it *well*, they will come."

Which is another way of saying writers believe in "quality."

Which gets us back to where we began. What *is* quality when it comes to writing? That's a question that has to be answered. Otherwise, what the hell are any of us—new writers or old pros— doing here? How the hell can writers write if we don't know what *good writing* is? How the hell can writers write if the only criterion is the result of today's market research or a statistical whim?

How do we write "what my boss will like"?

Piece of cake. We write with intelligence and sensitivity, with knowledge and skill, with the keenest possible grasp of what kinds of situations and characters and language will have the biggest impact on people.

We write with a control over our language, with literary style, with exciting situations and more exciting dialogue and with a sense that what we're writing means something, a firm belief that "even television" is important. Popular entertainment has the power to move people, to mold people, to teach them, change them, and thrill them all at the same time.

We write with a sense of passion about the present and a sense of the history of human culture. We take what works—what has always worked—and we redefine it and make it our own. We use it in a new way.

Build it well and the viewers will come!

We've already seen how this is done in the storytelling process, the structure and plot and outline of our work. Now we've got to apply ourselves to the teleplay itself.

In the teleplay stage, even more than in the outline, talent and sweat, the old "inspiration and perspiration" have to unite to create a script so well-written, so moving and powerful that even the most frightened executive *has* to buy it or hire the writer—a script so powerful that it's impossible for the showrunner or network D-Guy or D-Gal to say no.

And believe me, they're *always looking for a reason to say no.* Because if they don't buy they're not taking any risk. They can't fail if they don't give a project or a writer a "go." An executive who only utilizes the tried and true—material that's already proven itself in another medium, writers who've already written a thousand scripts— and turns down everything and everyone new no matter how great the potential may not become a studio head, but he or she has a better chance of keeping the current job than an exec who says yes, only to watch the new idea or new writer fall flat.

Writing a great teleplay takes energy and dedication. Your job as a new writer is to demonstrate your talent and potential in such a way that proves you're better equipped for whatever the execs decide they want than even the most highly awarded and respected established pro. No book can give you the talent; it must come from within. Having the personality traits common to most writers—the love of language, the ability to escape the vicissitudes of life via literature and media and daydreams with ease, alienation, or shyness—doesn't mean you have talent, but it's a step in the right direction.

Having a talent for writing means that self-expression via the written word comes easily, sometimes more easily than speech. Writers who are said to "have talent" have a pleasing way of forming sentences and paragraphs and—usually—are able to express feelings and insights by taking everything they've read and using the language patterns that have moved them in literature and reworking them to move others.

Having a talent for television writing incorporates this and then demonstrates even more. A "talented" TV writer is one who writes scripts in which the writer uses his or her mastery of language to create situations in which the characters become as real as any human being the reader ever has met and seem to be living fascinating moment after fascinating moment in their lives. A talented television writer keeps the reading easy yet creates exciting and sometimes very complex images in the minds of everyone who turns the pages of that writer's work.

The talented but untutored and unpracticed television writer who sits down and writes a spec script usually has one or two scenes in which everything comes together as described. One or two scenes where the reader—that same reader who's learned to love high-concept log-lines—nods his or her head and says, "Whoa! I wish I'd written that!"

When you're dealing with some insightful showrunners or executives, those one or two scenes out of your 45 or 55 or 110 page spec sometimes can be enough to propel you along further. I got my first break when feature film producer Jerome Katzman (now head of the television division of the William Morris Agency) read a spec TV movie I'd written, saw the couple of scenes that worked well, and, as he told me, thought, "This kid's got potential. With the right pushing he might be able to come up with this kind of work on every page. I'll have to meet him and see if he's the kind of guy who wants to learn more." It was Katzman who put me together with Arthur Dreifuss, creating a situation where I, indeed, "learned more."

In today's corporate showbiz environment most executives need more than a few scenes to make them jump up and shout. Over the years, I've continued learning and have acquired many techniques for demonstrating my talent and making *most* of the scenes of a teleplay strong and appealing. Now is the time for me to pass them along to you. So here come the tips, shotgunned in no particular order:

1) Scenes are more than a means to an end. Each one is a mini-story in itself, with a beginning, middle, and end. Scenes need to be structured so that the intensity within them grows and then climaxes, like microcosms of your screenplay or teleplay.

Just as a good story starts as close to the middle of the story as possible, so does a good scene. On the old *Hawaii Five-O* series, I learned the trick of beginning each scene in the middle of a confrontation between the main characters. Viewers very seldom saw a character enter a room and say, "Hello." Instead, the viewers reached the room after the characters had already begun arguing and because of that they were instantly drawn in.

The arguments would be played out to their fullest, reaching an emotional peak. Then we'd write an immediate ending. The ending was always something physical, not verbal, anything from a slamming door or a breaking mirror to a shooting, after which we were on to the next rising argument. In a good *Hawaii Five-O* teleplay— and that's most of them—each scene stands alone as an exciting and often violent character vignette. One way to accomplish this is to think of your scenes as short, two page stories. Do this and you'll see how much more immediate it will make your entire teleplay.

2) In TV writing, the key to the success of a series is to create characters the audience wants to come back and see again and again. Most writers make the mistake of thinking this means the characters have to be likeable. But was Andy Sipowicz of *NYPD Blue* likeable when the series started? He still took the airwaves by storm. How about Archie Bunker on *All In The Family*? Was he a loveable kinda guy?

Characters like Andy and Archie aren't people we like at all, but they are sympathetic, and that's what makes them work. For better or for worse, they've got attitudes we understand, and they're caught up in situations that give them the feeling of powerlessness we all have so many times in life. In reality, power may be like a drug, attracting people right and left. But in TV, *powerlessness* does the same thing.

Viewers become hooked on these powerless characters struggling to have some say in the world. They—and in all likelihood you and I, the writers—identify with them. This causes the viewers to come back every week to see how those they love or hate or love to hate are coping with events that usually are more serious than those which cause the viewers great anxiety and stress. This is true in every genre. Create scenes that demonstrate the characters' inner conflicts, as well as their conflicts with others, and you're way ahead of the game.

3) How do you show those conflicts? The way you show everything

else in a teleplay, with action primarily and to a lesser extent through dialogue. Having already created and positioned your scenes in terms of what part of the story they tell, you know to drop in the characterization within this context.

For example, you can show that a character is self-effacing and easily intimidated by having him or her defer to someone else while a plot point is being made. In a medical drama you can have Edie the intern start to give a diagnosis while on rounds with the rest of the interns and the supervising physicians—only to be interrupted by another intern after barely getting one sentence out of her mouth. (Make that a complete sentence even though it's going to be interrupted. Actors need to know all of what they're going to say. Otherwise they're likely to stop wherever you've put in your dash—before the other actor actually jumps in and cuts them off. Indicate the interruption by putting the dash at the end of the sentence spoken by the first actor and including the parenthetical "(interrupting)" for the second.)

Or you can show that a character in a sitcom is one horny bastard by writing a stage direction to the effect that Eddie the mechanic is always putting his face very close to that of any woman to whom he speaks, always getting in her space.

Adding the inner conflict to both these scenes is done by having another small event happen. To show that Edie the intern is furious with herself for allowing someone to interrupt her, you can have the thermometer she holds suddenly snap in her hand. To show that Eddie the mechanic is obnoxious but well-meaning, and bring in the comedy, you can have him be so pushy that when the woman he's with backs away he loses his balance and crashes nose first into a wall—and immediately asks if she's okay.

4) Remember that everything a character says or does sends a signal to the audience that says, "This means something." This means a character can't cough unless he or she is going to have a cold. And a character can't have a cold unless that cold is integral to the plot. In a fantasy series, the cold could keep the vampire hunter from being aware of an odor that would make another character a vampiric suspect. In a sitcom,

the cold could mean that no one can understand what the character is saying, leading to humorous but unfortunate consequences.

5) Characterization and story are interconnected. Your treatment of the characters in the teleplay is augmented by how difficult your story is making their lives. Viewers aren't going to know how your characters react under stress unless you give them some stress—which should be what your storyline is all about. The build-up is very important, so remember to start out small, with only one unmanageable stress which is the problem to be solved in the episode—and then turn the screws.

Pile more and more garbage on your characters' heads—the villains as well as the heroes. It's not enough that the daughter of the lead has been kidnapped; his mistress has to leave him as a result. And his sister has to let him know that if he doesn't make it to her birthday party with a good enough kid she's going to have her husband, who's the lead's boss, fire the poor guy.

With the right set of troubles, the audience feels for even the most otherwise unlikable lead. Remember Robert Altman's film, *The Player*? Tim Robbins's character kills a man who doesn't deserve it. (Does any man ever deserve to be killed? In films and TV, hell yes!) The only thing the victim has done wrong is become a writer, you might say. But his character's life gets so tough afterward that even writers rooted for him to succeed.

6) F. Scott Fitzgerald, not exactly known as an action writer, said, "In movies, characters are what they do, not what they say." That holds true in television as well. In a novel, the reader gets into the protagonist's mind and knows his or her thoughts. In a stageplay, the spoken flow of words is designed to both propel the story forward and illuminate the psyches of the speakers. But in a teleplay, the only way we can know what a character is thinking is by how the character behaves. We never hear his or her thoughts, and the only time we should hear a character speak is when he or she is having a conversation with someone else, to whom he could easily be lying.

Confession time: As a showrunner, one of my pet peeves is when a teleplay shows a character talking to him or herself. Almost always it's being done as a way of getting out some exposition, so the viewer will know why what's happening is happening. In real life, the only people I've known who talk to themselves are nut cases, so my advice is that unless you're trying to show that a character has gone off the deep end omit the thinking out loud and find another way to make clear what's going on.

In a well-written teleplay action is what gives us our characters' states of mind. An angry character throws a chair, breaks a mirror (I got that from *Hawaii Five-O*), squeals away in a car, and ends up wrecking it. A loving character holds a dear one tenderly, makes a self-sacrificing gesture, or "devours" the loved one with his or her eyes. A character who can't face life literally turns away, or runs away, or closes the garage door and turns on the engine to his or her car. Whether the action is large or small, it will always appear to come from within, caused by the needs of the character and, therefore, illuminating the character at the same time it fills the screen.

7) Don't overwrite in your action paragraphs. By that I mean, edit yourself. Remember that in television the writer has a limited number of minutes to fill and a limited number of pages in which to do it. Verbose descriptions of the settings and of the feelings and intentions of the characters, for the reader's eyes only, get in the way of the flow of the story and eat up the pages. Instead of writing this:

```
INT. DONALD'S OFFICE - DAY
It's a good-sized room, about 15 by 15, with two
big picture windows overlooking Manhattan 40
stories below. The office is walnut-paneled and
decorated in Early American, and a scale model
of the Liberty Bell on Donald's trestle desk is
actually a phone. This is expensive Early
American. Photos of Donald and a variety of
local politicians line the walls, and all light
comes from floor lamps.

Anxious about the way the investigation is going,
fearful of losing his license, Donald leafs
through a law book as he rocks on a recliner in
```

the far corner of the room. The recliner is on a small, circular American flag rug.

Write this:

```
INT. DONALD'S 40th FLOOR OFFICE - DAY
Bright and airy, with a view of Manhattan below.
Walnut-paneled and expensively appointed in Early
American décor. Walls lined with photos of Donald
with local pols.

Donald sits on a recliner, pages through a law
book as though looking for something.
```

This version takes up half the space and makes the same point. We don't have to know specifically about the trestle desk and the floor lamps and even the American flag rug unless those items literally play a part in the story. Was the trestle desk stolen, and will the original owner return to claim it in the next scene? Then it's needed. Is one of the lamps missing a bulb, which will cause a maintenance man to come in and utter a pithy epigram that will change Donald's life? Then it's needed. Did Donald and an underage woman make love on the rug, leaving a DNA sample that'll put him away for 10 years? Then it's needed. Otherwise— forget it.

Neither should the writer have to tell us about Donald's anxiety and fear. If the context of the scene and its placement at this point in the plot haven't made us well aware of his general state of mind, then this script isn't going to get its writer anything—not a sale, not a staff job, not an agent.

Come to think of it, the description can be even tighter. Here's the way it might be written by Shane Black, one of the highest paid screenwriters in the world, and a master at getting in and getting out:

```
INT. DONALD'S OFFICE - DAY
It's a law office — you've been there — you know
what they look like. Donald's into the Americana
thing, so think "set decoration by Ethan Allan."
```

```
He pages through a law book — sees what he wants —
picks up the phone.
```

And that's it, the writer's point efficiently made.

8) Don't underwrite the action paragraphs. Use your descriptive and narrative skills when they're needed. Many writers are so worried about overwriting that they don't say enough and fail to draw the reader into their world, or the characters' state of mind. If the reader of your teleplay doesn't have a clue of where things are or how they look, you're going to lose him or her posthaste. Too many writers write:

```
EXT. GARDEN - DAY
Miriam's tending her plants. Albert appears beside
her.

                    MIRIAM
          You startled me.
```

My first reaction reading something like this is, "Huh? Where's the garden? What kind of plants are in it? Where did Albert come from? Did he appear magically? Or did he walk over to Miriam but she didn't notice? Is Miriam really startled or is she lying? I mean, she didn't show any signs of being startled, did she? Oh, crap, do I have to read this again?"

In a word, I'm disoriented. And that disorientation pulls me out of the teleplay. Having to reread in order to understand reminds me that what I'm reading isn't real. It's created by a writer—a writer in whom I'm rapidly losing confidence.

You never want your reader to lose confidence in you. Your job as a writer is to make sure the reader feels in good hands. So a better way to write the above—without overwriting it—would be:

```
EXT. MIRIAM'S VEGETABLE GARDEN - DAY

She's staking tomatoes, Albert coming up behind
her from the house. Miriam turns to pick up
```

another stake and suddenly sees him beside her.
She gasps, startled.

MIRIAM

      Oh!

There. Now I'm secure as a reader. I have no questions and no reason not to keep reading on.

Similarly, although you don't want to write descriptions such as "Anxious about the way the investigation is going, fearful of losing her license, Miriam digs in the dirt as a way of avoiding the issue," there's nothing wrong with something like this: "Miriam's upset, tries not to show it." Or "Miriam's upset — tries not to show it." (Dashes are trendy; they mark the writer as young and hip.)

Always remember that you've got to use the tools that make you a writer. A brief sentence here and there, at moments of extreme emotion, telling the reader that characters' attitudes can be the difference between a hit and a miss. Even while trying not to say too much, remember the old theater adage: "If it's not on the page, it's not on the stage." And it certainly isn't in the mind of the reader.

9) Speaking of putting in bits of physical business, such as staking tomatoes, skillful usage of stagecraft can increase the effectiveness of a scene. One of the first things I learned when writing detective shows was to avoid having two people standing or sitting together in a room doing nothing but asking and answering questions. It's much more effective to put the characters into a more unexpected setting, and to have them doing something.

When I was showrunner of *Mike Hammer*, we worked overtime coming up with interesting places and things to be done in these places in order to put some physical excitement into what would otherwise be standard "Where were you last night? Did you know the victim?"-type scenes. We'd have Mike question a witness at the witness' place of employment—a loading dock, gym, racetrack—and have the witness engaged in his or her usual activity. The dock worker would be schlepping crates, the aerobics instructor leading a class, the motorcycle racer tuning his bike.

To make things even more interesting, we'd have Mike join in the activity, and make his part in it a little scene within a scene, building to its own climax occurring at the same time the necessary information finally—and always reluctantly because that was the conflict—came out. With the dock worker, Mike would help wrestle the biggest box—and Mike's back would go out just as he learned what he needed to know. With the aerobics instructor Mike would take part in the class—and two or three beautiful women (it was always two or three because the series was a "secret comedy") would fall into lust with the detective and drag him off to the locker room just as he learned what he needed to know. With the motorcycle racer, Mike would get on another bike and race a lap against him—and beat the champ just as Mike learned what he needed to know.

The latter form of activity—Mike versus the champion racer—is the kind of business that can also be expanded into a sub-plot: two men who, every time they encounter each other during the course of the main plot, immediately go into macho, mano-a-mano competition.

10) Speaking of setting things in unusual locations, here's something I learned from Philip Saltzman, supervising producer of *The FBI* and *Barnaby Jones*: vary your locations. Cutting from one interior to another to another gives a teleplay a claustrophobic feeling, and it feels even more closed in to the viewer after it's shot. Going from exterior to exterior to exterior makes the teleplay seem too generic and open-ended—and too expensive to shoot. On the long-running *Barnaby Jones* (*incredibly* long-running when you think about the fact that this was a series that did little more every week than answer the seldom-asked question: "What would my grandfather do if my grandfather fought crime?"), we would alternate locations religiously, going from exterior to interior and back again to keep from being too closed or too open.

11) Speaking of things being too closed or too open, have you ever watched a television episode or TV movie and felt as though you weren't watching the actual show but a very long trailer for it instead? As though you as a viewer weren't privy to what was really going on, especially in the mind of the lead? I've noticed that this happens whenever the script is comprised almost entirely of scenes

after scene cutting to another location and another time. The viewer feels like he or she is seeing only the public moments in a story. They are missing out on those private times just before or after what's already there.

To counteract this, I recommend mixing "continuous action" scenes with cuts to elsewhere and else-when, especially if you can make those continuous action scenes smaller and more personal than the others. Instead of having a scene between Will and Grace in their apartment, with Grace telling Will her latest problem and what she's going to do about it, and then cutting to Grace at work trying to do it, have that first Will and Grace scene and then stay with Grace after Will leaves. She's alone; no one's watching but the viewer. But what does she do? She practices the little thing she's going to do—the dance shtick or wisecrack shtick or whatever it is—and the audience gets a chance to see her earnestness, and to care for her that much more. And to laugh when in doing the dance step she falls flat on her behind.

(Note: Tips 10 and 11 could just have easily been included in the outline section of this book. The reason they weren't is that these particular problems usually go unnoticed when you're working out the story, and then leap out at you like demons when you're writing the teleplay. When this kind of thing happens, feel free to improvise and correct the situation. The outline isn't intended to tether you to a story or situation that doesn't work, so don't let it!)

12) No bumps. In the early 1990s Herb Solow, Janis Hendler, and I had a deal at CBS to develop an adventure series to be called *Justin Tyme*. The series was to be on twice weekly, a melding of the old Saturday afternoon serials that were in the movie theaters when I was a kid, with modern technology and techno-crime. After we'd written the first drafts of our first two episodes, Herb, Janis, and I went to a meeting scheduled with the D-Guy in charge of the project, an old pro named Tony Barr.

Meeting with Barr was always a pleasure because we could all trot out our war stories about the business and commiserate and gossip and generally have a good time. When we arrived for this particular gathering, however, we were surprised to discover that Barr had been summoned to the office of the president of the network to help handle some emergency or other and his secretary, Ruthie, was going to be giving us "notes" (the network executives' opinions, observations, and demands for changes in the script) instead of her boss.

I'll admit it. I was very tense. At that time I was of the "Oh hell, she's just a secretary. What can she possibly tell us that we don't already know?" school of ignorance and intolerance, not the enlightened, open-minded Mr. Sensitive I am now.

But Ruthie surprised me.

She changed my life.

In a general way, what Ruthie said at that meeting taught me to be a "better person" (at least if you like enlightened, open-minded Mr. Sensitive types). In a specific way, Ruthie taught me about "bumps." Solow, Hendler, and Brody sat on the couch in Tony Barr's office. Ruthie (if I knew her last name I'd use it, I swear) sat across the coffee table in Barr's chair and started going through the first teleplay.

Line by line. Sentence by sentence. Word by word.

She read something out loud—I forgot what it was—and said, "You've got to change this word. It's a bump."

She read something else out loud and said, "You've got to rephrase this sentence. It's a bump."

As Ruthie was giving her third "bumpy" note Hendler turned to me and mouthed, "What's a 'bump'?" I turned to Solow and did the same. "What's a 'bump'?" Solow, the senior member of our little "staff" turned to Ruthie. No mouthing this time. He came out and said it. "Uh, Ruthie, what's a 'bump'?"

Ruthie looked surprised. She spoke to us like a school teacher explaining to third graders. "Why, it's anything that's confusing when I'm reading. A misspelling, a typo, a word I've never seen before, a sentence so complicated I can't follow it. A hyphen! A multi-syllable word that's hyphenated and continued onto the next line throws me every time." She leaned in closer, more confident now that she saw she had our rapt attention. "A bump is a bump in my reading road. It's anything I don't immediately understand. Anything I've got to read twice." She leaned closer still, her bead necklace dangling dangerously close to my coffee. "You know," Ruthie said, "if I've got to read too many things twice too often, that's it, you've lost me. I've escaped your magic writing spell. And you don't want me to escape your magic writing spell, do you?"

She sat back. Her necklace and my coffee were saved.

And I had a new way of looking at my work. A way that took into consideration not just whether or not what I'd written succeeded in saying what I wanted to say the way I wanted to say it, but also if it could be read quickly and easily by busy executives and their support troops, who might be far less educated and aware of literature and media than I, or far more. (I never did figure out which applied to Ruthie, nor do I know where she is these days. Hope you're running a studio or network, Ruthie! Or teaching the hell out of third grade!)

The bottom line here (or "to cut to the chase," another exciting television term) is that you've got to keep your language simple. Keep it clear. Always spell correctly and fix any typos. Always use proper grammar. Always remember that even if the grammar is proper, if the wording is tough to understand, it's got to be changed. When you read your own work, always read it from the perspective of, "Do I have to read anything twice to understand it?" Because if *you* do, and you're the writer, you know it's never going to make it past Ruthie. It's going to be a big damn bump in the road.

13) It's corollary time again. While you remember to write with no bumps, also remember this: If the showrunner or executive who is reading your teleplay finds anything he or she can't follow or understand, he or she will always blame the writer. Readers of spec scripts—and assigned scripts too—are unforgiving. Confuse them in any way and the response is short and not very sweet: "This writer can't write!" And into the trash (metaphorically or, sometimes, literally) you spec script and your possible employment go.

You know how it feels when you shell out good money for a novel, and while you are reading you come across a paragraph where, suddenly, things don't seem to make sense? The author, either in the narrative or via a character's dialogue, is referring to something you don't remember. When that happens to me, I thumb back through the book and, with few exceptions, always find the info I originally missed by reading too quickly or because I was distracted at the time. I think to myself, "Brody, you dummy!" and then I go on. In film and television, however, this is a very unlikely event. The reader gets to an action paragraph or line of dialogue referring to something the reader doesn't remember and their reaction is, "This writer can't write!"

This holds true for intentional surprises as well as bumps. Any time you're setting up a mystery, you've got to be careful to reveal to the reader that this is what you're doing. If your character overlooks a simple clue because of something in the character's personal life and you're going to make that clear five pages later, you've got to write it so that a reader—but not a viewer—understands that now. If your character notices something that won't come into play until 10 pages down the (no longer) bumpy road, you've got to indicate that for the reader as well.

The best way to do this is overtly. I prefer the "Shane Black style." I don't know if Black's ever written anything like this, but he should have: "There's blood on the floor. The hero coughs — covers it with phlegm — doesn't see it. (This'll mean something later.)"

It's important to alert the reader without completely giving away what you're doing. Because if you reveal your full surprise upfront it won't surprise the reader when he or she gets to it later. And if it doesn't surprise the reader then, know what that reader will say? All together now: "This writer can't write."

14) Another corollary. If you're using Classic Format for your teleplay you can telegraph harbingers of things to come to both the reader and the viewer by a judicious use of camera angles. A few well-placed shots will tell the reader what's important in the scene, giving him or her a clue about how to regard and respond to what's going on.

In Classic Format, for example, you can tell the reader that the hero missing the blood is a plot point in this way:

```
INT. ROLANDO'S HOUSE - NIGHT
Det. Presley takes another look around the room.
He's been sniffling from his cold. Now he coughs.

CLOSE ON THE FLOOR BY THE TANNING BED
```

```
Where there's a spot of blood — but only for a
beat. If vanishes, spattered with phlegm.

PRESLEY
Sees nothing, goes out the door.
```

It's page-consuming, it's clunky, but it does the trick. Any time you show a specific camera angle you're telling the reader, "This is important. Watch for it." And with any luck the director will use the shot and make the same announcement to the viewer as well.

15) Your hero or heroes have to be heroic.

Television, more than any other medium, is one of heroes. I've produced or written about 2,000 episodes of TV and every one of them had a hero. Animated shows, shows derived from comic book-related material, and shows designed to breed new comic book-related material make it obvious. *Spider-Man, Superman, the Silver Surfer,* and *Spawn* have super powers. Ditto Steve Austin of *The Six Million Dollar Man,* the BBC's *Captain Lightning,* and *Automan. Diabolik,* the hero of a French-Italian series of the same name, is smart, skilled, tricky, and wears a super-style costume.

It's pretty clear in most one-hour shows as well. Mike Hammer is tough as nails and takes no nonsense from anyone. Ironside, Cannon, Barnaby Jones, Petrocelli, and Baretta of their various series of the same names, McGarrett and Danno of *Hawaii Five-0,* Tony Blake of *The Magician,* the two women known as *Partners in Crime,* the mother-daughter bounty hunting team from *The Huntress,* Pepper of *Police Woman,* Walker and Trivette of *Walker, Texas Ranger,* "Doctor Mark" of *Diagnosis: Murder,* Colt Seavers of *The Fall Guy,* and all the street cops and detectives of *Police Story, The Streets of San Francisco,* and *The New Adventures of Rin Tin Tin* were crime solvers and crook-apprehenders to the nth degree.

Janeway and the crew of starship Voyager of *Star Trek: Voyager,* Picard and the crew of the Enterprise of *Star Trek: The Next Generation,* Kirk, Spock, McCoy, and the gang of *Star Trek,* Super Force of *Super Force,* the psychic investigator of *The Sixth Sense,* and the intrepid explorers of Gene Roddenberry's *Genesis II* (a series I wrote for that never made it to the air) are all bold science fiction adventurers of one form or another.

The almost-angelic leads in *Heaven Help Us* are great little helpers of deserving living people. The docs in *Medical Story, Medical Center, The Bold Ones*, and *The Young Interns* will cure just about anything or kill themselves trying. The hard-working frontier families of *The New Land* and my old number one, *Here Come the Brides* would tackle any obstacle and work doggedly until it was an obstacle no more.

Sitcom and daytime serial leads are less obviously heroes because they operate on a smaller stage. In the main, they deal with emotional problems. I'm not a sitcom writer and haven't written a daytime serial since the days of an NBC soap called *Bright Promise*, so I won't force you to read through another list of "my" characters. But my love for television means that I actually watch these things, and I can say that the leads of *Friends, I Love Lucy, Will & Grace, The Donna Reed Show, Just Shoot Me, Ozzie & Harriet, Life with Bonnie, The Mary Tyler Moore Show, Everybody Loves Raymond, The Dick Van Dyke Show, Frasier, M*A*S*H, 8 Simple Rules for Dating My Teenage Daughter, Cheers, Sabrina the Teenage Witch, All in the Family, The Drew Carey Show, Days of Our Lives, Another World, The Bold and the Beautiful, All My Children, The Young and the Restless, The City*, and on and on, are as much heroes as the leads in other, more action-packed genres.

In a nutshell, then, we're talking about every show ever on TV, and one could argue that shows that have survived the longest and been most successful in terms of ratings, critics' approval, or both are the ones that delineated their heroes most effectively. That all-important network research, after all, says the main reason viewers regularly watch a series is because they love the family of characters, even the characters they hate.

As a writer and showrunner, I've had to create or present many, many heroes over the years, and I've spent more time than is probably healthy thinking about what makes a protagonist turn the corner and become more than someone the viewer is merely watching and, instead, someone in whom the viewer has a deep emotional stake, a character for whom the viewer roots and cheers.

While giving the character a hard time automatically gains the viewer's sympathy, there's more to it than that. On the one hand, viewers are moved by characters trapped in the same situations of powerlessness that the viewers are. But on the other hand, viewers are hooked by, and grow to truly admire, characters who seem in charge of their own destiny. To me, a hero is someone who is able to rise above all the forces that try to beat him or her down and take control of his or her life—or at least of the immediate action.

No matter how a character has become involved in the current situation, no matter how put upon or oppressed, that character becomes a hero to the viewer when he or she stops reacting to the outside pressures or the actions of the antagonist and instead takes steps that make the situation (via those who've created it) react to him or her. Even if in every other way the character is a schlemiel if, in this situation—this moment, this scene—he or she takes charge, a hero is born.

This is tricky, I understand. Think back to every book you've ever read in which you've loved the hero, every film or TV show you've seen in which you've wanted to cheer on the hero. The reason you loved the hero and wanted to cheer is because the hero was doing something you, as a real human being, probably couldn't. The hero was making everything revolve around him or her.

Yes, at last, the dread "it's all about me" finally isn't to be dreaded at all. Finally, it has validity—because for heroes it's always *all about them*. I could come up with literally hundreds of examples of what I'm talking about, but here's what to me is the best one:

Time: World War II (or the Korean War or Vietnam War or the Crimean War—it doesn't matter as long as it's a wartime situation).
Place: A prison camp, the dread Stalag Whatever.
The situation: Our Protagonist, a.k.a. the Lead, has been shot down behind enemy lines and is now being kept in solitary confinement. Our Protagonist is interrogated mercilessly—tortured—for hours at least twice a day. Between interrogations he's given only the minimum food needed for survival and deprived of more than a few minutes sleep at a time. He's in constant agony with no end in sight, but he doesn't

break. This torture escalates day after day, week after week, month after month, until at last the Protagonist is rescued.

"What?" you say. "Where's the heroism here? The poor chump's not in control of the situation. He's the ultimate victim! Brody's gone as mad as the poor Protagonist probably would."

If you say that you're right. There isn't any heroism in that situation. So let's twist it just a little:

Time: World War II.

Place: A prison camp.

The situation: Our Protagonist has been shot down behind enemy lines and is now being kept in solitary confinement. Our Protagonist is interrogated mercilessly—tortured—for hours at least twice a day. Between interrogations he's given only the minimum food needed for survival and deprived of more than a few minutes sleep at a time. He's in constant agony with no end in sight, but he doesn't break. *Instead, he schemes and plans, and although the torture escalates day after day, week after week, month after month,* at last the Protagonist makes a daring escape.

"Ah," you say, "got it." The scheming and planning are a form of taking control. The Protagonist is a hero because all the time they're working on him he's working on a way to turn the situation around."

And you're right. But if you're a perceptive reader, taking into consideration the fact that this is a chapter on the writing of the *teleplay*, you might also say:

"Hey, waitaminnit! This example is bull. You're not talking about a way to write the script, you're talking about a way to write the story. You're changing the outline into something more heroic. This is a cheat!"

And you're right again. The difference between being rescued and making a daring escape is indeed a story point. It's something that would be worked out in the outline and take several steps. I'm citing this example to illustrate the overt, plotline difference between being a victim and a hero. Now here's the more subtle twist, a twist that's entirely in and of the writing of the teleplay:

Time: World War II.

Place: A prison camp.

The situation: Our Hero has been shot down behind enemy lines and is now being kept in solitary confinement. Our Protagonist is interrogated mercilessly—tortured—for hours at least twice a day. Between interrogations he's given only the minimum food needed for survival and deprived of more than a few minutes sleep at a time. He's in constant agony with no end in sight, but he doesn't break. The Hero's strength and determination are driving his captors nuts. *They respond by escalating the torture day after day, week after week, month after month,* until at last the Protagonist is rescued.

"Wait another minute!" you say. "You've changed the perspective of the whole sequence! The Hero's strength and determination are forcing his captors to make his life even more horrible. On the one hand he's a bigger victim, but on the other hand he's a *hero!*"

Now you're really right. You've got it. Our Protagonist has morphed into the ultimate hero because his behavior is forcing the villains to change theirs. He's driving the scene. This is no longer just the bad guys' standard operating procedure; this is their reaction to something the hero is doing. The sequence has gone from being about the way being a prisoner is to being "all about him."

This takeover and the strength that causes it are, as plot points, relative intangibles. But you can write them into the teleplay simply by telling the reader of the look of determination on the face of the hero and the expressions of surprise and awe on the faces of his torturers, or by adding just a couple of lines of dialogue the gist of which would be:

SUB-TORTURER
How do we break him?

CHIEF TORTURER
Give him more.

I'd even bend the rules a little and underline "more." Whatever the actual dialogue—whatever the actual situation in the script you're writing—keep in mind that with a little ingenuity, a little creativity, you can write your Protagonist into a genuine hero and, in so doing, become a hero to your showrunner and the executives as well.

16) Speaking of heroes, every hero should have at least one overtly heroic moment, regardless of the genre. This is the moment when the hero's strength—either physical or psychological—comes to the fore in such a way as to totally satisfy the emotional needs of the viewer.

For a physical hero, such as a superhero, or even a cop, the moment comes when, although previously prevented from using his or her power, the superhero at last overcomes the chains that bind him or her and, like Samson, uses his strength for one mother of a good deed. The best way to accomplish this is to have the hero fail to rise to the occasion when it would help him or her but succeed because of the extra impetus he's given—the extra adrenaline or emotional strength—by seeing another, innocent character being menaced. The story of Samson bringing down the temple is effective because we think of it in terms of Samson destroying people who were mocking his God, and not because they were mocking Samson. This kind of activity should take one or two tries, with the viewer becoming more and more involved—and more and more frustrated by the failure—until at last … victory of the most satisfying kind.

For a hero whose greatest attribute is intelligence or skill, such as a doctor or lawyer, the heroic moment comes when all odds are against him or her. The surgeon is in the operating room during a blackout. Even the hospital generator is out. The surgeon and her team use their wits to find an alternate power source, and then she uses her skill to finish the surgery and save the patient in the nick of time.

For a hero in a more emotionally oriented situation, such as most sitcom and daytime serial heroes, the heroic moment comes when the hero defies the pressure and influence of all those around him or her and instead follows the dictates of his or her heart. In a situation along the lines of: "Marry that man and I'll disown you!" "For God's sake, don't you dare laugh. This is a funeral, even if it is

the funeral of a clown!" Or "Falsify this company's financial statement and we'll all be rich!" the hero struggles against the emotional
vise and then breaks through and does what's right. (This too
works best if the hero tries it two or three times and doesn't
succeed in being true to him or herself until the third attempt.)

Heroic moments are a combination of plotting in the outline
and writing in the teleplay. The language used in the teleplay to
describe the heroic moment has to convey all the tension and
difficulty presented by the situation, and all the strength, inner
and outer, that the Hero summons to do the deed. (That's why the
"three tries" technique works so well. There's something about
situations that occur in triads that automatically moves readers
and viewers. Try—fail—try—fail—try—succeed, or "I think I
can—I can't—I think I can—I can't—I think I can—I did it!" is an
unbeatable pattern when staging a scene.

Which, come to think of it, leads to:

17) Don't expect your teleplay to speak for itself.
I don't know how many times I've read teleplays where the writer
describes a powerful event in the least powerful way possible:

```
"Deedee is driving down the street. A meteor
plummets toward her. She stops, and it misses the
car, hitting the street in front of her instead."
```

Ignore the science (or lack of it) here and concentrate on the
writing. The writer (someone on the staff of a show who was paid
for this piece of work) obviously thought the event—the
impending strike of a meteor—was so interesting or powerful in
and of itself that there was no need to describe it in exciting
terms. The result of this thought is that the near miss reads as
anything but interesting or exciting. It's dull. Worse, it doesn't
"work." So out it went, replaced by a girder falling from a nearby
construction site.

Why was the girder more exciting than the meteor? Because
Mark Hoffmeier, the story editor of this particular series (an
animated show, or else meteors and girders would both be too
expensive to shoehorn into a script), wrote the sequence like this:

"Deedee drives down the street. Near the intersection is a construction site where a crane lifts a girder into place. Deedee drives. The girder rises higher. Suddenly, the line snaps. Looking out the windshield, Deedee sees the shadow of the girder plummeting toward her. She slams on the brakes, her foot going all the way to the floor, and the car skids to a shuddering stop—bouncing into the air as the girder CRASHES only inches in front of it."

See how the writing enhances the situation?

18) You can't overestimate the importance of good dialogue. One of the paradoxes of television writing is that, although the story is king, writers are judged by their dialogue. That's because stories can always be constructed by the entire staff, with everyone pitching in, but your dialogue reflects you, the writer. When reading a spec script, a showrunner may well forgive a weak story point or two (but only one or two), knowing how much the collaborative process can help a new writer in this area, but no one, showrunner, exec, star, or grip ever forgives bad dialogue.

The good news is that within the context of the teleplay, "good" dialogue has nothing to do with what anyone's boss will like. Good dialogue has a generally accepted definition. It's dialogue that is concise, witty, believable, and revealing of human character and emotion. Dialogue doesn't have to tell the story. The action paragraphs will tell the reader most of what's going on. But the dialogue should reflect the characters' interpretation of the story and do it in an entertaining and realistic way.

The TV writers who rise to the top are those who know what real people sound like when they talk, but also know how to edit that reality so their characters are more intense, more clever, and more expressive than real people usually are. Everyone's been through the real life situation where, after an emotional verbal confrontation, you wake up the following morning and think, "Damn! I should've said *this* last night instead of *that*." In your teleplay, all your characters, especially your hero or heroes, should say what you would if you had the time to second-guess yourself. Because, as the writer, you do have the time to second-guess and third-guess and fourth-guess the words that come out of your characters' mouths, and every reader expects that's exactly what you'll do.

Good dialogue always is original and sparkling, yet flows easily. The perfect comeback, wisecrack, or emotionally wrenching admission always flows easily in the reading and in the speaking. The speeches in a scene have to fit together as a unit, with no awkwardly phrased lines, no pauses in the conversational rhythm, and no accidental repetitions.

Think of poetry. Think of Shakespeare. You don't need to use iambic pentameter, but you do need to maintain a natural cadence that should be evident when you read your dialogue out loud. If you have trouble pronouncing a word, so will your actor—and never forget that you're writing for actors. If you're writing a spec script, one of the things you're demonstrating about yourself is that you can write dialogue actors can say. If a sentence or speech feels awkward to you as you say it, it'll feel awkward to even the best actor. If it sounds long to you as you say it, not only will it sound long to your actor, it'll sound interminable to the viewer. Spoken dialogue sounds much longer than it reads, which is another reason TV shows keep scenes short. A well-written two minute exchange will give the impression of being an entire evening's conversation. But even a well-written five minute scene will give the impression of being a week's worth of yadda-yadda.

One of the mistakes new writers frequently make is that they forget to use contractions, using phrases such as "He is going to the zoo," or "I am in deep trouble here," instead of the more natural "He's going to the zoo," and "I'm in deep trouble here." The only time to not use contractions is if you're trying to demonstrate this as a particular trait of your character. As in he or she is too stuffy to talk like "one of the guys."

Another common mistake new writers make is having your characters speak in long chunks. TV wants its scenes as conversational as possible. Repartee and banter are the keywords. If someone has a long speech, break it up by having someone else interrupt with a question or a comment (a clever question or comment, of course), or by having someone else deliver the second half. Seeing page after page of long speeches drives showrunners and execs insane with disgust, if not outright fury. A rule of thumb is to keep every speech at four lines or less. (Unless you're writing for animation, in which case two lines is the usual maximum. For that matter, animation execs get very, very nervous if they see any conversation longer than three speeches. They want to get to the action as quickly as they can.)

Daytime serials are another exception to the "four lines per speech" rule, but in the opposite direction. Let your characters rave on. There's seldom any action to get to anyway, and even though modern soaps move the story along much faster than they used to, compared to every other genre they still take their own sweet time.

The third most common dialogue mistake made by new writers is to put what I call "qualifying words" into speeches. Phrases like "I think," "it seems," and "kind of," and words like "pretty," (as in "pretty good") and "fairly" (as in "fairly certain") are common in real conversations, but you should avoid them like the proverbial plague when you're writing for TV. They take up space, they take up time, and when you hear them they always sound unnecessary and redundant.

Don't have a character say, "I think that maybe we can do such and such...." Instead, have him go straight to the heart of the issue: "We can do such and such...." The "I think" and the "maybe" and even the "that" are unnecessary because, if your dialogue expresses an idea cogently, an actor will automatically use a tone or attitude that conveys the same qualifying concerns as the extra words would.

On the subject of actors, remember that the reason we've got them isn't just for their looks. Actors are part of the collaborative process, not automatons who're on the set only to bring your vision to life. They're entitled to visions of their own, and take my word for it, they've always got them. You want the actors to interpret your words as only they can. That's part of their expected contribution. Don't try to force things by putting in "uh" and "er," or telling them when to laugh or cry. Let your basic words be their guide, and sit back and enjoy the actors' ride.

A few paragraphs up I mentioned "accidental repetitions." These are situations where a character says the same word or phrase more than once in a speech or in speeches that're close to each other. Or where one character uses a word or phrase and another character does also, in a coincidental, random way, as in:

>   OLIVE
> Hey, nice shoes. Sure like them.
>
>   CHUCKIE
> Yeah, I got 'em at Wal-Mart.
> Wal-Mart's my mom's favorite
> store.
>
>   OLIVE
> Yeah, my mom's a Wal-Mart freak
> too.

Aside from the fact that this makes the exchange sound exactly like a commercial or overzealous product placement, the repetition of Wal-Mart sounds unnatural and awkward. This kind of phrasing is the pet peeve of every showrunner and executive with whom I've ever worked, so if you're forced into a deadly dull conversation like this, make the best of it by avoiding the obvious mistakes:

>   OLIVE
> Hey, nice shoes.
>
>   CHUCKIE
> Yeah, I got 'em at Wal-Mart.
> It's my mom's favorite store.
>
>   OLIVE
> Oh, dude, I'm so sorry.

There we go. No more repetitions, and a little attitude (which everyone who has to read teleplays always loves) thrown in.

Speaking of repetitions, *deliberate* repetitions, which themselves demonstrate attitude, are also beloved by the same people who hate the inadvertent variety. Here's a short example:

                        DANZIG
            Better watch yourself with
            Angie, buddy. She's dangerous.

                        MANNS
            (temper flaring)
            What's dangerous, 'buddy,' is
            you mixing in.

There we have it, two theoretically clever deliberate repetitions in one speech. I'm a sucker for this particular technique. If you handed me a teleplay filled with that kind of stuff, hey, I'd forgive just about any mistake you made in the same script. An assignment would soon be winging your way.

19) Edit yourself. One of the most difficult tasks for any writer, no matter how experienced, is editing. In TV, the ability to edit your teleplay is crucial. That's because part of the magic of electronic reproduction is that it expands time.

Not only does two minutes of talk feel like much longer to the viewer, but a few minutes of action can seem like an entire military campaign. I don't know the psychological or physiological reasons for this, but anyone who's ever spent any time watching TV knows it's true. The trick, creatively speaking, is to make this effect work for you instead of against you. By editing your work properly you do just that, and increase your chances of writing a "good" teleplay and reaping the rewards quality can bring.

Skillful editing means deleting any word or sequence that isn't absolutely necessary. We've already talked about getting rid of those extra qualifying words, but often you've got to steel yourself to the pain of cutting out entire conversations. Speeches that don't simultaneously reveal character and forward the story should be the first things to go. Speeches that repeat anything that's already been seen or said should be the second deletions on your list. Any part of a scene where characters hem and haw and take too long getting to the point should be third. Unless that *is* the point, in which case you still should cut it in half, reread it, and then cut it in half once more.

Feel the need to have your characters tell each other something they would already know so you can make sure the reader or viewer knows it too? Resist it! People discussing a "plan" at a point where they would already have planned it or when they're already putting it into effect immediately sticks out as unrealistic. The surgeon who tells his assistant, "First we do this, then this, then this," when the two doctors have worked together on similar surgeries 600 times is guaranteed to make a showrunner shudder. Find another way to give the information. Or, better yet, re-examine the need for giving it at all. Most of the time you'll find that the reader or viewer can live without it quite easily, thank you.

Have the urge to have one of your characters talk to him or herself so you can be sure the reader or viewer is tracking with your plot? Resist that, too. Again, find another way to send out the info, or just shine on the explanation as unneeded. Look at it this way: If you're showing your characters in action, moving forward as though they know what they're doing, the reader or viewer will probably be satisfied to sit back and go along for the ride. Just make sure you get to the finish and deliver a big payoff that'll make everyone say, "Got it! I see what they were doing! All ri-ight!"

Overwhelmed by the desire to show or tell us every reason for every transition from one scene to another? Fight that off as well. In the 1930s, films often had scenes with someone like Bogie getting a phone call from a hot babe (he was the detective and she usually would be the client), telling him to meet her at such and such a place. He'd say, "I'll be there" and hang up the phone. Then he'd grab his hat, jam it on his head, and the next shot would show him leaving his office and getting into his car. Another shot would show him driving down the street. Another would show him arriving at a house, getting out of the car, and walking to the door. He'd ring on the doorbell, get no answer, try the handle, and discover it was unlocked. So in he'd walk— and find a dead body.

Today we make use of one of the most wonderful things about the human mind: its ability to create closure. Gestalt theory may be dead and buried in psychology, but it's very much alive in the media. Today all you've got to do is show Bogie answering the phone and saying, "I'll be there." Then, as he hangs up, you cut directly to the house with him ringing the bell and continue from there. The reader or viewer automatically fills in the blanks.

Remember: A teleplay isn't the final product. A production is. One of the ways I know I'm reading a really good teleplay is that throughout the experience I have this slight, nagging sensation that something's missing. Not a lot. Just the little extra oomph that a novel would have. If you get that feeling when you reread what you've written, don't despair. Instead, be joyful. It means you've left something for the production to supply. It means you've done your job.

20) Passion and energy sell. Never forget that no spec script has ever been sold just because it looked good or was easy to read. No TV writer has ever been hired just because the writer's worked "seemed professional." Those are necessities, yes, but they're not the whole package. At the heart of every sale, the core of every success, is something more. That essential characteristic is "*soul*."

I don't mean soul as in R&B or rock music. I don't mean it as funk or even angst. I mean it as passion. As in energy. As in strength, conviction, and integrity. Showrunners want to be moved. Executives want to be moved. Viewers want to be moved. They want to be involved. They want to be so caught up that they can't stop turning each page, or when they put down the remote they don't even remember it exists.

The best way to do this, to grab your audience by the throat and not let go, is to let yourself write with genuine feeling. Let yourself get just a little out of control, so your words go flying across the page. Write about subjects that mean something to you so your passion for them engulfs everyone to whom your material is exposed.

Create characters who feel as passionately about their chosen cause as you do about writing and then put them in a situation that tests their belief. Write it with language that races as quickly as your totally absorbed mind. Infuse your teleplay with idealistic and intelligent energy, with an outlook that bursts out of every word you put down, an excitement that sweeps everyone else along. Make your writing stand up and shout.

A great writer writing a great teleplay is like a great rider galloping on a wild horse. Don't break the beast; go with it and share the breathless exhilaration of the ride. Your audience—reader and viewer alike—will end up richer for it by far. And so, emotionally, spiritually, and—maybe, just maybe—financially will you.

section 3:
doing it

Some people change your work in order to make it better. They're producers. Some people change your work in order to make it different. They're writers. And some people change your work just for the hell of it. They're network executives. I like to think I'm in the first group. You're in the second. So let's make a pact here and now that we'll both protect each other from the third.

— Television producer Christopher Morgan to a young writer named Larry Brody in a meeting that ended with me going to work for him as executive story consultant of a new series in 1974. (The series, Medical Story, lasted only 13 weeks but won more awards that year than any other show, and established me as a "real writer" who could be trusted with running a show. I did my best to live up to our bargain, and so did Chris, teaching me a lesson in integrity I've never forgotten. Thanks, Chris.)

chapter 1 2:
getting started

On those rare occasions when I leave my Fortress of Solitude (a.k.a. my office/computer room) and go out into the world, I am always asked three questions by people I meet for the first time.

The third question is: "How do I get an agent?"
The second question is: "How did you get started?"
And the first question is: "Why is TV so bad?"

I seldom answer the "Why is TV so bad?" question because I don't agree with its premise. I don't think TV's so bad. It has a thin layer of good shows and another thin layer of bad shows, and sandwiched in between is a thick, juicy center of mediocrity... just like everything else in life. As of this writing the good shows I see are better than the good shows have ever been before. And the bad shows seem to me to be worse than the worst ever were. So, what else is new?

For many years I wondered about the people who asked question number one: doctors, lawyers, literal Indian chiefs (on the Lakota reservation in South Dakota, where I was spending some quality time), box boys in supermarkets, my kids' teachers, the mayor of L.A. People who would never ask each other that same question. "Tell me, Doctor. Why is medical care so bad?" "'Scuse me, counselor, why do lawyers all suck?" "Hey, Dr. Ph.D., why aren't you teaching my son to add?" But television was and still is fair game. Why?

I've got this theory...

I don't think it's because TV is all-pervasive, part of our bedrooms in most of this country—although it is.

I don't think it's because TV viewers have such high standards and expectations that they inevitably are disappointed by what they see—because they don't have such high standards at all.

And I don't think it's because TV makes everything it presents look so easy that my clothes dryer could do a better job of doing whatever it is that's being done—although it does.

No, I think it's because just about everyone—doctor, lawyer, Indian chief, box boy, teacher, mayor—*wants* to be writing TV. They read the financial statistics—almost 30 grand to write a one-hour show, as much as 30 mil to produce a few years of a hit—and even the most dedicated player of the state lottery thinks, "I could make the Big Score."

And then everyone sees the interviews with TV writers (or producers), or watches the shows that have characters who are writers (or producers), and there these men and women are, driving their Mercedes Benzes and Porsches and Beamers and living within walking distance of Rodeo Drive and staying home in their big, beautiful estates, doing nothing all day but giving telephone interviews plugging their new shows and, every once in a while, dashing off a clever thought via Microsoft Word. (Thank you, Larry David and *Curb Your Enthusiasm.*)

We won't even talk about the beautiful blondes. Or the boy toys.

Okay, we will. Let's talk about David Shaw, one of the great TV writers of the 1950s and 1960s and a force behind a series called *The Defenders*, which is still arguably the best lawyer series ever to have been on television. He was the younger brother of author Irwin Shaw, who was arguably one of the greatest short story writers in the English language—but that's another argument.

One day at a party in Malibu—yes, there really is a Malibu and there are lots of parties there—I asked David Shaw why he became a writer. He jerked a thumb over at Irwin Shaw, who at the time was being berated by a sweet looking old woman—Mama Shaw, it turned out—for not making a better deal when he sold his novel, *Rich Man,*

Poor Man to ABC. "Because of him," Shaw the Younger said. "It was right after the War [WWII, for those who don't remember], and there I was, the student living with our mother in lower Manhattan. And there was Irwin, the writer living with a blonde in a suite at the Plaza and driving a new Buick convertible!"

So almost everyone wants to write TV, even those who call themselves "screenwriters" and protest that they only want to make feature films. Am I really supposed to believe these creative men and women are laboring over their screenplays so they can be the auteurs of the next Dumb Teen Comedy? Or the next Rollercoaster Ride of an Adventure Film? Or one of a dozen uncredited screenwriters on the next Big Brand Name Superhero at Last on the Screen?

Each year, hundreds of screenplays become feature films, most of them aimed at the market of 14-year-old boys who love to watch their favorite movies over and over and, in the process, make the gross receipts grow.

And each year, thousands of teleplays become television episodes, most of them aimed at the market of hip young adults who love the feeling of being intellectually challenged by the same bedroom box that helps them decide what to buy.

Right now, creatively speaking, television's got feature films beat. Hands down.

And, as has already been mentioned, financially it ain't too bad either. So whether you're taking the high road (creativity) or the low road (M-O-N-E-Y), TV's got the heat. The magic. The glitz. The glam.

Which brings us back to the three questions. I believe most of the people who ask me, "Why is TV so bad?" already hear an answer in their minds: "Because you're not helping me write it." And I believe when they follow up with, "How did you get started?" what they really want to know is:

"How do I get started?"

Because if they didn't get started, they wouldn't need an answer to the third question:

"How do I get an agent?"

As a public service to all aspiring television writers (if you accept my earlier premise that I'm doing this for every living man and woman on the planet, which certainly ought to counterbalance some of the bad karma I *may* have brought upon myself by writing TV), I'll skip the personal story of my struggle to be discovered over 30 years ago (my former father-in-law knew this great agent…) and go right to how you can do it, now, today.

The first thing you have to do is become a player. Dedicate yourself to the Game.

Accept the fact that TV is a personal business. It's about you first and your talent and ability second.

Many of the rules that help execs rise to the top in the world of the corporate parent companies of the networks, studios, prodcos, and TV shows apply to rising to the top of the television writing world as well. The difference is that in addition to knowing how to make the best possible impression (and what the best possible impression is in TV), when you're called upon you've also got to deliver the writing goods.

If you've read this far and aren't cheating by turning to the last section first, you've got the basics of writing covered. You know what to do with the stories and the words. But how do you get there? How do you get to the point where someone wants you to write something for his or her network, studio, prodco, or show?

Your first step is to acquire the kind of knowledge you would need to acquire to enable you to succeed in any career. Which means you must adopt the "career" mindset. In television almost no one hits the jackpot with one script and then retires. In television we make a reputation for ourselves, amass credits and contacts, and get ourselves into a place where we can go to work everyday. Staff jobs, remember?

Sitting around at home in Beverly Hills looks good (and feels even better), but it's way up the road, for the showrunners with six series on the air, all of them paying royalties and fees and residuals. Going to work as a writer every day is what TV is all about.

As I write this, the TV biz is in the dozenth or so year of an immense youth jag. Not only is the target audience youthful—under 35—but so are the preferred writers.

As a child, my voracious reading and television viewing taught me that there are always two reasons for just about everything. There's the "good" reason, the thing people use as their public explanation for certain behavior because it sounds, well, "good." And there's the "real" reason, the true cause of what's being done. (My sources for this are impeccable—the young adult science fiction novels of Robert A.

Heinlein and the biting conversations between the cops on *Naked City* and David Shaw's baby, *The Defenders*.)

The "good" reason, often given for contemporary television executives wanting to work with young writers, is that they understand the times better and speak the language of the audience in a way older writers can't. This may be "ageist." It may even be unlawful under current equal opportunity statutes, but this is the "good" reason, because underlying it is a valid, if onerous, point.

That validity is based on this: Moral and ethical values remain the same, regardless of the age of the viewer or the writer and any discrepancy therein. Wisdom remains wisdom, regardless of the age of the viewer or the writer. But the attitude of fictional characters is shown by the language they use, and the language in which people's values and wisdom are expressed definitely varies between age groups.

For better or for worse, TV is all about attitude. The viewer watches shows that reflect and *validate* the viewer's attitude. If the language of attitude is off, there ain't gonna be no audience satisfaction. In the late 1960s and early 1970s, I became a hot young TV writer—because that was another youth-oriented time, the era of "relevant drama," of shows about characters in their early 20s, which was my age. As literally the youngest member on the rolls of the Writers Guild of America, West, I was one of very few professional writers who talked the talk…and could make my characters talk it as well.

Now, having said this, I also have to say I believe it's really only the "good" reason for TV's current love of young writers, and that the "real" reason is quite different.

Industrial psychology Professor Jack Feldman of Georgia Tech is a management guru whose most recent project has been to find a way for airline pilots to more effectively defend themselves against possible terrorist attacks. In a series of conversations with me, Feldman explained that his research shows "people with the power to hire almost always hire people they're comfortable with. It's a fact of corporate life."

According to Feldman, "Study after study shows that middle-class white managers who are men most often hire middle-class white workers who also happen to be men. They're at ease with one another.

They share a common background. A common culture. This makes working together in whatever pressure cooker they've been shoved into not only easier but more pleasant."

Feldman's finding is the kind of thing most people who work for a living recognize instinctively, even writers. Remember the film True Grit? Screenwriter Marguerite Roberts nails it in a sequence that helped John Wayne win a Best Actor Oscar. We're about a third of the way through the film and Rooster Cogburn, Wayne's grizzled old gunfighter character, can't stand the young woman with whom he's working, played by Kim Darby, until she does something that makes him utter the lines that are the ultimate seal of approval: "By God, she reminds me of me!"

In an era with an abundance of executives in their early 30s, it's plainly a big help to be that age yourself, but don't despair if you're older because you've still got something to offer.

You're new.

We've already been through the negative aspects of being a new writer. No track record. No reason to be trusted. But here's a strange, hidden plus regardless of your age. By virtue of being new, you can be "discovered." And being a discoverer of talent looks good in an exec's file. A new TV writer over 35 actually has a better chance of being hired than a more experienced writer under 35 if the more experienced writer isn't on the current hot list. And a new woman writer has as good a chance as a new man. (That wasn't always the case, but if I get started on that it'll end up being another book.) These days more development executives are women than are men. Which means, according to "Feldman's Law," the women doing the hiring will be much more inclined to want to work with women writers than with men.

Why haven't women taken over the business then? It might have to do with the fact that the bosses of almost all the women development execs are still men—but, again, that's another topic ready for a whole book.

Age and newness alone won't get you in the door, though. You've also got to be the right kind of person. In all likelihood you're already leaning in that direction. After all, why want to be in show business unless you like show business and are eager to embrace its *weltanschauung* or worldview?

It's best to be absolutely certain, though, which means your first homework assignment, when you feel ready to take the professional plunge into TV writing, is to learn as much as you can about the current crop of execs. You can't do much about your economic or educational background; if the execs and showrunners are Ivy League and you're not, or if they're not and you are. But you can find out what being—or not being—Ivy League means to those with whom you want to work (or what it *does* to them).

You can also find out what captivates the hearts and minds of those already in the biz by paying attention to the television shows and publications that report on them. Watch the *"E!"* network and *Entertainment Tonight* now and then. Read the show business trade papers, *Daily Variety* and The *Hollywood Reporter*, either at your local newsstand, bookstore, or on their websites. Supplement them with magazines such as *Entertainment Weekly, Movieline, Premiere*, even *People* and *Us*, and other magazines reporting on the showbiz scene.

These shows and mags are almost as intrigued by the showbiz power structure as is the power structure itself. They'll tell you who the people in charge are, what these people own, what they want. Is the in, hip, and trendy car this year the Mercedes or the Beamer? Which model Mercedes or Beamer? Know the "in" food, the "in" clothing, the "in" music, and the "in" people. And know the "outs" as well (so you don't make a mistake and join them).

People and *Us* will report all this straight, as though it means something in terms of the destiny of the world. *Entertainment Weekly, Premiere*, and *Movieline* will cover it ironically, with a tone bordering on the insulting, but they tend to be more in the know. Probably because their reporters and editors want to be TV (or film) writers as much as you do and they're keenly aware of what they need to know.

While believing in what everyone else in your chosen field believes is essential (how long do you think you could stand being around people who cared more for Armani than for God if you didn't kinda-sorta agree?), you don't have to have what everyone wants. As a new writer, you don't want to threaten your possible employers by seeming hipper, or better off financially, or even happier than they. Threatening or intimidating presences are out. Reassurance and respect are the two qualities people in the biz value. As you move up you can acquire more but, until you're at the top, beware of having too much.

How much am I exaggerating and how much of what I'm saying is dead on? Let's put it this way: A writer friend who has asked to remain nameless (for reasons that will become clear) got a job as a producer of a new one-hour series that was getting a lot of good buzz at the time. Excited and feeling the need to celebrate, he went out and bought a new Porsche 911. After he took delivery he drove it to the studio and told his boss, the executive producer/showrunner, that he'd gotten a new car. "Want to see it? Want to? Huh? Huh? C'mon, I'll show you…"

The showrunner wasn't all that interested but allowed my friend to take him out to the parking lot, where he was introduced to the shiny Porsche. My friend looked at his boss eagerly, waiting for the showrunner to say something admiring about his new pride and joy. There was a moment of silence. Then the showrunner shook his head. His voice was a grating whisper. "You son of a bitch," he said. "You son of a bitch. You've got a better car than I do!"

Six weeks later, when the option on my friend's contract came up, he wasn't renewed. He was dropped as a producer and kicked off the staff. No one ever said why, but he knew. "You've got a nicer car than I do…" Oh how he knew.

I know what you're going to say. "Brode, waitaminnit, slow down here. I get what you're telling me, but what's the difference does it make what kind of human I am? I'm in Little Rock and the people you're talking about, the execs and the showrunners, are all in L.A."

You're right. They're in L.A.

Which means you've got to go there, too.

To get what you want, to work in the genres about which we've been talking, you've got to go where the genres are. You can't be a cowboy and herd cattle if you live in the Bronx. And you can't be an intelligence analyst for the CIA if you live in Des Moines. And you can't be a TV writer if you don't live in L.A. This isn't a freelance business anymore, remember? You've got to go where the industry is.

And why wouldn't you want to? What's better than living in a place where no one mocks your dream because everyone shares it? Where the desire for stardom is right out there, all-pervasive? Where on every street you can find some role model, a man or woman who's tried what you want to try—and succeeded?

If you love showbiz you'll love L.A. It's the company town where you'll make the friends and contacts who'll help you create your career, and for whom you can do the same. That's right, I said "friends," because your friends will be your best contacts. They're the ones who'll go out of their way to help you. They'll do it for love, and you'll give love back the same way.

L.A. is alive with show business electricity. No matter where in the area you are—as far south as San Diego, or as far north as Santa Barbara—you'll hear the keywords of show business existence being used all around you: "option," "deal," "pay or play," "pitch," "pick-up." They're all there and you'll be part of it. Remember how on a TV series everyone's a detective regardless of job title? In L.A. everyone's a salesman regardless of job title. As a writer you'll be working the world's largest deal-making shop because you're surrounded by potential buyers at all times.

Where else can you turn to look at the car beside you in a traffic jam and see Mel Gibson behind the wheel?

Where else can you find yourself entering the department store dressing room as Jennifer Aniston is leaving?

Where else can you bump into someone on the way into a football game and discover you've just collided with Aaron Spelling?

In the film *Shakespeare in Love*, a boatman hands Shakespeare a script to read after taking him across the Thames. In L.A., you're positioned to do the same. Hand your spec teleplay to Dick Wolf or David E. Kelley or Steven Bochco, showrunners supreme. All you've got to do is keep your eyes open. They're around.

The best way to move to L.A. is with a few prospects. You want to get as close to a writing job as possible, which means you want to be in or near the TV biz on a daily basis. If you can arrange an apartment in advance through one of the area's many rental agencies, do it.

Make a realistic budget for yourself, taking into consideration what savings you'll have and your likely salary at an L.A. job, and get a studio or one-bedroom or guest house in West Hollywood, Venice, maybe Santa Monica. Or move a little farther out in the San Fernando Valley—Studio City, Burbank, Woodland Hills. San Diego and Santa Barbara may be within the spiritual city limits of "Showbiz Town," but they're too far from the action to do a newcomer much good. So are Ventura, Riverside, and Orange Counties.

If you use an agency and rent a place before you move, you'll probably be able to pay by credit card. If you wait until you get to L.A.

to start your search, you can still use an agency and pay by credit card. But if you go out on your own you'll need a check—and not just any check. It'll have to be local, from an account with an L.A. area bank. In all likelihood you'll be dealing with apartment building managers who are so cynical they make Norman Powell seem like Roma Downing.

L.A. building managers will make you fill out a credit application on which Donald Trump would have trouble looking good. Then they want first month's rent, last month's rent, and a security deposit. They may also want a personal letter of reference or two, preferably signed by someone living in the area, so have those ready in advance. The building managers are lousy at answering their phones or returning inquiries, so don't expect to be able to sit in a friend's house or motel room, look through the want ads, find what you need, and set up your new life via your cell phone. (You don't have a cell phone? Get one. If you're planning on living in L.A. proper, get one with a Beverly Hills prefix; if you think you'll be sacking out in the Valley, get one with a Studio City prefix.)

The best way to find a place to live is to hit the streets. Drive through the area of your choice. (You don't have a car? Get one. How're you going to do all the driving any entry-level job demands without a reliable automobile? How're you going to get any place without a car that'll allow you to clog up your share of the road?) In L.A., even the grandest apartment complexes have the presentation of the cheapest motels; there's always a sign in front announcing a vacancies and letting you know how many bedrooms and bathrooms those vacancies have. They won't tell you the price, though. For that, you've got to go inside.

Even in the best parts of town, you'll find yourself driving past building after building, vacancy sign after vacancy sign. My advice is to look for the place that seems to have the busiest swimming pool. (No pool? "Pass-a-deena," as one of my former agents would say.) A busy swimming pool is a great social center. It gives you a chance to meet your neighbors and get to know those who are working or trying to work in the biz. Not only is this a great way to start networking, it's also a way to make real friends with common interests and have an instant support group as well.

Security buildings also abound, and in a city with as many comings and goings as L.A., living in one can be a plus, if not a necessity.

Finding safety for both your car and your body in your own gated garage isn't exactly a bad thing.

When you find a place with a good pool, security, and an appropriately sized apartment that you want advertised, get yourself buzzed in and talk to the manager. Know, though, that while you're doing this for yourself—finding out the price, seeing if you like the place—your meeting with your first apartment building manager is likely to be your first experience in being judged in L.A. The building manager doesn't care one iota if you rent the place or not. But he or she does care what kind of person you seem to be. He or she is screening you from the moment you meet, and appearance counts. If you look like the kind of person who can afford the rent and who won't terrorize the other tenants, you're fine. But if the first impression you create fails either one of those tests, the apartment about which you're inquiring will mysteriously have been rented between the time you rang the bell and the time the manager opened the door, or the security deposit you're quoted will be in five figures—before the decimal point.

This is where the research you did before coming to L.A. starts to pay off. The appearance for which the apartment manager is looking is the same one any and all future TV employers will want to see. The entry-level dress code is casual but not sloppy. Hair should be cut and neatly combed for both men and women. Clothing should be inexpensive, clean, and middle-of-the road for both sexes. Your wardrobe should be what you would wear to talk to your senior advisor in college, and not what you'd wear to go to an employment interview. This means no suits or ties for men, no business skirts and ruffled blouses for women. Unless...

Unless your natural appearance falls into the category of "threatening stereotype." The stereotyping on which the advice I'm about to give is based makes me insane with fury, and I hope when you take over the media you'll be able to change it. But until then, knowledge is power and knowing reality does give you a chance to manipulate it in your favor. So, if your particular look is one that attracts the attention of racially profiling cops and airport security men or would get you cast as an extra in an inner city street scene without a second of hesitation, then you've got to go a step further to accomplish the reassurance thing for the building manager as well as

for showrunners and execs. Scary men and women have to dress
a little more "up"—conservative sports jacket and slacks for men,
corporate separates and nylon stockings for women.

A note to those of you who are asking, "What's the preferred L.A.
and showbiz mode of dress beyond entry level?" As you move up
economically and careerwise, the casual look will always be *the* look,
but the cost of your clothing has to go up as well. Thirty years ago I
wore T-shirts from the Gap that cost $4.95 apiece. Now I've got a
drawer full of designer T-shirts from boutiques on Melrose Avenue in
L.A. that cost from $99 to $150 dollars each.

This reminds me of a story. One day when I was 31 or 32
and producing the series *Police Story*, I had a budget meeting with
Seymour Friedman, the VP in charge of production at what then
was Columbia Pictures Television. It was shortly after Fathers'
Day and I was wearing a new watch my eight-year-old daughter had
picked out.

Friedman had a habit of circling the room as he tried to figure
out ways to pare down expenses, circumnavigating behind those of us
who were at the conference table. As we tried to bleed another few
thousand dollars out of our budget—which was about $500,000 an
episode for a one-hour show, as opposed to today's going rate of three
times that much—Friedman stopped behind me and looked down at
the new addition on my wrist.

"Rolex?" he said.

"Seiko," I replied, proud father that I was.

Friedman sniffed. He didn't speak to me for the rest of the
meeting. In fact, the way I remember it, he never spoke to me again.
I'd let him down by wearing the wrong watch, loving the wrong thing.
I'd proven myself to *not* be his kinda guy.

Getting your living quarters is easier than setting up your day
job, but sometimes you get lucky. Before you go, put out the word
that you're going to L.A. to family and friends and ask if they know
anyone who knows anyone who's in the biz. Cousins of cousins
are good. In-laws are better. Old college roommates' ex-wives will
work too. If you're a film school graduate, time to get out your class
list and track down your old pals. See who's doing what, and who's
in L.A. Remind them all of how your contribution saved their first
student film. (Of course, if you're smart, you never got out of touch

with film school buddies to begin with. They're the people with whom you have the most in common in life. They're your real friends.)

Get the names and numbers of everyone in L.A. who has even the most remote connection to the TV industry and call them all before you leave on your Big Move. Don't ask for a job. Don't impose. Just explain who you are and what you're up to and ask if you can get together once you get to town. Those to whom you're speaking will understand. They know what it's like to relocate. They appreciate the loneliness of the long distance mover. They're aware of the *need*.

As soon as you've gotten your apartment on Beachwood Drive, under the Hollywood Sign, or your converted garage in Burbank, within sight of Universal City's Black Tower, call back those you've alerted and let them know you've arrived. Take them to lunch or breakfast. Dinner's reserved for "important" meetings with people who can help the people you're turning to for help yourself, or for sexual seduction, and you don't want to get into that. (Sorry, but the "casting couch" isn't what it used to be. Never was, for writers. Think of it this way: Using your sexuality in order to obtain any kind of professional courtesy is *threatening* to whoever you approach, and they're looking for reassurance, remember?)

Now's when you hit on these men and women for help getting a job. Do they know of any openings? Do they know anyone else who might know? Do they have any names at all for you to call?

Please understand that the jobs about which you should be asking aren't just any old jobs. They're jobs that'll get you into studios or network offices, that'll put you in the trenches alongside other writers, showrunners, and actors. They're jobs that will automatically lead to networking and take you another step closer to the staff writer position that's your Holy Grail.

If you're a computer specialist or stockbroker, it may seem sensible to get a computer company or brokerage house job, and it might even be fairly easy. It's your area. You've got references and recommendations. But this is L.A. This is your new life, your chance to hitch a ride on the rocket to stardom that takes off there a hundred times a day. And a computer company or brokerage house isn't going to put you anywhere near enough to the launching pad.

In the "Dark Ages" when I was starting out, no one who could hire writers wanted to consider for one moment that the writer might be

covering the rent by doing something else. Secretaries who wanted
to write were almost never given the chance. Today, though,
the corporate culture that has taken over the TV business endorses
the concept of moving up from within the company. This means the
primo job—your first choice—is to be the lowest of the low on a
series that's already on the air or is about to debut.

The number one best day job by far is being a production
assistant. Or a writers' assistant. Or a studio messenger. Or an assistant
anywhere along the chain—series, prodco, studio, network (but not
corporate entity; that's too far away from the action you want), or
talent agency. Is there an opening in the mailroom of a production
company with a zillion shows (or even just one) on the air? Go for it.

Production assistants are gofers. They get lunch for the production
staff. They make pick-ups and deliveries on and off the set of the show.
Writers' assistants are gofers, too. They get lunch for the writing staff.
They make pick-ups and deliveries in and out of the offices of the
show. Studio messengers, by definition, are also gofers. They get lunch
for the execs and make pick-ups and deliveries for them as well. The
mailroom staff, of course, picks up and delivers the mail, including
inter-office communications. In fact, just about everyone with the
title "assistant" is an errand runner of some kind. (Unless you're
an "executive assistant," or "personal assistant" to a producer or exec.
Then you're a secretary, scheduling the gofer assistants and running
your boss's life. If that's your job, you probably don't want to be a TV
writer; you've got much more power right where you are.)

Internships in these same areas are also good ways to start. In the
TV business, "intern" translates as "unpaid," so as an intern you'll need
a day job to support your day job. But although you'll be unpaid, as an
intern you're in the thick of things, meeting the people you need to
know, learning the things you need to learn, and running the errands
that need to be run.

I know one writer who began by working as an intern for several
employers at once. Three mornings a week he ran errands for a
series I produced. Three afternoons a week he ran errands and wrote
"coverage" (reports on unsolicited manuscripts that had been
submitted) for a small talent agency specializing in representing
writers. Two mornings a week he ran errands, wrote coverage, and
answered phones for another series in production at another studio

and on another network. Two afternoons a week he ran errands, wrote coverage, answered phones, and did computer data entry at the biggest actors' agency in town. After a few months this guy knew just about everyone there was to know—and we all knew he was a writer with energy and ambition. (How did he earn money? His paying job came on Saturdays and Sundays, when he sold new Nissans at a dealership in North Hollywood.)

Other desirable jobs in which you'll be directly employed within the biz include studio guard; assistant caterer; network, studio, or prodco accountant; tutor (for underage actors); and the ilk.

To the uninitiated these may not seem like wonderful employment opportunities, and the pay's not all that wonderful either. But access to men and women who can hire you as a TV writer is what they're all about. In today's showbiz, none of the writers or execs with whom you'll be interacting expects for one minute that you're really a food server or a typist or a messenger. They can see right past your secret identity to your inner self, your inner writer. (Although they may misinterpret the signs and think you're an actor. If you see any indication of this set them straight as soon as you can. Actors are by nature insecure and demanding, and having to face a would-be actor on a daily basis is almost as frightening to most of the people you want to impress as having to face someone who might want to have sex.)

Of course, it's one thing to know you should get the right job in the right place and another thing to get it. The first thing to do for your job hunt is follow up on whatever information you got from all those folks with whom you've been having breakfast and lunch. Call those they told you to call and make friends with whomever answers. Keep the charm flowing when your target finally takes the call. If he or she doesn't take the call, leave a specific message saying you're looking for a job. There's no need for trickery here. If your call isn't returned within a couple of days that's an answer in itself. Not the answer you wanted, but you won't be able to change it so move on.

When you do talk to the person you've called and explained that you're a writer looking for a way to start out, listen closely to the response. Even if the person on the other end of the phone doesn't have a job for you he or she may have valuable advice, or another person or place for you to call. If there is an opening, find out how quickly you can come in and discuss it. Be ready to make your move right now, today, and don't be afraid to give way to your natural inclination to whimper, "Can I come in and interview? Please please? Huh huh?" It's okay to sound desperate. TV people know they've got plums to offer and are upfront about their appreciation of job hunters who grovel and beg. They regard this kind of behavior as "enthusiasm" and applaud your "energy."

If you haven't come up with anyone to call, or all your calls have failed, don't despair. Start working your neighbors. You know, the ones you're meeting at the pool. Get all the leads you can. Get more leads from the want ads—not in the *L.A. Times* but in *Daily Variety* and *The Hollywood Reporter*. You can also check the various websites that list showbiz job openings. Use the telephone directory too, and a publication called *The Hollywood Creative Directory*. Call all the networks and studios and prodcos and agencies you can find listed and ask if they need an experienced assistant.

Even if this set of phone calls doesn't work, you're still not out of the running. L.A. is home to literally thousands of companies, and only about 10 percent of them have the kind of security that keeps job seekers out. Most of the others are in accessible office buildings just like any other company, so it's time to make the rounds. Go to Century City in L.A. proper, Wilshire Boulevard in Beverly Hills, Venice Boulevard in Venice, Ventura Boulevard in Studio City, Sherman Oaks, and Encino. Walk into the lobby of every building— especially those that are named after banks—and check out their directories. Look for company names using the words "Productions," "Entertainment," "Agency," and "Management." Then get on the elevator and walk in. Throw yourself on the mercy of the receptionist. He or she will understand your situation. Odds are that a week ago, he or she was *you*.

Sooner or later, you'll get an interview. You're dressed the way your were when you rented your apartment, so you're okay on that score. You've done your homework about the biz and its tastes, so you're okay there too. And your personality is tuned up to 10 on the charm scale. (But you're not too slick or too smarmy. You're real. You're sincere. Hell, you *are* real, aren't you? You do want this job.)

If you get the chance, one more thing can put you over the top. Unless the interview comes immediately, as soon as you make a cold walk through a cool door, you should have time to do one more bit of research. You should find out everything you can about the specific company where you're interviewing. And about the specific person who's interviewing you if you know who that'll be.

By this I mean you should know as much as possible about what kind of shows this company or person produces or talent it, he, or she represents. You should know the titles, genres, ratings, and stars. If possible, you should have seen an episode or two so you can comment favorably ("adoringly" won't hurt but don't be too obvious—well, not too too. Well…). Be eager. Be bright. Be the kind of person you'd like to mentor if you had the chance to mentor someone. Because, in effect, a mentor is what whoever hires you is going to become. Be someone worth your mentor's time, prestige, and position. Someone who obviously will benefit from what you're taught and who'll reflect well on the boss. Someone who'll remember to thank him or her in your first Emmy Award acceptance speech.

But, Brode, you say, what if this doesn't work either? What if I can't get one of these simultaneously terrific and terrible show business jobs?

Ah, says I, to quote Lawrence Gordon, producer of *Tomb Raider*, the *Die Hard* series, and many other highly successful action films, "Don't think negative until they say no." And after that see what you can do about getting another kind of job that gives you contact with the great and the near-great, such as being a driver for a private messenger service; or a script typist; Kinko's clerk; wait person in the right hang-out (preferably in Malibu, Beverly Hills, Brentwood, at the kind of eatery that's always full of celebs even though its phone number's not listed).

Or get a hobby that brings you into contact with working writers and execs. Being in the right basketball league has done wonders for several people I know. So have such activities as walking their dogs in the right park at the right time and jogging around the public outdoor track at UCLA.

Classes can work too. If you haven't been to film school, now's a good time to take a TV writing class at any one of a number of places in and around L.A. that offer them. For that matter, it'll help even if you've been to film school. You're not going so you can learn about writing. You already know how to write and have your spec scripts ready to show—that's why you're here to begin with. You're taking the class to meet other new writers who may have information you can use (about staff openings or a better place to be an assistant) or who can become friends with whom you'll trade favors for the rest of your professional life…and to get in good with the teacher, who almost certainly will be a working pro who could—if he or she wanted to—help you get your first assignment or staff job, or at least get your specs read by someone else who could.

Whatever avenue puts you into contact with possible employers the behavior you exhibit has to be the same. The "you" you are has to be, above all, a Get-Along Guy or Get-Along Gal. Respectful and reassuring come first, followed by eager and bright. You must be the absolute best at whatever job you're doing, hobby you're pursuing, or class you're taking, distinguishing yourself with your energy and constant performance above and beyond the call of duty.

You may know damned well that bringing the latte to the writers' room with just the right amount of milk and at the perfect temperature, a big smile on your face, and a biting yet worshipful wisecrack on your lips, has nothing whatsoever to do with your potential as a sitcom writer, and the writers who drink the latte and see the smile and nod at the wisecrack may in their heart of hearts suspect that as well—but this is still how you're going to get your big break. This is what's going to make one of the writers or producers or whatever give you that edgewise look people with good TV jobs give people without good TV jobs and say, "Did you say you want to be a writer? Got anything I can read?"

And, if what they read is as good as you think it is, that same demonstration of assistantship skills (or the way you get the Caesar salad just right at that fancy bistro or your great jumpshot in the gym and so forth and so on and on and on) is going to get the first person who reads your material to show it to someone else and eventually to the showrunner or development exec and say, "You should read Maria's *Law & Order*. She's a really bright gal."

Notice that no one said you were a "really good writer." The "bright gal" or "bright guy" thing is what counts here. It means working with you will be a good experience and that whatever you don't know you can learn. It also means that whoever said it thought you wrote a hell of a good script but doesn't quite have the courage to go on record saying so in case the boss disagrees.

In recent years many production assistants and writers' assistants on shows that have been picked up for another season have been rewarded by being given a writing assignment. Provided, that is, that they're Get-Along Guys/Gals. This has become the main point of entry into television writing, so much so that the most common answer to our last question—"How do I get an agent?"—has become, "By being an assistant on a current show."

Don't shoot the messenger. I'm merely giving you the facts. Pat Quinn, an agent at the Paradigm Agency, puts it this way: "We're looking for self-starters." Paul Weitzman of the Shapiro-Lichtman Talent Agency says it more directly: "The last client I took on was a writers' assistant on a sitcom. He's got friends. He's connected. In my book that's a self-starter."

How did Weitzman's writers' assistant client get to Shapiro-Lichtman? By referral. I don't mean the client was referred to Weitzman (although that did happen). I mean Weitzman was referred to the client. An existing client who happened to be one of the writers the WA was assisting told Weitzman, "Sign this guy. He'll make you some money." Pat Quinn gets the majority of her new clients that way also. "If a client I respect recommends somebody to me, I'm going to give them every consideration," she says. "That's how it works."

That's one of the reasons why, even if you aren't working as an assistant, you can still get fairly easy access to an agent. As long as you know a writer who already is agented. Where do you meet another writer who already may have an agent? How about your building's swimming pool? Or the basketball league? The park? Or that swanky restaurant in Bel-Aire where you're working? (You can also meet agents there directly if you keep your ears open.)

If you don't have direct access or know any agented writers it's time to return to the telephone directory and the *Hollywood Creative Directory*. Or you can get a list of agents from the Writers Guild of America, West, conveniently located in, of all places, L.A. The Writers Guild will provide you—free!—with the names and numbers of all the agencies who have signed the Guild's Minimum Basic Agreement. The Writers Guild of America is the union that protects screen and television writers from exploitation in the marketplace. The M.B.A. is the Guild's basic contract and the screen and television writers' bible.

The M.B.A. sets up minimum payments for writers working for

companies that are Guild signatories. It also sets up minimum working standards and rules for the awarding of screen credit, residuals, and royalties from those companies. The Writers Guild health insurance may well be the best in the United States, and its pension plan is up there as well. The Guild also governs all dealings between agents and Guild members, protecting members from having to sign on for too long with agencies that aren't really helping them, and from conflicts of interest involving employers and clients. Writers Guild members aren't allowed to work for any company that hasn't signed the M.B.A. Neither are they allowed to employ any agency that hasn't signed it.

The Writers Guild M.B.A. doesn't cover artists' management companies, by the way, and as long as we're on the subject of artists' or "personal" managers you should know that although technically there's a big difference between what agents do for you and what managers do, in practice managers can be just as helpful to a new writer as agents.

Technically, agents get their clients work and negotiate the deals, while managers plan careers and bring people and projects together. Practically, managers usually end up helping their clients get a specific job just as much as an agent does, and they can arrange for someone else, such as a lawyer, to negotiate the financial part of the deal.

I'm telling you this because as long as you're looking for representation you may want to consider getting a manager. This gives you more places to contact, and often it's easier to attract the interest of a manager than that of an agent. Why? Primarily because representation of writers is a new area that managers are only now beginning to enter. This means they're not jaded. In many ways they're as eager as are you.

You may not know it now, but you want to be a Writers Guild member. All the major networks, cable channels, studios, prodcos, and agencies are signatories. Being a signatory is a sign that these entities will do the right thing and that if they don't you'll have free recourse against them; the Guild's legal department loves to enforce the M.B.A.'s compulsory arbitration clauses. If your career takes off, the stage that comes after getting an agent and a job is joining the Guild. The shows on which you want to work are almost all owned by Guild signatories, and as soon as you qualify for membership by having done the minimum amount of work for Guild signatory companies (the equivalent of writing the story and teleplay for one one-hour episode on assignment), not only will you be eligible but you'll be contacted with instructions on how to get into the "club."

The Writers Guild's list of signatory agents indicates which agencies are actively looking for new clients and which aren't. Don't waste your time contacting those that aren't. They mean what they say, and you're not going to talk them out of it unless you've already got a job and need the agency simply to come in, negotiate, and collect its 10 percent. (That's a Writer's Guild rule, by the way. No signatory can collect a commission of more than 10 percent of your fee. Ever. No matter what. The percentage usually asked for by managers, who aren't signatories, is 15.)

Concentrate on the agencies that say they're open. Call them. Don't write. As a general rule in the TV business you should always call people instead of writing to them. That's why you won't find any chapter in this book on "Query Letters." I don't believe in them. I've never seen them work. Letters get lost. Letters get thrown into the wastebasket. Letters get ignored. They're impersonal, and the people who write them are nonexistent, since their lives and personalities don't impinge on anyone at any agency. If you write a letter, you don't make an impression.

But if you call you become real—a living, breathing person with a voice. In this personal business you become a person with whom an agent—or showrunner or exec or whatever—can do business. So get on the phone and call the agencies. Tell the receptionist what you want and ask him or her to whom you should talk. Since this receptionist was also you just a week or two ago, odds are you'll get some sympathy here and your call will be directed to the proper place. Talk to the assistant who answers next. Turn on the charm that you're probably sick of using. (Charming those with whom you want to do business, also known as "schmoozing" is an important skill in TV. More than a skill, it's an art. Study it. Practice it. You'll never go wrong by forcing yourself to schmooze.)

Tell the assistant your situation. You're new in town, you're a writer, and you've got three sensational spec scripts. Listen closely to every word of acknowledgement, and make it work for you. What you're listening for is any phrase that can be interpreted as, "Okay, send us your specs." As soon as you've heard this make sure you've got the name of the person who said it and, if it's different, the name of the agent to whom you're going to send those specs. Then get your copies made (you can do it yourself if you're working at Kinko's) and mail or hand deliver those suckers to the agency.

And then be prepared to wait.

And wait.

And wait a little more.

Terry Porter of the Terry Porter Agency is one of the most open and accessible agents I know, a man who genuinely wants to help new writers. But according to Porter, "I'm so backed up that it takes me months to get to scripts from new writers. I owe my first allegiance to my current clients, servicing them the best way I can. Potential clients have got to wait."

So don't take it personally. Don't get angry. Don't get depressed. And, for that matter, don't be dependent on this mailing or delivery. There's nothing that says you can't approach two or three or 300 agents simultaneously. Okay, 300 might be a bit extreme. But if I were starting out now, I'd have my material with two or three different agencies, and I'd call them every month or so to remind them I exist and am a terrific guy—and that they've got my scripts.

These follow-up calls are important. Don't screw them up. Don't call too frequently and don't let your charm fade. Keep schmoozing and make yourself a delightful part of the day for whoever takes your call. As time passes with no word it'll be harder and harder for you to avoid trying to bite the head off the neck of the agent or the assistant. Nevertheless, you've got to avoid it. In this busy, overbooked day and age, give the agents six months reading time. That's six follow-up phone calls worth. On the sixth call, tell whoever has become your contact you're sorry but you're going elsewhere and ask if the agency can mail back your specs. As soon as you've said that, "get" a better idea and suggest that you save the agency the effort and come by and pick them up.

This suggestion carries with it three possible outcomes:

1) Your contact apologizes profusely for the delay and actually reads the scripts.

2) Your contact says, "No, that's all right" and pops your scripts in the mail even though you never included return postage. (Why should you? Wouldn't that be a sign of thinking "negative?")

3) Your contact says, "Sure. When can you come by?"

The middle answer isn't what you want, but the last answer is as much a winner as the first. Because if you "come by" it's only polite for you to drop into your contact's office and say hi. And once you've done that you're even more real. And you know an agent or an agent's assistant, for crying out loud. Take him or her to breakfast or lunch. Make a friend. You'll get your work read.

If your spec scripts are good enough to show an agent who reads them that you've got the potential for a TV writing career (which means the potential to earn both yourself and the agent a bundle), you'll eventually get the call that says the agency wants to sign you. Most agencies want two-year contracts. In a good agent-writer relationship two years is a fair amount of time for the agent to do his or her job. In a bad agent-writer relationship two years could be hell. Can you imagine how terrible it would be for you, henceforth called "the talent," as your contract will say, to be saddled for two years with an agent who didn't do a thing for you?

Terrible indeed. Demoralizing and destructive.

But not something you need worry about. Because with a Writers Guild of America, West signatory agent you've always got a way out. Every contract approved by the Guild contains boilerplate language to the effect that if your agent doesn't get you something more than Writers Guild minimum employment or Writers Guild minimum for a sale of your literary property during any period of six months, you can declare your contract with the agent null, void, over, finished, kaput. You've got an escape clause. You're free. Free to do what? Why, look for another agent, of course. Free to go through the whole process all over again and come up with a better agent-writer fit.

Once again, notice my word choice. I didn't say "free to find a better agent." I said "a better agent-writer fit." Translated from Brode-speak, that means "an agent who understands your work and you."

This is important. In all my years in the business I've been with five different agencies—but have changed representation about nine times. My first agency was the William Morris Agency. Then I went to the Major Talent Agency. Then I moved over to Lou Weitzman and Associates, Lou having been one of my agents at William Morris. Then the Shapiro-Lichtman Talent Agency, working mainly with Mark Lichtman, one of the partners there. Then International Creative

Management. Then Shapiro-Lichtman, working mainly with another partner, Marty Shapiro. Then Lou Weitzman, working mainly with Lou's son Paul. Then Shapiro-Lichtman and Mark Lichtman again. And then, while staying with Shapiro-Lichtman I turned mainly to a "new" agent there—Paul Weitzman again.

See a pattern here?

"Horses for courses," Leonard Hanzer of the Major Talent Agency used to say. Different writers have different needs. An individual writer's individual needs change depending on what's happening with the writer's career, and the writer's personal life as well.

I began at William Morris because at the time that agency had the hands-down best agent for new writers in show business. Her name was Sylvia Hirsch, and she'd been in the business for years. Everyone in power knew and respected her, and if she said, "This kid's good," that meant the kid was good. Sylvia's word was enough. No sample necessary.

I went to Major Talent as my career was taking off in a direction that would make me a producer. Leonard Hanzer was a no-nonsense ex-paratrooper who knew how to get the highest dollar possible for his highly respected hot clients.

I went from Major Talent to Lou Weitzman because I was going through a divorce and needed a professional partner who would lessen the stress in my life and, having worked with him before, I knew Lou was just the right guy.

I went from Lou Weitzman to Shapiro-Lichtman because I wanted an agency that would strike terror into the hearts of my employers and talking to Shapiro or Lichtman whenever I hired their clients had always struck terror into me.

From there I went to I.C.M. so I could have access to that agency's acting and directing clients and use that as leverage in creating new series and getting them on the air. I wanted big agency politics in my corner.

I returned to Shapiro-Lichtman because I was being lost in the crowd and the big agency politics at I.C.M.

I returned to Lou Weitzman because his son Paul was young and energetic and was on top of the new trends in the business

I returned to Shapiro-Lichtman because I was tired of hearing my employers tell me how much they enjoyed making deals with the

Weitzmans. If the deal-making process was so pleasurable how could I be getting paid enough?

I latched onto Paul Weitzman when he joined Shapiro-Lichtman because Shapiro and Lichtman terrified me and Paul was such a nice guy.

There you have it. Each change of representation satisfied a need I had at the time. I can truthfully say no agent I've ever had was "better" than another. They were just different, and they all fulfilled my expectations for their services. They performed as I needed.

When you're looking for an agent, try to know enough about the people with whom you'll be dealing to be certain you're suited for each other. Don't just grab onto one because he or she will take you. You'll be very unhappy if you do.

You'll also be unhappy if you assume that your career is made because you're agented. Or even if you assume you agent will get you work. Agents don't get their clients work, and any honest agent will be upfront about that. Instead, agents create opportunities for you to get work. Even Sylvia Hirsch didn't call me and say, "Okay, darling, you've got an episode of *Ironside* to write." She called and said, "Sweetie, I've set up a meeting for you with Cy Chermak, the executive producer of *Ironside*. He needs good writers and knows that's what you are. So go in there and give him a great idea or two."

A good agent knows everything that's going on regarding current series and shows being developed. A good agent knows which showrunners and execs need writers and what kind of writers they need. A great agent knows the kinds of writers with whom the various showrunners and execs like to work, and understands his or her clients well enough to put together compatible people and then sit back and let the chemistry take effect. All the great agent has to do is negotiate the deal.

All you have to do is not blow the chemistry.

And write a great script.

chapter 1 3 :
the pitch meeting

Congratulations! You've used every trick in the book, calling
and writing agents, producers, executives, old and new friends,
neighbors, and distant cousins. And now your old college roommate
has talked to his old girlfriend, and she's talked to her sister-in-law,
and the sister-in-law has put out some feelers with a client's uncle and
the client's uncle has put a call in to his broker whose sister is just
finishing film school and interning at a television production
company—and the impossible has become possible after all. You've
been invited to:

1) Pitch your idea for the hottest possible new network or cable
channel TV series.

or:

2) Pitch your idea for the greatest, most exciting, and most
meaningful (talk about heat) network or cable channel TV movie!

or:

3) Pitch your idea for a genuine, already hot, big deal network or
cable TV series!

All right! Way to go. This is good, very good. There's only one
little "uh-oh" involved. As in, "Uh-oh...now what do I do?"

Don't worry. Pay attention and you'll get through this just fine.
Regardless of whether you're talking series idea, TV movie idea, or

episode idea, and whether your genre is one-hour action or drama, sitcom, or kids' animation, these "official" pitch sessions all include pretty much the same cast of characters and play out just about the same way. Here's the step-by-step breakdown of how you should act and what to expect as you walk through that door where you've just jammed your foot. Armed with this knowledge, even the rawest novice is on a par with the most seasoned pro. (And maybe you pros can pick up a pointer or two as well, since this knowledge comes as much from time I've spent in the showrunner's chair as in the writer's.)

First of all, you've got to get the nomenclature right. This is a "pitch meeting." Not a "look-see" or a "how do," or any of the many other possible kinds of meetings. There was a time when the name didn't matter so much, but there also was a time when people looked for nice, cozy caves carved out of limestone in which to make their homes. The days when you could call a showrunner or exec and say, "Listen, Lydia, I've got this idea. Let's get together and talk" are long gone. Try that now and the response will be, "Idea? Get together? Talk?" Followed by a beat in which, if you listen very closely, you'll make out the whirring of mental gears, and then, "Do you mean you want to pitch to me? You want to set up a pitch meeting? Is that what you're saying?" Followed by another beat. This time, if you listen very closely you'll make out not gears but a disdainful mental voice silently adding, "Fool."

So whenever you talk to anyone in the business and they ask what's up, make sure you've got the lingo down and say, "I've got a pitch meeting at ABC next Thursday," or wherever and whenever it is. Knowing the language shows you're one of the gang. It means you deserve this pitch meeting, although others probably won't think you deserve it nearly as much as you do.

Whether or not you deserve this opportunity of course isn't the issue. In fact, before you get into your car to head for the office where the meeting will occur—before you even brush your teeth or take the Xanax you may think you need in order to survive (don't take it, by the way; my psychiatrist friends tell me anti-anxiety medications can cause temporary short-term memory loss and you don't want to forget your idea halfway through the telling)—you must recognize this all-important point:

No matter what anyone's told you, you haven't really been

"invited" to pitch at all. You're merely being "allowed." Why is that? Glad you asked. In a series idea pitch, you're meeting with broadcast network or cable channel development execs who've committed nearly 90 percent of any time slots opening up in the foreseeable future to already proven showrunners. Specifically, to the half-dozen or so major writer-producers who already have a successful series or two or three on the air. The development executives love these men and women who've risen beyond their natural writers' shyness and alienation to become gregarious salesmen who wine and dine the execs, and promise them cushy, high-paying jobs when their network careers end—with the unspoken proviso that the execs continue to give the major showrunners a big slice of the pie.

Proven track records, seats on the floor at Lakers games, and the promise of future job security are pretty powerful sales tools, but your cause as a beginner isn't hopeless. Although series development execs aren't actively ferreting out new ideas from unknown writers, they are willing to listen to you. Because they're smart enough to know they can't be sure from where The Next Big Thing will come and if you have it, they want it. Some writers say the execs want your idea not so they can use it but to keep you from giving it to the competition, but I've seen too many unexpected deals end up with series that got on the air. Shows such as *The X-Files, Power Rangers, South Park, News Radio, The West Wing, The Sopranos,* and many others all came from the fertile minds of total or relative unknowns.

Besides, look what points the series development suits can make with a major player like Dick Wolf or Steven Bochco or James Brooks if they put you together with him and another hit is born. And it won't exactly hurt *you* to be involved in this situation either. Just as it didn't hurt David E. Kelley, Les and Glen Charles, Steven J. Cannell, and other current Big Guys to get hooked up with other major players early in their careers. Always remember that although it may be closed, the door isn't locked—and if you've got that perfect, execution-proof high concept logline you've got a good shot.

Executive thinking in the television movie arena is pretty much the same, but your odds are a bit better. Although TV movie development execs have what they call "white lists" of approved writers who've written highly rated TV movies in the past and who therefore, get "first dibs" for their projects, there are no contractual commitments with these writers per se, which leaves new writers more room to wriggle inside. Also, more and more TV movie scripts are being bought instead of developed, which means you can go in there, wow 'em with your song-and-dance, and then, if the execs are interested, leave your impeccably written script behind to do the rest of the talking for you.

Pitching an episode of an existing series is a little different. Here, your meeting will be with all the members of the writing staff who haven't been able to come up with a good excuse for not attending. (In other words, all those without an imminent deadline for a first draft or rewrite.) This means that instead of talking to execs who specialize in developing new material you'll be pitching to rival writers, who, whether they're called executive producers, supervising producers, consulting producers, executive story consultants, story consultants, or plain old story editors, would prefer to write every episode themselves.

Their reasoning is the same reasoning originally used years ago to create all these big writing staffs, so it may sound familiar:

No one anywhere, no matter how talented a writer he or she may be, knows the show and its needs better than the members of its staff do. No one anywhere, no matter how gifted, knows the characters better than those on the staff do. No one anywhere, no matter how dedicated, knows the actors who play those characters and their personal likes and dislikes in material better than the the staff does. And, when you get right down to it, in the eyes of most staffers, no one deserves the money for writing each episode more than they do. Especially since they're certain they're going to have to rewrite every word a freelancer puts down. (And, to tell you the truth, regarding this rewriting thing, they're probably right.)

Why, then, do ongoing series hire freelancers at all? Try this for a reason: The staffers have been working twelve hours a day, seven days a week, since they were hired. They're under the gun with nothing to shoot next week and everyone is jumping in to gangbang the new script together simply to get out some pages, and they're just plain out of time to get the next script started. Or here's another possibility. The same working conditions as described above, coupled with network sharp shooting and cast rebellion have completely robbed them of workable ideas, so the show is in dire need of an infusion of fresh blood in order to complete the current season.

And yes, casts do rebel; it's common for stars to decide they want more control—and why not? As Robert Blake, one of the first TV leads to become showrunner of his own series, once said to me, "You can write the words and then duck. But it's *my* face up there on the screen. If the audience is disappointed, it's disappointed in Robert Blake!"

Oh, there's one more possible reason for an episode pitch meeting to be held. The Writers Guild of America rules mandate that a certain number of freelancers must be interviewed, and another number (lower) actually be hired, on every series over which the WGA has jurisdiction. So every once in awhile the writers of *Frasier* and *NYPD Blue* and The *Simpsons* take time away from their own scripts and get together to listen to outside writers and remind themselves of how lucky they, the staff members, are to be regularly employed.

Given these facts, is it possible to get anywhere at an episode pitch meetings? The answer is yes. Although there may not be a desire for your services, there is a need. Your mission is to prove beyond a shadow of a doubt (a.k.a. "unreasonable" doubt) that you're the one to fill that need.

In other words, no matter whether you're pitching a new series premise, a TV movie, or an episode for an existing series, be *in control* of your material. *Be smart.*

If you're trying to get an assignment creating a new series, know it inside and out. Be able to explain everything you've got in mind clearly and succinctly, starting with the high concept and expanding outward like the universe after the Big Bang. Be able to rattle off the basic premise, the setting, the main characters, and the loglines of half a dozen possible episodes without pausing for a breath. Be able to tell anyone who asks what happened in this place to these people and regarding this situation before the first episode of the series and what will happen long afterward. In a word, make it *real.*

Creativity isn't the only essential here, though. You also need the equivalent of an MBA's business plan. That means finding out all you can about the network to which you're pitching so you can tell the execs exactly where your series can fit into the network's future. Where is the network in the ratings? What are its highly rated nights? Its bad nights? Has it been developing mostly drama or comedy? How are its recent projects doing? How can your shows help improve the network's situation? Who is the target audience for your series? Is it the demographic generally desired by advertisers? Is it the demographic desired by this particular network? What can your series do in addition to attracting an audience? Can it sell merchandise? What kind of merchandise? Clothing? Toys? If merchandising millions aren't in the offing, will your show instead create audience good will? Critical acclaim? Will it increase the network's prestige in a way that translates into dollars?

Where do you get this information? The info about your own shows and their potential comes from you, of course, fashioned out of your awareness of what attracted you to the ideas you're pitching in the first place, and what holds you to them now. For data about the networks, you have to reach out a little. Read back issues of the trades Check out the Entertainment sections of *The Wall Street Journal* and the *Los Angeles Times*, and the *Arts and Leisure* section of the *New York Times*. Remember how you were watching *Entertainment Tonight* in order to prepare for your move to L.A.? Watch it some more, and as many of its imitators as you can find as well. When you know how to look you'll find that what the *Los Angeles Times* calls "Entertainment Business News" can be almost as available as the box score for your local team.

Preparation for a TV movie pitch meeting should be almost the same. Think of yourself as a public speaker ready to do at least 20 minutes on each of your TV movie ideas. Since TV movies are, for the most part, one-shot presentations (except for the inevitable—and profitable—reruns) you don't have to do the business major analysis you do when you're trying to sell series ideas, nor will you have to come up with potential episodes. But not only do you need to be able to sound off on the high concept, basic premise, setting, and main characters of each film you're presenting, you also must be ready to tell every twist and turn of the plot. Yep, each of your ideas is *The Odyssey* and you're Homer, King of Raconteurs, relating the story in such an exciting way that all who listen become so involved that they feel like they've just seen the whole film.

When you're pitching episodes to an existing series, the most important thing is to know as much as you can about the show on which you're trying to get the assignment. Make sure you've watched a million episodes, and read as many scripts as possible. You can get the scripts straight from the office of whoever you're pitching to. For this moment, at least, you're on the inside, so if you don't have an agent who can call and ask for sample scripts of the series, you can do it yourself without fear of being hung up on, ignored, or otherwise embarrassed.

What exactly is "knowing the show"? It's being aware of the stories that have already been done. It's knowing the kind of problems the series usually tackles. It's knowing the storytelling pattern through which the stories usually unfold. Not only do you have to understand the characters' names and relationships to each other, you have to be aware of their strengths and weaknesses as people, the hopes and dreams they have addressed during the series' run.

Armed with this knowledge, your job is to think of what you'd like to see the characters do. What interaction? What adventure? What tragedy would you enjoy seeing them thrust into? Be very careful not to stray far from the parameters of the episodes you've seen and read. If the producers and executives who ran, say, *I Love Lucy*, had wanted Lucy to go into space, or meet Dracula, or drop Ricky and take up with guest star John Wayne, they would already have done it before having you in to talk. (Oops, I mean "pitch.")

Stay to the premise of the series and keep the crazy redhead in the apartment, coming up with a new way to convince her husband to let her sing with his band. Like everything else we've been talking about, your series episode ideas should be easy to state in one carefully worded, high concept sentence. You should know the beginning, middle, and end of each story, and be able to speak on the subject without faltering. If you can do all that and come up with a notion that fits in perfectly with the series and its characters but is far enough out of the box that the harried members of the staff just plain would never be able to think of it themselves, you will succeed.

Regardless of whether the upcoming meeting is for your own new series, a TV movie, or an episode, always have three ideas with which to regale the execs or staff. To test them and yourself sit down and write the basic high concept sentence for each. Then write a page and a half telling the basic continuity of each series idea or the story of each TV movie or episode. Study what you've written. Think of what problems someone could find in them, what holes a showrunner who wants to pass on your work could poke. Write them again and again, fleshing them out and expanding them to no more than the equivalent of three double-spaced pages, stopping only when you get rid of those problems and holes. In all likelihood, no one ever quizzed Homer about possible loopholes in the plot of *The Odyssey*, but you'll be questioned as mercilessly as a wannabe lawyer forced into taking an oral exam for the bar.

Now you're ready to go into the meeting. Notice that I said go. Other media may welcome telephone or fax or e-mail pitches, but in TV everything is up close and personal. Gene Roddenberry put it best when he said, "They want us to be right there in front of them when they reject us. Otherwise what fun is it to say no?" You should have the dress code down by now, but here it is in case you've forgotten: Dress well...but not too well. Casually, but not sloppily. (Too well is threatening. Too casual means you don't really care.) The image you project should be the image the execs and staff writers want to see. And what they want to see is someone just like them.

Figure out which of your ideas is the strongest in terms of the kind of thing you've already seen on the network or the series you're meeting with and which one is the weakest. This is important because it affects the order in which you'll present these little gems. Now head for the studio, and make sure to bring the neatly written three pages for each idea along in an inexpensive but tasteful folder. Leather is nice, but not leather that's too thick or that smells too rich. Remember, outdoing, or seeming to outdo the people you're trying to impress doesn't impress them. It just makes 'em mad.

At the studio you'll have what I think of as "the usual parking problems" and "the even more usual getting lost while trying to find the office problems," so give yourself plenty of time. It isn't fashionable in this instance to be "fashionably late." Of course, it's important to know that even if you were to come late you would still be early. Some crisis will have come up that the person with whom you're meeting has to solve, and you'll have to wait.

While you're waiting, the assistant to that person will probably be cordial although not necessarily pleasant, making you one of the gang by rolling his or her eyes at you for sympathy when speaking over the phone with someone—usually another writer coming in for a meeting—who's making "impossible demands," such as wanting to have a word with the boss. A few moments waiting in the outer office like this and you'll very clearly see the true power the "gatekeeper" has over the likes of mere mortals such as thee.

Don't worry about making small talk. There won't be time for that. Other network, studio, prodco, or show personnel will be going in and out, and to them you'll be as not one of the gang as possible. They'll ignore you completely. To the various assistants, interns, gofers, and casting directors (on a side note, casting directors always have to discuss emergencies with showrunners and execs. Usually the problems have to do with actors who've gotten a better part and want out of their pilot or TV movie commitment or next week's episode, depending on what kind of office you're in, or managers who think they deserve a bonus for getting their clients to show up for the shoot), who pass by, you and the couch on which you're sitting will be one inanimate and invisible object. Don't take it personally. Just sit back and rehearse your loglines and pretend to read the trades that will be sitting on the coffee table before you.

Eventually the meeting will start. For a series idea and pilot or TV movie pitch, your audience probably will be three or so middle management types. One will have a VP title. The others will be directors of development. An assistant or intern to take notes will also be present, scribbling like mad on a yellow legal pad. The meeting will take place at either a network or studio or prodco headquarters and most likely be in the vice president's inner sanctum, an office that's "nice," but not "too nice." Bright. Airy. A good view. Modern furniture interchangeable with that in the office of any comparable executive in most other businesses. Family photos and symbols of the VP's hobbies on the desk and the wall.

If the meeting is for a series already on the air it'll be at the studio or prodco production facility and the person running it most likely will have the title supervising producer. Two or three other writing staff members will show up, often wandering in and out while you're talking, and an intern will also take notes. Be warned: The office will be disappointing. Small. Drab. Overstuffed furniture of the type that usually comes with a furnished apartment on the campus of most major colleges. A window that looks out at the parking lot. Few touches of personal décor on the desk or wall.

The real development power, a.k.a. the *senior* vice president, and the real power on a show, the showrunner, almost never come to a pitch meeting unless the writer is a personal friend. Then, of course, the meeting is held in their conference room, which is usually an outrageously ostentatious room in an office suite larger than most homes, and more expensive than most homes as well. Such suites are decorated precisely to the taste of the boss or his or her interior decorator, per one of the most important clauses in the boss's contract.

As the meeting begins, the vice president of development or supervising producer will make the obligatory offer of a drink of coffee or Snapple and the rest of those in attendance, development directors or the remainder of the writing staff, will treat you to the small talk you didn't get while you were waiting, usually exchanging news about traffic and weather and then turning to your background as a writer and human being. Then, just as you start to relax, the person in charge will ask what you've got to pitch. This is the official announcement that it's showtime, with you at center stage.

Take your cue from the attitudes of the others and, again, be casual but not so much that you don't seem to care whether or not you get the assignment. Try to communicate and make eye contact with everyone, but spend most of your energy on the boss. This isn't as easy as it sounds. Odds are the VP or supervising producer will be the least personally accessible person there and the intern will be the most. You'll feel comfortable pitching to the intern, but don't do it. Low man, least eye contact. You want to be viewed as a force with which to be reckoned, not just another schnook. (But don't ignore the intern completely. Someday he or she may be ruling the world.)

Tell your best idea first. If you're very lucky, it's the only one you'll have to tell because it'll immediately be snapped up. If you're not so lucky, the vice president or supervising producer will say, "Hey, that's good, but we're already doing something very similar." Or, "Hmm, not bad. What else've you got?" If you're unlucky you'll get, "What're you, nuts? The last time anyone tried to do something like that it tanked worse than Michael Richards's [or Jason Alexander's, or Ice T's] career!" followed by a shake of the head and a dismayed, "And I heard that you were a *good* writer..." The simultaneous headshake and ejaculation of disappointment will be repeated once or twice just to make sure you get the point. I've never been the speaker, but I've been the unfortunate listener a time or two (or ten).

Either way, move on quickly. This time give your weakest idea. As a sales technique, this is crucial. Psychologically, it gives everyone else in the room a chance to feel very superior and even more smug than usual and say, "No!" in unison. Try to keep calm. Ignore the gales of laughter. The truth is they'll all love you for giving them that chance to be so "very very." Your weakness makes you their pal, because they're living in constant fear that their own inadequacy will be exposed; finding what they consider to be your inadequacy marks you as one of them in a way they can't consciously acknowledge.

While your audience is still lording it over you, tell them your third idea. They'll stop, and they'll think. The underlings will turn to the VP or supervising producer, who will enunciate the obvious. Which is that while this one has its merits, it isn't quite as good as the first. Under the leadership of the vice president or supervising producer, the development or writing staff will start bending and shaping and rearranging idea number one. If this happens, smile. It's what you want. Whatever you do, don't get defensive and defend your original point of view. On the contrary, sit back and let the others run with your idea. Let them play with it. Change it here. Alter it there. No one in that room will be upset because they're doing all the work instead of you. They like it this way because it proves their value—as long as you interject an occasional expression of delight and amazement at the way they're improving your concept and thereby proving your good judgment and taste.

Occasionally, as an alternative to going back to the first, best idea, the VP or supervising producer will do a little grandstanding and pick idea number two, the weakest, to work on with the others, trying to put some great spin on that one and thereby establish a position as almost—but not quite—ready to move into the senior vice president or showrunner office suite whenever it's vacated. Either way, your job is the same. Let the gang have at it. Watch and listen and smile and learn.

If all goes well, your new friends on the development or writing staff eventually will put together a series or TV movie or episode they like. It may be exactly what you came in with, or it may be completely different in every way (but even so, they know it's "yours" and that if they do it you've got to be hired as the writer. This is, in a strange way, a "gentleman's game," and very little material is ever misappropriated— if for no other reason than it's a lot cheaper to let the new guy do it than to steal something and turn it over to a highly paid old pro.)

The vice president or supervising producer will tell you the group has to kick the idea upstairs to get it approved...even if he or she in fact has the power to approve things. (This arbiter of all things television wants time to think it—and you—over.) You'll be told you can expect a call in a couple of days, and to be optimistic. If the idea is just like one you came in with, now's the time to leave the appropriate three pages (your leavebehind, as you of course know). If not, just smile and make your exit, and hope you can find your car.

(Note: If you're pitching a new series concept or a TV movie you'll probably be pitching to a studio or prodco and not directly to the network—unless you're one hell of a fine sales person, in which case I want to know how you did it. However, if the studio or prodco likes your idea, they'll be taking it and you to the network to pitch it there. So you get to go through this all over again!)

And that's it...well, not exactly. Because after a couple of days pass you won't be called. And a couple of days after that you won't be called either. This isn't the same situation as when you were giving an agent six months to read and respond to your samples. This is a situation in which there's a definite timetable, especially for TV series development and existing series writing.

There's a definite "series development season" for new series, usually late Spring through Fall, and after that no new series concepts are considered until the next series development season. (Don't confuse series development season with "pilot development season." The latter occurs after the pitches have been heard and pilot scripts have been commissioned, read, and—a few of them anyway—approved. At that point pilot development season becomes another four months or so of pre-production, production, and postproduction of the pilot episodes themselves for the decision-making fun that occurs in May.)

There's also a definite "series episode writing season," although no one calls it that. A series that's been given a 12 or 13 episode production commitment for the current season shoots from June or July through November. A series that's been picked up for the usual full 22 episodes shoots through February, or March if it falls behind.

You've got to get your assignment and deliver the goods within these temporal windows, so wait a full week but no more and then call the VP or supervising producer. When you do call, remind the assistant of who you are and say you're checking on what happened with that idea everyone liked so much. Make sure to say they *liked* it so you won't be confused with the writers who were dismissed outright at their meetings and are calling back to try and get in all over again. The assistant will put you on hold and then get back and tell you the VP or SP will call you back soon. (In the office, he or she is probably rolling his or her eyes about you at another waiting writer. Try your best not to let that realization get to you.)

If the call you've been promised doesn't come within another week, call again. Even if you've got an agent, let your fingers do the dialing so this stays all about you. It'll be a difficult phone call to make, I understand, but making yourself do this is the kind of thing that builds strength for future efforts, reminding you of the personal aspect of the biz. The odds are that when you make this particular call you'll get the same response you got earlier—and never hear from anyone at that network, studio, prodco, or series again. This means one of two things. Either your idea wasn't approved by whoever has the power to do so, or as soon as the meeting was over everyone forgot what you said. Something else came up and the VP and SP never got around to mulling over your great concept or kicking it upstairs. Whichever way it went, the outcome is the same. You didn't get the assignment. No deal. No check. No calling the people who said you'd never make it and letting yourself gloat.

Now's a good time to talk to your agent if you've got one. A good agent—one who's right for you—will commiserate and give you the pep talk you need. A bad agent—one who's not right for you—will blow you off and immediately write you off too, not trying to get you more meetings. If your agent reacts this way, don't ever think it's your fault. You didn't let down the agent—the agent is letting down you. Look for someone else, someone who knows how difficult a new writer's life is.

As grim as this may seem, the way I look at the situation, even if your pitch session ends this way it's still not over. My point of view is even more hopeful than Larry Gordon's. I say, "Never think negative even if they say no." Perseverance prevails in this game. Something about *you* got you in the door—your spec samples, your agent, your pal, your father-in-law. The TV gods let you enter once, and unless you did or said something so humiliating the VP or SP had you thrown off the premises by a security guard, you've still got a little leverage.

The way to use it is to wait a few days and then call and ask if you can come in and pitch again. Make the call yourself and don't beg, wheedle, whine, or do anything else that could possibly make that damn supercilious assistant's eyes roll. Be a mensch. You'll be put on hold, and then you'll get the verdict. If you get a shot at another meeting, make it for as soon as you can, run in, and do your song and dance—only better this time, using what you learned about yourself and your audience the last time in. If you're told there are no more openings, that the development or episode slate is now full...take the hint. If your agent's one of the good ones, call the agent and vent. If not, you can still do the venting. Just call your mom.

(Note: Never—absolutely never—lash out at the assistant who gives you the bad news. And don't stalk the VP or SP and their staff or scream at them if you run into each other somewhere. Even in a business where just about anything goes, that's considered unprofessional. Worse, it ruins any chances you might have had of ever working for or with any of these people—or people they know. Save the expressions of hostility and contempt for later, when you're a showrunner and these losers come in begging. Although by that time you really shouldn't care. If you do, I'd suggest you take a big chunk of the big bucks you'll be making and seek competent professional help.)

On the other hand, if you've presented the kind of material those with whom you met can't live without—and there's no reason to think you haven't—the vice president or supervising producer or another member of their gang will indeed call back. If they do it's almost always to tell you the idea is a *go*! They're ready to make a deal to have you write it! If they're not ready to make a commitment, then the call is to let you know the idea was shot down but you should definitely come in again.

This is "the stuff dreams are made of." This is what you came to L.A. to hear. If the message is the former, jump up and down and celebrate! You're almost in! Call your agent or your mom and share the good news. If the message is the latter, it's still time to jump up and down and celebrate and call. It means you've still got a chance. One of the tricks I've learned to help me keep myself relatively sane is to celebrate whatever I can, whenever I can.

In a business where the "no" answers outnumber the "yes" responses by as much as they do in TV, I regard every meeting from which I emerge alive as a good meeting, and every phone call where no one zapped me over the wires as a good call. Even the most important showrunners get pet projects shot down and write scripts that don't get approved for production. Even the men and women with multi-million dollar guarantees come back from meetings with higher-ups saying, "What's wrong with those people? How can they possibly not see how good this thing would be?!" Take my advice. You've had a near miss? Hooray! Go out to dinner! Take someone you love! They want you to come back and see them again? Take a bow! Have a bigger dinner. Take two people you love.

Whichever way things turn out (and if you stick with your career you'll get the good and the bad—ever see those old campaign buttons for Richard Nixon: "You Can't Lose 'Em All?"), you must keep the following in mind: The pitching process can be so long and laborious and painful it often begins to seem like an end in itself. After all, don't millions of people earn their livings as salesmen? But never lose sight of the fact that success here is only the *beginning* of your job.

If the network or studio or prodco or show has decided to use your idea, the real work is yet to come. Ahead of you lies the labor of writing what you've pitched in such a way that everyone involved thinks you're the greatest writer who ever walked through the network double doors or the studio gate. Which means you have to write it so each of their bosses will like it. Which in turn means you have to write your pilot or your TV movie or your episode just the way the people in charge would've written it if they had the time—and the talent. Only *better*. The trick is to write like an angel and play the game with devilish delight because if you do someday you'll be the creator with multiple commitments, the one on the "white list" for TV movies, the showrunner of the megahit series going into its fifth or tenth or fifteenth glorious year.

chapter 14:
fulfilling the assignment

Regardless of the genre, what happens after you get a writing assignment will be just about the same. From the moment the VP or SP to whom you pitched your ideas six weeks ago finally calls and says he or she loves one and wants you to start writing, the creative aspect is pretty much "engraved in stone." You'll write an outline, a first draft, and various subsequent drafts as has already been discussed. But what's really going to happen to you the writer? What should you expect in terms of your dealings with the network, studio, prodco, or show?

First, of course, you've got to make a deal. If you're "agented up" (kind of like when a suspect on a cop show is "lawyered up" except a writer has higher expectations than a suspect, although a suspect may well have more rights), call the assistant to whoever called you and tell him or her who represents you so the business affairs person (remember this all-important link?) can start the negotiations. Then call your agent so when the overworked, harassed, and impatient BAP doesn't get around to making that call your agent can step in and make the first move.

If you don't have an agent and don't want one, get the name and number of the BAP person from the assistant and call him or her directly yourself. Chances are the business affairs person won't have the slightest idea about what you're talking. Don't get paranoid. No one's reneging. The authorization for the deal simply hasn't gone through yet, which is par for the course. Now the BAP knows who to bug on his or her end to get the paperwork and start the ball rolling.

If you don't have an agent and do want one, now's the perfect time to make your move. Just about any agent you call will be glad to sign you up and do your negotiating for you. After all, haven't you just proven you're a "self-starter?" You don't get more self started than getting your own job. (And yes, getting an assignment means you can think of yourself as being employed. You can call home and tell everyone, "I got a job!") Not that there's much to negotiate when you're a new writer. This is the phase of your career where the words "take it or leave it" may never be uttered, but they're certainly implied.

This is because although some people liken deal-making to a courtship, it's a strange courtship indeed. The first move is the "we want to do business call" you've already received, where the conversation usually goes something like this: "This is going to be a great project [or episode]. All of us here love it. We love you. Where have you been all our lives? Thank God you came to us. How has this network [or studio or prodco or series] ever gotten along without you?"

Smile when you hear this, pardner. Grin and laugh and dance around the room.

Because the next conversation, the one with the business affairs person, is going to give the compliment you've received a spin that'll make you feel as though you're the top: "Nobody at the network [or studio or prodco or series] is all that excited about this project [or episode]. We've got a lot of misgivings about it and the writer. So we're talking as little financial exposure as possible all the way down the line."

Sometimes I think the reason everyone gets an agent is just so we don't have to hear that statement directly, although agents always end up passing it on even though they know how devastated the client will be. I believe they do that for the same reason that a lawyer always tells you how high the odds are against you prevailing in the litigation, no matter what the circumstances actually are. ("You were sitting in your living room watching TV and a bulldozer came smashing through the wall with its millionaire driver yelling, 'I know this is the wrong house, but I don't care anymore!' And he knocked down the entire structure, burying your whole family, breaking all your limbs, and destroying your life and future? I dunno...sounds like a tough case.") That's right. They tell you how worthless you are so that when they get you Writers Guild minimum you'll be so grateful you won't invoke the Guild's "If your agent doesn't get you work for more than minimum in any six month period you can declare your agency agreement void" clause.

And that's something to remember. The deal itself is usually pretty straightforward, with very little negotiation needed, because if it's a Writers Guild show, Guild minimum is what you'll get. That's what everyone gets except the established creator-showrunners or top feature film writers "slumming" in TV. These writers can get twice as much per script deal because they've got the clout to do so. But for most merely mortal writers, and all new writers, minimum means "maximum" as well. Since the early 1970s, Guild minimum has evolved into the "going rate" because it has also evolved, as we've seen, into quite a nice hunk of change.

I remember talking with Paul Playdon, an amazing storyteller who was one of the primary writers responsible for all the twists and turns of the original *Mission: Impossible* series and the producer who guided *The Night Stalker* to cult status. "Ah," he said (he was British and always said things like "Ah"). "The good news, boys and girls, is that we've raised minimum to a new level. The bad news is that you're never going to get a penny more." He was correct, but, fortunately, minimum has continued to climb to new heights. (You can check on the latest numbers at the Writers Guild of America, West website.)

If the negotiation is for a non-Writers Guild job—and most animation and other kids' shows falls into that category—the BAP may make a half-hearted attempt to offer less than that company's going rate—which will be the same as that of every non-Guild company in that genre and about half what the Guild rate would be—but the "going rate" is called that because it's what the companies are prepared to pay.

A note here about animation and the Writers Guild. Although Guild rules forbid members from working for nonsignatory companies an exception is made when the entire genre is non-signatory. Animation as a genre is considered non-signatory, even though most if not all primetime animated series have been brought into the fold. The daytime serial as a genre is also considered non-signatory, even though many soaps have consummated a wonderful relationship with the Guild.

Whether or not the project comes under Writers Guild aegis, the deal you'll be offered will be "story with option for teleplay." This means the company is employing you to write an outline, and that once the outline has been completed to the showrunner's satisfaction, the option the company has on your teleplay will be picked up. Or not, if it isn't completed to the showrunner's satisfaction. In which case you just take the money, as a few people have said before, and run. Speaking of good news-bad news, the good news here is that as long as you write the outline in good faith and the rewrites for which your deal calls, you'll be paid for it, no matter what happens next. The bad news is that even if your option isn't picked up, the network or studio or prodco or series now owns the idea and can assign another writer to do the script.

This stems from the fact that from the minute you agree to the deal, verbally or in writing, the copyright on any material that comes out of your concept belongs to your "employer" and not to you. The story or script and everything they contain—characters, settings, *attitude*—are in the eyes of the law "work for hire." From this point on you, the lucky employee, are a wage slave even though you're not being paid wages but a single fee divided into a few payments. You're also not eligible for benefits from your employer, although you are building up your benefits account in the Writers Guild on any Guild job.

(Note: All the above is true even when what you've pitched has been an idea for a new series. In that situation, the company will be optioning the series concept and hiring you to write the pilot, or first sample episode, of the show.)

Some new writers are insulted by the "story with option" provision of the usual contract, but you've got go get past that. This is another situation where everyone works this way except a creator-showrunner or feature film writer who's so hot he or she can push the BAP to the wall. If you're negotiating for yourself it doesn't hurt to try and get the teleplay guaranteed, but by no means should you let that point be a deal-breaker. Let's be honest. As a newcomer, you shouldn't let any point be a deal-breaker. You need this assignment so you can become a "pro," not only in the eyes of the industry but from your own perspective as well.

For most writers, negotiations for the writing of one episode of a series customarily take only one phone call. Negotiations for a pilot or TV movie can take longer. I've been involved in pilot and TV movie negotiations that took as long as three months. But that's because I was in a position to demand (I like to think "expect") more than minimum for royalties in the case of a pilot or potential royalties in the case of a TV movie that might spin off into a series of its own, and because my agent and I also had to negotiate my "potential continuing involvement" (a.k.a. my showrunner deal for any resulting series) at the same time. New writers can—and should—try to get more than minimum in those areas but need to face the fact that you probably won't.

Most of the time you'll find that the development vice president or series supervising producer with whom you're working will want you to start immediately, regardless of the status of your deal. In the television business, as in most businesses, a deal is considered official as soon as the contracts are signed by both sides, which can be months after the negotiations have ended with everyone's verbal agreement, and long after the window of opportunity for the project, even an episode, has closed. For that reason you'll receive a preliminary document called a "deal memo," which is like a letter of intent, stating the points of the deal in clear, non-legal terms, and which also must be signed by both sides.

Many times, the deal memo also takes too long to prepare (the business affairs people are busy, busy, busy, remember?), so in TV we abide by a simple rule: If they want you to work, do it. It's common for an outline, and sometimes the whole script, to be finished before the deal memo is signed. Don't worry. With the exception of a handful of companies that your agent will know, no one's trying to cheat you. You'll get paid for what you do. (This is one of those times when having an agent is handy. If you don't have one you can call the Writers Guild and talk to the legal department there. They have a list of bad guys who are signatories. For crooks (who don't see themselves as crooks at all but as justified in withholding payment) who aren't signatories, the unagented will have to rely on gossip, hearsay, and innuendo, which are usually a bit more reliable in show business than in most others, and which are available at your apartment building's pool.

When you get started what, exactly, will you do? If you're writing a pilot or TV movie, first you'll have another meeting with the VP of development and the VP's staff, where they'll tell you exactly what they liked best about your idea, and what thoughts it's triggered in them. In other words, they have a lot changes for you to make that they believe will make this a better series or film, which means one that better fits their needs.

Sometimes the changes are minor. I once had a pilot deal for a series about two cops who become unlikely partners—one is by-the-book, the other a ex-outlaw biker. The only change requested by the development people was that I describe the ex-biker in a more attractive way when I wrote the outline than I had at the pitch meeting, so they'd have a better chance of landing the star they had in mind.

Sometimes the changes are major. I once had a pilot deal for a series about an idealistic young lawyer who practices an individualized brand of criminal law from an inner city storefront because he can't get along with anyone who, to him, seems at all "establishment." At the "request" of the development people, he became an idealistic young lawyer who creates a public service division of the firm and works it with the crusty old senior partner whose life is reinvigorated as a result. Was the change for the better or for the worse? To this day I still can't decide. The series didn't get on the air. But if I hadn't made the change I never would've written the script, which led to a later "job" writing a TV movie for Valerie Harper that did get made, and was good enough to win several awards.

(Note: If your original series pilot deal or TV movie deal is with a studio or prodco, be warned: You'll have to go through every step here twice, once with the studio or prodco, with the execs there trying to second guess what the network execs will want, and once with the network itself. Know the old saying about too many cooks spoiling the broth? In this situation there are so many cooks you're lucky if you even get to *smell* the broth.)

If you're writing an episode of an existing series, your first move also will be a meeting, again with as many members of the writing staff as can make it, and, possibly, with the showrunner as well. At this meeting the showrunner will tell you exactly what your story idea has become since you pitched it, and believe me, it'll have become something quite different. Elements you never imagined will have been added because the showrunner believes they're necessary to maintain his or her vision of the show. These will be elements with which the other staff members never could've come up with either.

Your position as an episode writer is more than a little like being the living incarnation of a Rorschach test. You say, "Black!" and it makes the showrunner think, "Beige." So beige is what the concept becomes. But it couldn't exist in any color, shade, hue, or tone unless you hadn't walked in with basic black first.

When I was running *The Silver Surfer*, for example, Dorothy Fontana called me with an idea for an episode in which the Surfer stopped an interplanetary war. (I let writers do as much pitching as possible by telephone because I knew how difficult and painful just driving to the office for a pitch meeting can be to a nervous writer.) I told her we already were noodling with something like that (because we were!), and she said, "I should've known. It's a staple. Some things always stay the same."

"That's it," I said. "We're buying your idea."

"What idea?"

"The one where the Silver Surfer meets up with another super character who's been caught in a time warp, reliving the same battle for thousands of years. He can't figure out how the Surfer fits in—and neither can the Surfer."

The idea became "The Forever War," co-written by D.C. Fontana, Mark Hoffmeier, and myself, and it was considered one of our best episodes by Marvel Comics cognoscenti. Was the idea for it really Dorothy's? Was it mine? Or both of ours? It didn't matter. What was important was that we got an episode out of it that most viewers liked. And that's what should be important to you.

In addition to concept changes, the first meeting—or second if there are many changes—on your assignment regardless of whether it's a pilot, a TV movie, or an episode, will also be a time for everyone involved to work together and plot the story. Whoever's in charge usually has a precise idea of what story points the project needs—specific scenes, plot twists, character arcs—and if you don't put them into your outline you'll have failed in your assignment and instead of your option being picked up you'll be "cut off." So ask questions. And *take notes.*

If you're a particularly insightful person, now's the time to give full rein to those instincts because you'll do very well if you can be more than a parrot regurgitating specifics dictated by the boss. If you can put yourself into the exec's or showrunner's shoes and figure out what's behind the instructions you're being given—what professional or, yes, personal need of the individual involved the change will satisfy, and figure out an even better way of doing it, you'll be perceived as a genius, or at least as an up and coming new star. Don't wait and try to do this later, after you get home. Make your contributions in the meeting, where they immediately can be yay-ed or nay-ed. Otherwise you stand a good chance of wasting a lot of time—and losing a lot of good will.

How long and detailed this meeting will be depends on the individuals in charge. (As Cal Clements has said, "We hire writers in order to torture them. Which is fair if you look at it that you're being paid to take all those meetings and not just for the writing per se.") As a rule, series development execs like to lay out a few general guidelines and a specific scene or two they "hope" you'll incorporate into your outline for the pilot. TV movie execs, on the other hand, usually want to cover the film scene by scene by scene. Since they seldom have a block of more than two or three hours of time available this means you can end up taking a week's worth of two-hour sessions. (The plus side to this is that by the time it's over you'll actually know your way around the office and get a genuine smile or two from the security guards.) Many existing series also keep you coming back for days, working out the precise beats. Others will give you the teaser and the act breaks and tell you the remainder is a "w.p." That stands for "writer's problem" and means: "You're on your own, kid. But you'd better come through."

Eventually everyone will run dry, and you'll be sent home to write. At this point you should ask exactly *what* you're supposed to be writing. Do the people with whom you're now working want a beatsheet? A treatment? How detailed should either of these be? Even after you get your answer, try to make sure you're all on the same wavelength by asking for copies of other outlines they've liked. Series and TV movie development folks usually are unable to oblige. The arena in which they're playing is so competitive that everything they're developing is "secret," "hush hush," and only for those who need to know. But they'll appreciate your interest.

Showrunners and series staffs will be more forthcoming and eager to load you down with examples. While the assistant is putting together your package ask for some finished scripts as well, even if you already got some before the pitch meeting. Say you want to read episodes that everyone especially liked so you'll know where to aim. And don't be surprised when all the scripts you get are those written by the showrunner. Everyone likes the showrunner's work best. That's what the entire staff is being paid to like.

Now, regardless of what you're writing, go home and turn the story you've worked out into an outline. If you've been given the scenes point by point, use them, changing things only if they absolutely don't make sense to you. "Grace takes off her top and dances on a table at the office party." Whoa, hold on. Sure, this sounded great when you were sitting at a big table with the *Will & Grace* staff. Sure, everyone in the room laughed until they fell out of their chairs. But now, one-on-one with your computer, doesn't it sound dumb? What happens next doesn't even stem from it. If Grace is going to do something like that, don't the action and its consequences merit an episode of their own? Maybe you can sell the show that episode after this one is done...

There's nothing wrong with this line of thinking. In fact, it's the way your mind should be working. But don't just throw that scene away and come up with your own replacement. Call the network, the company, or the show. Specifically, call the one staff member to whom you felt closest when you were in the meeting or meetings. (Just don't make it the intern.) If you're lucky that person will be the VP or the showrunner. (My mother was always telling my sister, "It's as easy to fall in love with a rich man as a poor man," although neither of them did it. In theory it's as easy to feel comfortable with the boss as it is with an underling. But I know that's only in theory.)

So talk to whoever doesn't scare the pants off you and explain the story problem. Ask his or her opinion. And then do what he or she says. You'll get big points for this behavior in two ways. Questioning one of your marching orders shows you're thinking of the good of the project and not just taking the easy way out. And following the advice of the person you call shows you're thinking of the good of the project and not just your own creative needs. You'll have made the person whose advice you've sought feel necessary and smart and will have an ally for the rest of this assignment, and longer if you don't blow it another way.

You will probably have been given a target date for delivery of this part of your opus. Usually it'll be three or four weeks for a pilot or TV movie, and ten days to two weeks for an episode. This won't be the same amount of time you've been guaranteed contractually. It'll probably be less. But it doesn't matter because one of the ways you prove yourself in TV is by delivering early. In a deadline-driven business, writers who consistently beat the deadlines can be more valuable than writers who consistently write brilliantly. Complete your outline and deliver it a couple of days early. More than a couple of days would give the impression you didn't give the piece enough thought. Delivering it late would mean—well, just about everything bad that you can imagine.

Until the mid-1990s, everything had to be delivered printed out and by hand. Sometimes a freelancer on assignment could convince the employer to send a messenger, but most of the time the writer had to drive in and drop it off at the office. The positive aspects of this outweighed the inconvenience because as long as the writer was there he or she could have a few minutes of conversation with the various staff members, all of whom wanted to hear one thing: "I love this outline. It's great. Everything flows. That meeting was so damn helpful. Thanks, thanks, thanks."

As of this writing, e-mail is the accepted mode of delivery. For an outline you'll probably use Microsoft Word or Word for Mac or another Word-compatible program and send in the file as an e-mail attachment, either to a specific assistant in charge of such things or to your pal the staff member with whom you feel comfortable. This takes away some schmoozing time, but you can compensate by noting in the e-mail that "I love this outline. It's great. Everything flows. That meeting was so damn helpful. Thanks, thanks, thanks." Of course, you'll have to be a little smoother than that, and less effusive, in writing because as all writers know it's a lot easier to seem foolish via the written word than the spoken one. (Another of life's injustices we've all got to overcome.)

After you've delivered the outline sit back and wait. No matter what terrible time crunch you were told existed, it'll most likely be a couple of weeks before anyone gets back to you with a verdict about what you've written. And, as Richard Nixon might've said, "Make no mistake about it," a "verdict" is what it is. Judgment will be passed.

And if the outline is found wanting, you'll feel as though you've been damned.

In most cases you'll be called by your pal and told that what you sent in is good but some changes need to be made—by you. You'll feel bad when you hear this. You're damned, remember? But considering all the people who will have read the outline, believing for one minute that it would be universally acclaimed would have been the height of foolishness, so take this result in the most positive manner and go out and celebrate your survival. Then relax and go to the "notes meeting" with all the confidence you can muster and consider it deserved.

You'll meet in the same place you met before, and with the same people who were there before, unless some of them are busy, in which case your audience will be smaller. Everyone will have opinions— "notes"—about every sentence you wrote, and those who aren't attending will be represented by the intern or another member of the staff to make sure you don't miss any input.

Don't be surprised if those at the meeting disagree with each, with some of them finding problems with beats others like. Don't be surprised if much of what you're asked to change is material originally given to you by those who now don't like it. (Did I say "asked?" Think of the television business as Wonderland and you'll understand better when I tell you that "asked" means "told.") Don't be surprised if characters are added or taken out, if men are transformed into women, and women into men. And above all, don't be surprised if you're "asked" to completely change the story so that it bears no relation to what it was. No one likes to admit it, but the name of the game is hindsight. It's much easier to see if something will work if you write it down and read it than if you try to imagine what it'll read like before it's written down.

Once again, take good notes. By the end of the notes meeting, your mind will be reeling. You'll find it difficult to keep track of everything that's been said, and the pleasure you felt when you first got the assignment, that flash of heat and excitement when you were able to say, "I'm really a writer!" may now be replaced by dread. Fight it off. Remind yourself that they told you it was good. That to them these are just a few minor alterations. A facelift. And they're still looking to you to be the chief of surgery.

Odds are that revising the outline will seem more difficult to you than did originally writing it. Quite honestly, I don't think that's true. In a rewrite situation you're not facing a blank page. You have pieces you can move around and specific scenes or moments that have been okayed as and where they are. Revising the outline is a *daunting* but far from insurmountable task.

Although the notes meeting may have been filled with good-natured (and sometimes not so good-natured) give and take among the staff members, you'll be way ahead if you keep this in mind: Your future on this project hinges on doing a rewrite that works for the boss. Always go with the money. In any case of conflicting notes, make the changes preferred by the highest paid and therefore highest ranking person in the room—the VP or the showrunner. Or, if the boss disagreed with those who thought something should be changed, *don't* make the changes. Keep it as it is.

In fact, it's a good idea to keep an eye on the boss throughout the entire meeting, and try to get into his or her head. The VP or showrunner's facial expression may be a clue to the thought process behind a note, and if you can ferret out the source and address it throughout the outline you'll be a hero. You'll also be a hero if you can figure out the politics of the office and address those in your changes as well. Does the VP frown every time one of the directors makes a point? Does the showrunner wince every time the story editor speaks? This could be a sign these people are on the way out. It's certainly a sign that the boss doesn't agree with what they've got to say.

You'll only have about half the time you had originally to make the changes, so get to work. You probably won't be able to finish early this time, but you must turn in the changed version on schedule. The reason this particular rewrite is so important is that when you're working under a Writers Guild contract you can only be asked to do two versions of the story, so this is when the decision will be made regarding whether you'll get to write the teleplay. Or, sometimes, whether there'll even be a teleplay.

On a non-Writers Guild deal, the situation's a little different. Non-signatories, including animated series, tend to demand more of the writer even though they're paying less. Fortunately, they also expect less, so no one's holding it against you if it takes five versions of the outline to satisfy them. (And in animation it often does because there's no immediate, "Oh my God, we've got to get the next script shot right away!' kind of pressure. Animated scripts are written so far in advance of production that they almost never fall behind.)

For now, let's say you've finally done the last possible version of your outline. What happens next? You guessed it: You wait. After a wait so long that you're convinced your employers hated not only the outline but also despise you, the call finally will come. No, they weren't spending those weeks interviewing hitmen so they could find someone to keep you from inflicting your writing on anyone else ever again. They were just... "busy." What happened—it's inevitable—is that an emergency came up.

In the pilot and TV movie development business, disaster may have struck in the form of a legal challenge to the rights to something else being developed, or a big star who was being wooed demanded even more attention, or the in-house political situation destabilized and there's a new network president. Or the worst possible outcome of all for a writer: the VP in charge of your project got canned. Which always means that his or her successor has to write off, cancel, and if possible lift a leg on all of the former VP's projects—because if the son of a bitch had been any good at his job he'd still have it, wouldn't he?

For an existing series, the disaster is usually in the production area. (Budget crises are the number one probability.) Or ratings may have changed dramatically. (If they plummeted, everything stops while the staff tries to figure out why and how to fix it, each member alerting his or her agent that it's time to start looking for another job in order to avoid career ruination. If they soared, everything stops while the staff tries to figure out why and how to duplicate it, each member alerting his or her agent that it's time to start looking for another job in order to capitalize on this career success.)

When I was showrunner on *Mike Hammer* we had a more unusual, ahem, *situation*. Our star, Stacy Keach, was convicted of trying to smuggle cocaine into England and was sentenced to a year in Reading Gaol. Commencing immediately, as of the bang of the judge's gavel. No going home to say goodbye to his family or finish the season on the show. Think I got back to the writers waiting to hear about their outlines in a timely fashion? Of course not. I was busy trying to figure out a way to save the series—and myself.

The series was saved for the season because we had only a couple of episodes left to shoot. For one of them the staff quickly team-wrote ("gangbanged") a script in which the current mystery could only be solved by "remembering" past mysteries, and then another in which Mike Hammer had disappeared and the other regulars were trying to find him. Both episodes relied heavily on re-using footage from previous shows, and on having impressionist Rich Little duplicate Keach's voice for the new dialogue and voice-overs. Each script was written in approximately four days—from idea to shooting draft. Not a good time to turn to freelancers or writers whose work I didn't already know.

When you get the call after your final set of outline revisions, you'll get one of two possible messages. Either it's the worst of all worlds and you've been cut off, or it's the best of all worlds and it's time to go into teleplay. If the news is bad, try not to cry so the caller can hear you, and also try not to scream and threaten the caller's spouse, kids, and parents. Every writer's been cut off at one time or another, and certain shows always cut off outside writers.

I was very upset a few years ago, for example, when the showrunner of a certain name brand science fiction series called me to say, "Congratulations! Everybody loved your outline. It's a go. There's only one little thing…this episode has to shoot next week so I'm going to write the teleplay myself."

My reaction to this news was to assume that somehow I'd failed, that I hadn't given the showrunner what he wanted and what he was really saying was, "Everybody hated your outline but we still like the idea so I'm taking over."

Then I spoke to several writers and producers who had worked on this particular series recently, and they all said the same thing: "Don't worry. It's got nothing to do with you. They go to outside writers whenever the idea well runs dry, but then they always push them out the door and do the script in-house. The pattern was set years ago."

Keep a stiff upper lip, then, if you're cut off, and try to find out why, either from the caller or from friends. Or ask your agent to try and get the word. Being tied into all the TV industry gossip is part of an agent's job. Insider knowledge, after all, is the agent's lifeblood. Usually the agent will get to the bottom of things without a problem. Use the information you get from this experience—and the totality of the experience itself—for your benefit. Learn from your mistakes if you've made any. And make certain you don't let them happen again.

(I sure as hell didn't pitch any new ideas or write anymore outlines for that s-f show, even though the showrunner kept calling and asking me to come back in.)

If the news is good, and you're going "forward," go out and celebrate. Your "story money" has probably arrived by now so you can afford a good meal, maybe even scalper's prices at an already over-priced rock concert. Then gird your loins and head back to the network, studio, prodco, or series headquarters because it's time for another meeting, boys and girls. Time to get the notes on the changes in the storyline you've got to incorporate into your first draft. Most of the time this is a short meeting, and instead of being with the whole staff it's with the one person assigned to work out these little kinks with you. More than likely, the VP or showrunner, and probably the SP, will be nowhere in sight. That's because usually these are, indeed, merely little adjustments. After all, if not, you'd be out. Sometimes, in fact, the changes are so minor you can be talked through them over the phone, or get them in an e-mail. This is another important turning point. Once again you have to make sure you understand not only the changes that are being "asked," but also the thinking behind them. At this stage of the game the notes may strike you as odd, as belaboring an obvious point, or telling you to do something in the teleplay that you intended all along. Don't protest and don't explain. Remember, it's the other person's ball. You've got to play the way the owner wants if you want to be allowed to play again.

While we're on the subject of not protesting or explaining, let me stress how important this is throughout the process. From the first notes meeting on any project to the last, you'll be sorely tempted to make statements that sound something like this: "The reason I did that was…" or "What I was trying to do was…" Whatever the reason, and whatever you were trying to do—*don't tell anyone*. Don't try to justify or defend your writing. Not because it's indefensible, because I'm sure you've got a valid point, but because the people at the meeting just plain don't care. What you wrote didn't work for them, making its cause irrelevant, and they're so busy they regard any discussion as belaboring the point. Rightly or wrongly, nodding and letting the note givers move on are regarded as signs of your professionalism. Anything else is considered arguing, even if you don't mean it that way, and arguing is a sure way to lose any note givers' respect.

At the end of this meeting, you'll be given another due date. For a pilot, it'll be about six weeks away. For a TV movie, it'll be about two months down the road. A series episode will be expected in two to three weeks, with two weeks preferred. This is another time when you want to come in a little early. For a pilot or TV movie find out what the preferred script format and software program are, and use them. You should already have seen scripts for an episode if that's what you're writing. If you haven't, get 'em now. And find out about the software. Use the format, whether or not you're comfortable with it. And definitely use the software, no matter how much it costs. It's up to you to accommodate your employer, in this case, by delivering an easy to use and read file when you're done.

As you write the first draft you'll find that even though everyone and her brother has been through the outline with a fine-tooth comb, there still are elements that seemed fine when viewed as beats in the story but don't work when you try to make them into scenes. You'll also find that the new changes you were given are more difficult to incorporate than you thought they'd be. Again, pick up the phone and call for advice. Explain your problem, and then do whatever is suggested.

(Note: You can't do this too often, or you become an annoying writer, and annoying writers don't repeat with the same employers unless what they turn in is brilliant—and a huge hit. Your best bet is to call once, with a couple of these issues. Then, using the way your staff contact handled those problems, figure out what he or she would do the next time you have one and do it on your own. And if you called more than once during the writing of each version of the outline you may have used up your "get advice free card" even before you start the teleplay. So be careful: play it smart.)

Try to pace your writing so that after you're done, you still have a couple of days in which you can go over what you've written and revise it until it feels perfect. That way your official first draft is actually the second draft you've written and will be more polished. And the more polished the better. Over the years I've found that I average seven pages a day when writing a first draft of a pilot or TV movie, and eight or nine when writing an episode as a freelancer. (When I'm on the staff of a series, I write 15 pages a day and get that sucker out of the way. That's because I'm usually the showrunner and have a million other things to do, all of which are easier and more fun than first draft writing.)

After you've e-mailed the first draft, it's time to play the waiting game again, but you've padded the first hurdle so everyone with whom you're dealing will be friendlier now and they'll usually get back to you more quickly on your first draft than they did on the first version of your outline. Unless they hate what you've written. Then whoever was your main backer for the assignment will be busy trying to figure out how to justify your hiring so he or she can keep his or her office and title. If you start getting that "time is dragging on" feeling while waiting for a response to your first draft, it's okay. There is, unfortunately, a good chance it's more than mere "writer's paranoia."

When the call comes regarding a pilot or TV movie first draft, the most likely possibility is you'll get what has already become to you the usual response of: "Nice work. C'mon in and we'll give you notes on the changes." When it comes to an episode first draft, it'll be a little different: "C'mon in and we'll give you notes on the changes."

When it comes to your writing on a series, you seldom hear anyone say what you wrote was good, and in the meeting that follows you probably won't hear about one page or line in the script that anyone on the staff liked. Sometimes this is because everyone on a series is feeling so rushed and overworked they want to get the meeting over with as quickly as possible, and praise takes up time. At other times, it's because the staff members have no social grace—hey, they've been concentrating on their imaginations all their lives. And still other times it's because they're complete bastards deliberately trying to keep you on the defensive so you don't get too confident and try to take away their jobs. (As if.)

The least likely call you'll receive is the one where the person at the other end says words to the effect of, "Thanks very much. The script doesn't need a rewrite. You're finished. We're sending out the rest of your fee, so just sit back and smile." If this happens with a pilot script or TV movie it means your worst fears have been realized. They hate what you did and have waited until signing a new writer to rewrite you before letting you know. In many ways, this is a more bitter pill to swallow than being cut off, because the first draft is when you pulled out all the stops and gave these people everything you had, utilizing each wonderful tip from Part Two of this book...and in their eyes it wasn't enough. I have no advice, either flippant or sage, on how you can deal with this particular disappointment. It seems to me like another time to cry with someone you love—and then figure out what you did wrong (or ask your agent to go right to the source and bring you back the info) and absorb the lesson so you'll never fail this way again. (That's right, you can still fail, but you've got to find a new method. And you will. Sigh... all of us do.)

On the other hand, if you get this message about your first draft for an episode, it doesn't necessarily mean the worst. This could instead be "The Call You've Been Praying For," a.k.a. "The Gift From God Call." If it is, the showrunner or other staff member who called will get right to the point and ask if you want to write another episode—more quickly this time because whatever emergency they've been having that got you this opportunity in the first place is probably getting worse. Usually the staff already will have a story idea waiting to go. No pitching needed.

Or, this could be "The Call You've Been Praying For Even More Than The Other Call You've Been Praying For," a.k.a. "The Gift From God That Proves There's A God Who Really Loves You A Whole Lot Call." This kind of call is very unusual, and the showrunner or other staff member who called will have a problem getting out the words but finally you'll hear something that sounds like, "So, you all booked up for the season? Or can we get you here on staff?"

You know what to do if you get either of these. Jump up and down and scream and yell and say, "I'm ready. Let's go." Call your agent. Treat yourself to another big dinner and a night of Bruce Springsteen or Sting. (Don't buy that new car just yet and don't get a new apartment. But you can let yourself have some fun window shopping.)

Even when you're doing an episode, however, there's still a chance that the "Thanks Very Much. This Script Doesn't Need A Rewrite" call is from the Devil instead of God. You'll know it's bad news and not good because if you treat it like a compliment and ask if the show has another assignment for you the phone'll go dead. Or the person who called will "fumfer" all over the place, stuttering miserably. Just give him or her a "I understand," hang up, and go into mourning and the learning experience thing.

If your teleplay experience goes the way of most teleplay writing experiences, you'll have that next meeting mentioned earlier. We've already talked about what'll happen in the meeting on an episode. In the case of a pilot or TV movie it'll be the best meeting of the assignment. You'll go through the teleplay line by line and everyone will laugh at the good lines and compliment you on the way you riffed on the twist one of them suggested during the outline phase. You'll muse out loud about the series or film potential, tossing out the names of possible stars and the numbers of possible ratings, and muse further about what you could write for this group after this is done. They'll also have a ton of changes for you, some of them in the dialogue, others involving a restructuring of the storyline, but no matter what they may be, and how difficult making them may turn out to be, you'll be having the time of your life. This is showbiz! This is TV! In the words of Sally Field, "You do love me. You really do!"

The actual rewrite is a lot like rewriting the story. You've got less time in which to do it than you had for the first draft, and trying to get in all the changes will be maddening at times. Just do your best and keep in touch with the staff. It helps if after the meeting you go over everything that was said and call with any questions or concerns. Then you won't have to call again while you're writing. Then do the writing and send it in on time.

If this is a pilot or TV movie, your deal probably says you'll owe them another couple of drafts, one of which is a what we call a "polish," which is a rewrite in which you go over the dialogue shortly before shooting starts on the project. This is so you, the original writer, can make the changes necessitated by production problems—or production opportunities, if a location of which you've always dreamed suddenly is available after years of saying, "No!" to Hollywood—or to accommodate or make use of the special qualities of the stars. This is a great opportunity for both fun and education, and one that's much more likely to be available to television writers than writers of feature films. Feature films routinely are rewritten by new writers brought into the project. TV movies routinely have one or at most two writers. Is it because television production companies are more honorable? Or because television budgets don't allow for infinite writers? My experience leads me to think it's a combination of both.

If this is an episode, your deal usually entitles the series to ask for one more version of the script, calling it a polish. This is always the case in Writers Guild deals. In many non-Writers Guild deals and all animation deals you more likely have had to agree to write as many drafts as you're requested to write, or until the production company approves the teleplay. Nothing to do for it except grin and bear it and continue being a Get-Along Guy/Gal while hoping the staff takes over as soon as possible.

In practice most shows almost never ask a freelance writer to do a polish because the showrunner does the polish instead. That's the main reason he or she is there—to give each episode that special flavor only that showrunner can give. You're there to get the script close enough so that the showrunner's once over doesn't take too much time and effort. No showrunner expects any other writer's work to be "perfect" for the series. But the closer you get to perfection, the more beloved you become.

After you've finished your last version of a pilot, TV movie, or episode, you're entitled to know where you stand. Is your career going to barrel along as a result of this assignment? How fast? How far? Give everyone a week or so to digest your final draft and then call and volunteer your services again. You've got another great series idea to pitch. Another sensational TV movie. The best episode the series could ever show. The reaction to your excited call will be an honest one because you've advanced another level, to "known commodity." If your pal at the network, studio, prodco, or series communicates the same eagerness you have, you're doing just fine. It means it's only a matter of time before you're writing two or three pilots or TV movies a year, or replacing the next departing member of the series' writing staff.

It means you're a pro.

chapter 15:
working for a living

In days of yore, the top TV action and drama writers made
their living by coming up with concepts for series and writing two or
three pilots a year, or by writing two or three TV movies during that
same time period. Often they did both because the line between the
two arenas was blurry. During that era, pilots were usually two hours
long and presented with great fanfare as movies of the week or specials.

These writers were treated with great respect by their fellow
writers and by the TV industry as a whole. For their three pilots or TV
movies a year they were paid more money than any writer-producer
could make working 40 weeks on a series in a single season (40 weeks
being the usual term of employment for a show that had what we
called a "full order") and earned the equivalent of what a freelancer
would've made writing 15 to 20 episodes a season—which was an
impossible chore.

The action-drama pilot and TV movie writing gods of that time
came from two major sources. A small minority of them were feature
film writers after whom the networks hotly lusted. (Wouldn't *you* want
the writers of, say, *Bonnie and Clyde*, or *The Graduate* to come up with
something equally impressive if you were a network VP?) The others
were writers who'd worked their way up from being freelancers to
story editors to producers of successful, or not-so-successful series.

Many of them, including myself, were victims (if that's the right word) of young heart attacks. Others had watched the long hours they'd put in on the shows destroy their marriages and families. Others were just plain exhausted, and if we could make more money by working less it certainly seemed the right thing to do. Your pilot sold? Great, let some workhorse sweat it out, making the concept work while you sit back and collect the royalties. Writing a TV movie? Great, put down the words, consult when it's shot, and go home and recharge.

In television today, the situation is much different. The action-drama writer's best chance for creative and career fulfillment comes from being on the staff of a broadcast network, cable channel, or first-run syndicated series. No longer is being a writer-producer a means to another, brighter end. It's the end to which every writer aspires.

Why? For one thing, pilots aren't two hours long anymore. Payment for a one-hour action or drama pilot is still much more than for an episode—one and a half times as much according to Writers Guild of America, West rules, but this is one time, perhaps the only time, in which "minimum" isn't the going rate, so pilot writers customarily get two or three times that sum. However, it's still not as high for the freelance writer, proportionately, as it once was, and there's no longer the likelihood that any freelancer will obtain two or three assignments each year. There isn't even the likelihood the freelancer will get *one*. The openings are simply no longer there.

Instead, as we talked about earlier, the first choice writers for one-hour pilots are the showrunners of series currently on the air. These writers' multi-million dollar deals include network commitments to pay for and broadcast more shows created and produced by the same showrunner. Them that's proved themselves gits. Them that schleps themselves to work everyday to ramrod a show or two gits more shows and more schlepping. They gits to work harder than writer-producers ever did before, and to reap financial rewards that would boggle the minds of those who came before them.

To be honest, many writers who used to write two-hour pilots are willing to damn the current situation and its politics at the drop of a hat, yet are glad they're out of the pilot business from a creative point of view.

The creative challenge involved in writing a one-hour pilot is much different from writing a two-hour one. In two hours a writer has a chance to fully—and artfully—set the stage for the entire series premise and incorporate into that a good, strong sample of what the viewer will see every week. Lethal Weapon, although a feature film, would have been the perfect two-hour television pilot because of the way it presents the who, how, and why of the characters and their general environment at the same time it lays out one specific, hard-hitting story. Not once do you feel a shifting of gears.

A one-hour pilot, however, has just enough time for the writer to give the viewer either the backstory or a sample of the weekly story. There aren't enough pages to do justice to both. As a result, for those who experienced the "old days," the creative satisfaction in writing a one-hour is much less than in writing a two-hour. In a sense, the challenge may be greater because the degree of difficulty is higher, but with the end result more limited and the end "product" viewed as an inherently lesser one, fewer top writers are inclined to devote all their artistry to this form. The bottom line: Many of those who created your favorite action or drama shows in the 1970s, 1980s, and early are now writing novels instead.

For another thing, TV movies have changed direction both creatively and businesswise. In an era of "branding," where feature films based on properties that've been established in other media (characters such as Batman, Spider-Man, and James Bond; properties such as books by Crichton, Clancy, and Ludlum), television networks and channels also are looking for pre-sold commodities to turn into TV movies, especially books, and more and more frequently the adaptations of these books are entrusted to known feature film writers. (Want to make it big in the TV movie or mini-series business? Here's a tip: Get hold of the TV rights to as many books as you can that tell the true stories of ordinary men or women who have triumphed over extraordinary problems—or even not so extraordinary problems. Shop those and insist that you write the script.)

For sitcom writers the situation is different—which is to say it's the same. Nothing has changed. Sitcoms always have had half-hour pilots, and the majority of those pilots have been written by experienced sitcom writer-producers, usually men and women who already have shows on the air, or whose series was recently cancelled. Financially, sitcom pilot deals are as lucrative as ever, and creatively the challenges remain what they always were: Set up the characters and the situation and be funny, dammit, funny! As far as television movies are concerned, TV has done very, very few comedy films and still is doing very, very few comedy films, which means there are no fewer TV comedy writers working in that arena now than before.

To cut to the chase (as execs are always telling writers to do when they're bored with the writers' pitch—so if a VP says that while you're talking, know that you've lost him or her, relax, and move onto your next high concept), in the sitcom arena being on the staff of a series has always been the road to El Dorado, and in the one-hour business (and animation, et al) that's where it now is.

In television today, being on the staff of a broadcast network, cable channel, or first-run syndicated series is how you make your daily living. It's also where you get your advanced training and experience as a writer and producer. And it's where you make friends and contacts not only with other writers and writer-producers, but with network, studio, and prodco execs who will be able to advance your career if they like your work and you. These days, networks have to approve all above-the-line personnel on every show and, in most cases, the execs in charge of different shows have no problem recommending writers and others who they believe will do a good job—which in this case means the ones they think their bosses will like.

Fortunately, these days it's easier than ever before to get a staff job. Large writing staffs mean a larger need for manpower, and the manpower comes from the freelance pool. In bygone years a writer might labor for five years or more, writing dozens of freelance scripts, before being offered a story editor job. Today a freelance writer who does one good script for a show will be asked to write another one for that show. If he or she writes two good scripts, the writer will be asked to be on staff. If the show stays on the air long enough when it's over that writer—you—could have become its showrunner.

If you want to become a television writer it behooves you to know what to expect. So exactly what happens when you're on staff? What's it really like?

For many writers it's heaven.

And for others it's hell.

It depends on how well you handle pressure, how you feel about living your life in the trenches, because to most showrunners running a TV series is like running a war. The objective in this war is to get a good series on the air week after week for a whole season and be renewed for more. In this situation the definition of "good" is a series that pleases the various people who pay its bills and the showrunner's artistic and career aspirations as well.

What will please those paying the bills? Let's take a look:

If the deep pockets belong to a broadcast network or basic cable channel, the bill payers will be happy if the show gets a high enough rating (total number and percentage of viewers as determined by the A.C. Nielsen Company—more info than this would be best served via the writing of yet another book) with the population demographic sought by the advertisers the network or cable channel is trying to attract—because these advertisers are the primary source of income.

If the bill payer is a premium cable channel, Deep Pockets, Inc. will be happy if the show gets the kinds of positive reviews that in turn attract enough viewers to achieve a high rating, which demonstrates to cable systems that aren't carrying the channel that they should be, and creates enough buzz to cause more viewers to sign up for the channel—because subscribers are the primary source of income. That's why shows on the HBO and Showtime families of cable channels are—or give the perception of being—"better" in terms of quality than those on so many other networks and channels. Because there's a direct relationship between the supplier and the viewer. If HBO and Showtime don't attract subscribers by presenting shows that are more appealing than those of their rivals, HBO and Showtime will be joining defunct dotcoms in Wall Street Hell. And research has shown these two companies that artistic quality is the best lure for new sign-ups.

Also coughing up some dough for series production are the studios and prodcos that make them. The "license fee" paid by the networks is never enough to cover the entire cost, so these companies pay the deficits. Therefore, what makes them happiest is when production costs are kept down and each episode is made for less than has been budgeted. This almost never happens, so the studios and prodcos usually have to be satisfied with their shows coming in on budget, which is happening more often as the world's overall economy tightens. The studios and prodcos also react merrily when the network execs seem to like the shows the studios and prodcos are producing because that means these buyers will come back for more.

Wait a minute here. If the studio or prodco has to deficit finance each episode of each series, how does it make a profit? The easy answer to this question, often given by people in the TV business, including studio and prodco execs, is an eye-rolling, "God only knows." The more difficult and more complete answer is more complex. The studios and prodcos make money on their shows because they're allowed to sell them more than once. In fact, they're allowed to sell them as many times as they can, except in specific instances where the contract for a series forbids it.

Most broadcast networks and cable channels pay for a specific number of runs, usually between one and five. If they want to show the series more than that they've got to pay another fee. And if the studio or prodco wants to make a deal with another network allowing the second network to present the show after the first network has, hey, sure, be our guest—just pay the fee. And then there's syndication, where the right to broadcast an entire package of episodes from a given series or from several series a predetermined number of times is sold as one entity to as many local stations as the salesmen can find. That's where *Seinfeld* made all its money for its backers. And where Warner Brothers, the studio that produces *Friends* hopes, as of this writing, eventually will go into profits on that series.

Another way for the studios or prodcos to make money on their shows is through "creative accounting." It's becoming more and more common for the networks, studios, and/or prodcos to be under the same corporate umbrella, in which case many of the costs are simply payments from one pocket of the big corporation to another pocket. In one set of books these are expenses. In another set they're income. These also happens on a smaller scale with studios that aren't network-owned. As full service production organizations, the studios supply everything to the production—offices, stages, set decorations, dressing rooms, cameras, sound equipment, you name it—and charges the show's budget for each item. Yet, again, the money, in fact, is only going from one pocket to another. According to auditors specializing in TV accounting, the result of this practice is—at worst—that the studios or prodcos break even—and at best they make money right off the top by using expenses that don't really cost them anything to defray profit participation payments to outside participants. That's why they so often are sued by their shows' stars.

What will please the showrunner's artistic and career aspirations?

That's not so complicated. Look at it this way: What would please *you*? The best showrunners I know put out shows they'd like to watch and are so in tune with the viewing audience that enough viewers feel the same way to make the shows hits. Glen Larson, Steve Cannell, and Gene Roddenberry are or were all of this type. During the times when they were at their peaks they loved every show they produced—and so did millions of fans. Most other showrunners I know are aware that their personal tastes and those of the audience may not always mesh. As a result, they're constantly striving to attain the perfect balance between their need for artistic self-expression and the related need to entertain others. How well they succeed depends on each showrunner's talent, taste, and judgment.

In terms of their careers, most showrunners view the ultimate reward the same way Norman Powell does—getting the chance to do what they do again. Or, in the case of the most ambitious, as getting the chance to do *more*. Glen Larson and I worked together at a time when he was the official executive producer of three different hit series on the air at the same time: *The Fall Guy, Knight Rider, and Magnum P.I.*

I was supervising producer of one of them, during an era when supervising producers *produced* as well as wrote, and I was exhausted all the time, but whenever I went into Larson's office and he wasn't doing work related to any of these shows, it was because he was trying to come up with his next series. "Remember *I Spy*?" he'd say. "I think I've got a new take on that." Or, "Remember Lou Ferrigno, the guy who played the Hulk? I've got a terrific part for him." And the next season he had four more series going: *Automan, Manimal, Emergency 911*, and *Masquerade*. Larson was the official showrunner of seven series—and he was still creating and trying to sell more.

If producing a series is like a war and these are the objectives, who's the enemy? What's standing in the way? Money—rather, the lack of "enough" money—is the big enemy for those working in series TV. The budgets just never seem to have enough money in them to pay for all the great ideas and significant moments the showrunner and staff put into each script. And, working hand in hand with money and creating a kind of "axis of evil," is time. In fact, on the day to day, moment by moment experiential level, the lack of enough time is the enemy whose eyes staffer's stare into every day.

The problems begin the same day the show does. Most shows get their writing staffs in place and start working on scripts in early to mid-June, and the first episode starts shooting in August. This gives the showrunner and staff approximately six weeks to come up with a script and get it approved by everyone with approvals—the network, the studio or prodco, the stars. As difficult as this might sound on its face, the situation is compounded by the fact that five to seven or eight work days after the first script starts shooting not only does all photography have to be finished so film or tape editing and other postproduction can begin, but another script has to go before the cameras without a single day of downtime. Then another and another, without let-up, in an unending cycle until the season is done—because everything and everyone in the budget is being financially compensated by the day or by the week, and the payments have to be made whether or not the stage is used or the crew or even the writing staff is working.

Postpone just one shooting day and the show is at least $50,000 over budget. Take one day too long to shoot and the overage is at least three or four times that. Plus the overall season schedule—which includes planned catch-up days or days off because of holidays or other commitments to be fulfilled by the stars—now no longer may be valid, and the production manager will have to take extra time (at extra cost) to rearrange it.

No one can prepare anything without a script to break down so a final draft must be ready for all the departments to read—even though it may not stay "final" for long. One-hour shows are scheduled so that after the script is written the showrunner, director (usually a freelancer, only there for the one episode), and the production staff have as many working days as it takes to shoot an episode to get every-thing in place for the next shoot. Depending on the series and its budget, that can be six, seven, or eight days—seven's the average—to come up with a schedule the director can meet. Rewrite pages to make meeting that schedule possible. Build new sets. Rewrite pages to make the set-building situation more affordable. Find necessary locations. Rewrite pages to account for the fact that a desired location is unavailable, or that an even more interesting and appropriate one has been found. Cast the guest stars and other "this episode" only actors. Rewrite more pages to make the part more attractive to a particularly valued guest, or to cut down the number of speaking parts and make the casting process simpler. And more and more...

Except in the case of the first and last episodes of the season, all aspects of production are scheduled to save time and money by continuously overlapping. One episode is "on the stage" (TV jargon for being filmed) while the other is being prepped. And another episode is in post being cut together, with music, sound effects, and visual effects being added. The shooting and the postproduction also take an average of seven days. And, during all of this, members of the staff, either singly or working together, and perhaps some freelance writers as well, are writing the next script and the next and the next. And getting the ideas for the one after that and after that and after that.

Sitcoms are in the same bind, with time a more serious obstacle than money. Sitcoms are almost always shot indoors, using the same sets every week and with only one or two outside cast additions. This saves a ton. No one likes to talk about it, but the biggest single expense on the average sitcom is the salary of the stars.

Sitcoms that don't perform before a "live audience" (if there's any other kind of audience I don't think I want to know) also have to accommodate the seemingly infinite loop of "prep," "shooting," and "post," and most of them have only five working days for each part of the cycle. On the plus side, these sitcoms usually have two regular directors instead of having to depend on freelancers.

Like staff writers, the staff directors are paid weekly salaries and receive "producer" titles as well as "directed by" credit, and they alternate episodes so one is prepping while the other is shooting. These shows are always filmed and, just as a matter of information, usually use film teleplay format, or some variation thereof.

On sitcoms that do perform "live," that is, that are shot on theater-style stage before an audience using Desi Arnaz's three-camera technique, the performance is the culmination of one single very intense work week. Each episode's script, which is probably written in taped format, has to be a ready to go final draft on Monday. That's the day of the "table reading," in which the cast gathers around a conference table with the showrunner, writing staff, and director. Shows like these often have only one director, who is also is a staff member and usually receives an "executive producer" credit as well as "directed by" for every episode.

Under the guidance of the director, the cast reads through the script out loud. This gives the writers a chance to see how everything sounds when spoken by those for whom it was intended, and to take notes on changes that'll have to be made to make the script funnier. The cast and director also contribute suggestions for improving dialogue or plot points they think are weak.

Many times the script is rewritten right there, "at the table," and then further refinements are made by the showrunner the next day. Other times the actual changes are made later, by the showrunner or another staff member designated by the showrunner, and based on the comments and suggestions made during the table reading.

The staff comes to every rehearsal and performance. Wednesday usually is a daytime rehearsal of the revised final draft on the stage with the director "blocking" (as in "choreographing," not "preventing") the actor's movements. More script changes are made. Thursday is an evening dress rehearsal before an audience, with more changes made in the script, taking into account the reaction of the audience. The dress rehearsal is filmed or taped, with the director in a separate control room deciding which angles and shots to use as the performance is in progress. Network reps also attend.

After the dress rehearsal everyone meets to discuss the script and the staging, and more changes are made. After four days of familiarity lines that seemed funny at the table on Monday can sound flat and dull, so new jokes are written, with the actors making significant contributions. Then, the next day, the show is shot before an audience again—twice. Two performances. Two different audiences. The rehearsals and performances don't go straight through, by the way. The situation isn't, "We're here for half an hour and then we go home." It can take as long as four hours to shoot a half-hour "live" sitcom, with retakes to cover acting or camera mistakes and instant rewrites to save scenes that aren't having the right effect. That means that on Friday the staff can be at it on the stage for eight hours, plus all the time put in at the office earlier in the day.

During the daytime on Thursday and Friday, and during as much of Wednesday as they can grab, the staff writers are working on the next script so it can go to the table on Monday. In effect, prep, shooting, and post all are compressed into one week. But not quite: The episode that's broadcast is actually a combination of the best versions of the dress rehearsal and the final performances, with music and titles added and, if necessary, the laughter and applause "sweetened" (as in enhanced). So this means the showrunner is supervising two or three days of postproduction while polishing the current script and supervising the next one.

Live-action kids shows usually fight the Money and Time Battle the same way one-hour shows do, except that their schedules are compressed to three or four days instead of six, seven, or eight. Animated shows face the enemy a little differently, though.

On an animated series, after a block of episodes is ordered, the head writer (who is usually the de facto showrunner, although the animator-producer more often than not is given that title) assembles a two or three-person staff, augmented by more freelancers than usually used by one-hours, sitcoms, or live-action kids shows, and the scripts for the entire season—or for more than one season because the order can be for as many as 65 episodes at a time—are planned out, approved by the powers-that-be, and then written.

At the beginning of any animated series, time isn't a problem for those on the writing staff. That's because it'll be several months before "production" starts. On animated shows, prep is a long, involved process involving several separate stages. After a script is approved, it's storyboarded by a group of artists who decide how it will look shot by shot, and who draw each "master shot," co-ordinating the images with the appropriate chunks of dialogue.

The storyboards go through the same approval process the scripts do and while this is happening, actors are hired to record the dialogue. Unlike actors who go before the cameras, these voice actors are paid to be ready to speak into the microphone whenever it's convenient for the series, so no one has to keep feeding them scripts on a regular basis. When two or three final drafts are ready, and only when they're ready, a voice recording session is scheduled and the work gets done. Only *after* the voices are recorded and the storyboards approved is the actual drawing of the thousands of images that make up an animated episode begun.

The animation process takes weeks, the length of time varying from series to series and even episode to episode. After it's finished, the episode goes into postproduction. The writing staff seldom is involved with anything to do with the series after the voice recording of the scripts, but time eventually starts to compress and crunch after about a third of the scripts have been written. That's when the storyboard and animating machines are in full swing and must be fed as continuously as all the other production beasts.

The money monster raises its head earlier, and is more direct in animation than in other genres. The first financial obstacle has to do with the writing of action scenes, and since most animated shows pack as much action as possible into their pages, that's a lot of writing. Many new writers think that because sets, locations, and living, breathing stuntmen aren't involved, they can write just about anything and then have it animated. Don't make that mistake.

The fact is that yes, you can write the end of the entire universe (and I did, on *The Silver Surfer*), but you must present it in the most abstract way. At current budgets the artists don't have time to draw a billion, or a million, or even a hundred individual faces screaming in terror because Galactus is "eating" their planet. But they can draw two or three people here, four there, and another two or three in another place, all registering their panic.

Similarly, certain types of locations seem to be "undrawable" because they would take too many man-hours and too much money. Amusement parks cause big art problems, for example. And certain small physical activities have to be avoided at all costs because in TV animation costs are kept down by using animation processes that are, to say the least, not quite as sophisticated as feature film animation state of the art. What do I mean by "small physical activities?" Try this one: Animating a human being—any number of human beings— *walking* is almost impossible to do with any degree of realism. Running, jumping, flying, and swimming work just fine, but a walk across the room is a mess. If I hadn't been there, I'd never have known.

The only genre that seems to be immune to the obstacles of money and time is the daytime serial. Soaps are about regular people in regular places doing regular things. (Okay, they're about beautiful people pretending to be regular people in regular places doing outrageous things, but the point is they're not involved in car chases or battling super villains.) They're shot the way sitcoms are, on standing sets, only rarely venturing out to expose the viewers to an exotic locale. And although a new script is shot each day, the writer of that script usually has three or four days in which to write it. It may not sound like it, but having been there and done it I know this to be a low-pressure situation—because the writer doesn't have to do any editing. The whole idea of soaps is for the characters to sound natural, which means the sub-writers can more or less write the first thing to enter their minds. And the story editor has a day to go through and fix any out of character or too-clunky lines.

But there are a couple of other big enemies as well, and from them no genre, not even the soap opera, is exempt or immune.

When I was a kid, one of the top comic scripts of the day was Pogo, and one of the catch phrases that made it so big was Pogo's remark that, "We have met the enemy and he is us." In TV, that often is true in the sense that those the staff is trying to please are the ones we end up having to fight.

That's right. I'm talking about the network.

And the studio or prodco.

They don't mean to be stumbling blocks, intention and result aren't always the same thing.

What's am I talking about? Here. Have a war story or two:

Let's start with the network. *Police Story,* which I produced, was *the* TV critics' favorite series during its time. A pile of awards. Praise from civic groups. General acclaim. And its ratings were Top 20, averaging about 35 to 40 million viewers an episode. Based on true stories told to the staff by working LAPD officers still on the job, with first novelist/detective Joseph Wambaugh and then former LAPD Chief Thomas Reddin as technical advisors, *Police Story* created the "cop-works-on-the-case-and-case-works-on-the-cop" style of story-telling that since has become obligatory for cop shows.

An anthology where no one had to worry about saving the hero so he could return next week, the series often featured downbeat endings, unresolved issues, and tragic personal consequences from professional heroics, and in spite of its success, the execs at NBC always were trying to get those in charge of the show to change it to something safer, quieter, warmer. Mark Rodgers, who was an executive story consultant on *Police Story* before I came on staff, told me about a meeting he'd been to early in the first season with various network suits in which the execs laid down the law. "Our research shows that you're doing everything exactly right," he quoted a VP as saying. "But we don't care. We want it changed."

"I'll go to the press," Joe Wambaugh replied. "I'll tell the whole country you're destroying your own show."

The suits backed down that day, but even though *Police Story* became a major hit, those for whom we were winning the ratings and quality battle still functioned adversarially. When I was producing the show, a common script note was, "Can't we let the good guy win, just once?" In fact, the good guy always won. That is, he always solved the crime and brought in the perp. It was just that at the same time he did that he was likely to come home to an empty house, his wife having left him because he was too devoted to the job.

The studio or prodco usually ends up functioning as an enemy as well. For example, I was executive story consultant of *The Magician*, a cult show so influential that part of the mythology of another series, *The X-Files*, is based on the "fact" that the hero's sister was abducted by aliens while he was watching a Magician episode. Paul Playdon was the showrunner for this series, and at least once a week he'd go to a meeting with the production execs at Paramount, the studio producing the show, and then stomp back to our suite of offices. "These people won't be satisfied until we have to shut down the show!" he would shout. "They say we're making the production too complicated. They're saying we're putting in too much magic. I tell them the name is *The Magician* and they just wince and say, 'Don't remind me.'"

Over a decade later, execs at 20TH Century-Fox were saying the same thing to me about *The Fall Guy*. "Do we have to have so many stunts?" Mark Evans, the vice president of production, would say after reading each script. "They're too difficult to shoot." But they didn't stop there. Very seldom were any two executives on the same page. Invariably, the same day I heard from Evans I'd also get a call from Lee Stalmaster, one of the studio's TV programming VPs, saying, "Larry, don't you think this would be more exciting if we had more stunts? The hero's a stuntman. Can't you give him another big action scene?"

To be fair, some networks and studios or prodcos are easier to work with than others. This is a function of both corporate policy and the individuals implementing it. In my experience, HBO execs, for example, would never think of dumbing down a script, not even one scene. In fact, their tendency has been to go to the other extreme and urge the writers to push the creative boundaries.

On *Spawn*, which was a product of HBO's own HBO Productions prodco as well as being shown on the cable channel, the director of the series, Lenny Brown, was always saying things like, "Do we really want to do anything anybody's seen before? Isn't there a more original way to show the guy's mad?" Or, "I didn't understand what was happening in the last scene, but it had me riveted. That's good! It's just what we want."

And his boss, CEO Chris Albrecht, was even more encouraging and helpful when my former partner and I were developing another project, called *Rock City*, for him. "I like the story," he said at one meeting on the first of three episodes we were writing. "I like the writing. And I like the characters. But I've got an idea. Every show on TV is written so that, in each scene, first you come up with the reason for a character to do something and then you have him do it."

"Sounds like a natural progression to me," I said.

"Sure it is," Albrecht said. "But what if you write every scene so that first we see what the guy does, and then we see *why* he did it? The thought process is the same—he had the motivation first—but we make the audience wait a beat to find out what it was."

An experiment, suggested not by a hot showrunner, but coming from the brain of a corporate nabob instead. Did it work? Kind of. Did HBO put the series into production? No. But what a joy to stretch our creative muscles by attempting what was literally a new method of storytelling. What a pleasure when those you're trying to satisfy actually give you a hand instead of standing in the way.

So now you know the objectives and the enemies. What's the campaign itself really like?

Daytime serial sub-writers stay home and write their scripts, just as freelancers do. But members of the staffs of one-hour shows, sitcoms, and animated shows are expected at the office. The hours are deceptive. You don't start till 10 in the morning, which usually makes everyone you know who's not working in TV envious. "You call that work? Waking up late and writing? C'mon!" But many nights you don't knock off till eight or nine, and on dress rehearsal and performance days sitcom writers work past midnight.

Need new clothes? Send your spouse, boyfriend, girlfriend, or an assistant. Be prepared to remotely take part in any number of corrective exchanges. Haircuts? They're a thing of the past. Until the show's canceled, you're lucky if you find time to trim your nails.

The office suite, or bungalow, or trailer, depending on whether you're located at a studio or a prodco and how big the prodco is, becomes more of a home than the place you wake up at every morning. The downside of this is that typical staff members usually don't have great offices. You get more than the cubicle you would if you worked at one of the parent corporations, but don't count on a view or even a window. You'll get a desk, a chair, a computer, a sofa, and a bookcase, all shoved back against walls painted the same drab color they were back when you were in elementary school—which could well be when the painting was done.

However, it's easy enough to bring in some personal items. Paints, photos, posters, plants if you've got the touch. And the really big bonus is—hell, you're *"on the lot!"* If you're a lover of television or show business in general—and why would you be writing TV if you weren't?—there's an unbeatable thrill to driving to the gate of Universal City or Warner Brothers or Sony or whatever and being waved through by a guard. The guard's only looking at your sticker, not you, but you'll still feel validated. You'll feel *honored* by the fact that you're about to park in the same lot or garage where writers and directors and actors whose work you've admired—for me it was Billy Wilder, John Wayne, Rod Serling, Clark Gable—parked before you.

And if you're not at one of the old studios, you can still feel a sense of tradition. "Wow! *The Man From Uncle* was written here. Man! The offices of *Homicide: Life In The Street* used to be right upstairs!" I admit it. I'm a sucker for this stuff. And so are all the other writers and showrunners I know.

So there you are. Your car is in a parking space with your name on it, beside a car in another parking space on which is stenciled the name "David E. Kelley" and just down the aisle from a space reading "Aaron Sorkin" or "Aaron Spelling." Sure each one of these people is closer to the building or the elevator than you are, and their cars are, well, a little "grander" I suppose we can say—but you're here. You've got your little piece of the turf.

And you're in your little office, but not for long. Because the first thing that happens is every morning is that the staff gets together, either in a meeting room, the office of the supervising producer—if the showrunner is busy elsewhere—or of the showrunner him or herself—if he or she is there. The meeting room or office will be much better than yours, but you won't have time to think about the décor. You'll be too busy with the business at hand: ordering coffee. An assistant or an intern is standing by, wanting to know exactly how you take it. Is Starbucks all right? Or do you want yours from The Coffee Bean? Or, if this is one of the better office suites or bungalows or trailers, you may be able to get your coffee yourself from the show's kitchen, directly out of a machine that carries only top "designer brands." Hey, this is Hollywood. TV Land. Sure, you work your ass off, but these're the perks. (And the coffee's paid for by the company, as is any breakfast you may think you need.)

Once you've gotten your coffee order out of the way, or you've emerged from the kitchen with your cup, you flop on a chair or couch and take part in the second major discussion of the day: the improvements just made, or yet to be made, on the currently shooting script. Another assistant makes sure everyone has a fresh copy, and the whole staff starts reading. (It's a little like being in church, with the showrunner as the preacher, uttering all the new lines out loud as though they were prayers.) You don't read the whole script, only the changes, and in all likelihood when the showrunner hears them he or she will turn to the computer keyboard and do a little fine-tuning right then. Especially since it's more than likely that while you're all at this, someone from the network will call with "just one more little note."

During this meeting the phone will ring constantly. Most of the calls will be for the showrunner, and most of the showrunner's calls won't be about this series but about another one he or she is commanding, developing, or selling. Names of writers who could help out with the new show will fly from the showrunner's lips, along with authorizations to make deals with them. Or not, depending on how everything is progressing. You'll listen closely and wonder why your name's not being mentioned. After all, you're a good writer. You've proven that by your work here on staff. Don't be disappointed. That's precisely why you're not being mentioned. You're too good. You've made yourself too valuable—possibly even indispensable—here.

By now it's almost noon, which means another big discussion— this one about lunch. On some shows the staff always eats together in the office, so everyone has to agree on what restaurant should supply today's meal and then choose salad, entrée, and dessert. Or, if the showrunner's in the mood for deli, what kind of combo does each staffer want from Jerry's Famous Deli up the street? (There's a Jerry's Famous Deli up the street from every studio or prodco, just as there's a Starbucks or The Coffee Bean. How do you think it became so famous?)

On other shows, the staff always eats together but goes out for lunch. This means that instead of discussing what to eat, the talk turns to who should drive. Usually the designated driver is the showrunner's favorite writer on the staff. What do you think? A millionaire writer's going to entrust his or her life to someone he or she doesn't like? This is an example of office politics at its finest. Keep your eyes peeled so you know who to like—even if you don't like that person at all.

After lunch—which is either paid for or unquestioningly reimbursed by the studio or prodco—it's usually time for you to get to work on your own individual script. Or, if this is a sitcom, to gangbang on the next script. As you sit there, trying to think of the right beat or the right word you should be inspired by what you've been hearing so far today. By that I mean your writer's ear should have been paying close attention to what the other members of the staff have been saying...because TV writers are for the most part very clever people. You don't get ordinary table talk in any aspect of showbiz, and writers especially seem to take great pride in their sharp and cutting one-liners.

On TV, even ordinary people don't speak ordinarily. Don't "steal" what someone else has specifically said—because in all likelihood he or she is going to incorporate it into his or her own script. But be aware of the rhythm and flavor of the dialogue you've been hearing, of the quick banter and subtle, or not-so-subtle interchange of ideas and, yes, insults. Let this mode of expression guide you as you write your characters' exchanges. Think also of the way your fellow writers tell their stories. Of how they shape and pace them. Of how they bend the truth to make every experience more interesting to the listener. (This drives spouses crazy, but this is TV.) Adapt that approach and shape the scenes of your teleplay so they too are little tales all their own. The best television writers are those whose work reads as though they're creating urban legends.

Tom Greene, who was one of the producers of *Knight Rider* while in his early 20s, is a master of verbal storytelling, partly because he's also a master of self-deprecation. In his stories he never has the last word and never tops the other guy. He's the victim, a Charlie Chaplin-esque Everyman. And he succeeds as a writer because his characters are the same way. We love his heroes because they always speak with great humor. Someone else is always a little funnier. David Hasselhoff may have been the Knight Rider, but Kit the car always topped him whenever they spoke. And it took both of them working together to stop the bad guy and save the day.

I'll never forget the time Greene stopped in the middle of the charming tale of his most recent misadventures. "Shit," he said.

"What's the matter?" I said.

"This story doesn't have an ending." Then he smiled. "But it will next month, when I tell it to you again."

And it did.

The dynamic of working with a group of writers who get along with each other is a wonderful thing, but what happens when you don't get along so well? Believe it or not, such situations are rare. That's because as the series moves on a real sense of being in the trenches together takes over. You're all buddies, hanging tight because you're under fire. That war analogy, remember?

What happens as you get deeper and deeper into the production schedule is that the afternoons, which originally were fairly routine occasions for writing, become more stressful. Emergencies abound, more and more of them every day. The network people call and voice complaints about material the staff thinks is fine. Or worse, these cold-hearted execs e-mail their negativity, copying everyone at the network and the studio or prodco, so your newly precarious situation is totally exposed. The studio and prodco execs invariably overreact to network "disappointment," and their calls and e-mails have been known to make grown men cry.

"My goal in life," a Universal exec once told me, "is to make Don Bellasario cry."

I've only met Bellasario, who has been showrunner of such hits as *Magnum P.I., Quantum Leap,* and *J.A.G.,* once, and he didn't strike me as someone to whom tears would come easily, so I asked the exec if he'd succeeded.

"No," he said. "But Bellasario's done it to me."

Stars like to get into the act too. They'll decide they hate something in the script they loved yesterday and refuse to leave their dressing rooms until "someone gets their ass down here and fixes this crap."

This kind of mortar fire cements the staff, bonding its members together so that you find yourself almost *loving* men or women you otherwise couldn't tolerate for a second. You pull together to handle the emergency and back your showrunner. Eventually every show turns into "us against them." The writing staff is "us." Everyone else in the world is "them." I find this a fascinating phenomenon because, as the conflicts with "them" intensify, each staff writing job becomes not worse but better. You're energized, adrenalized, testosteronized. You can't wait to get to the office and fight, fight, fight.

Another strange phenomenon that occurs around this time is the, "Hey, this show is even better than I thought!" phase. There's something about putting in so many hours and fighting so many battles that changes your perspective. You start believing that what you're doing is more than a job. It's a divine mission. And deservedly so—because your show is the best show ever on television. And your star is the best star ever to perform anywhere any time.

How else can I explain sitting in a screening room at Fox, watching dailies of *The Fall Guy*, and shouting out, "Hey, Lee Majors is a hell of an actor! Who would've thought?"

Or Cal Clements doing the same thing on *Dallas*, "Hey, that Victoria Principal—she'll be a superstar."

How else do we justify *Will & Grace*'s Jeff Greenstein confiding to a friend, "Debra Messing's the reincarnation of Lucille Ball."

Energy. Adrenaline. Testosterone.

No matter what happens, you'll love your job.

You gotta love your job.

Ain't nothin' else there.

Sure, once in awhile everyone gets discouraged. Showrunners are always quitting and then being talked into coming back. I used to quit *Police Story* once a week. I'd stomp out of the office angrily and go home and rant. Then David Gerber, the head of the studio, would call and make nice. The next day I was back.

Not because he'd called.

Not even because he'd added a new pilot to my deal.

I was back because the pressure is addictive. I got to hobnob with the show's guest stars, both on the set and at dinner and parties. I went to charity events where I could sit at the same table with Goldie Hawn and Harrison Ford. (No, they weren't together.) My friends and neighbors were jealous. My family was snowed. And most of all, I was doing what I'd always dreamed of doing.

I was in the TV biz!

And I love TV.

Beside my computer monitor, taped to the wall by one corner, is a piece of paper. On one side—the side that's usually showing—it says, "Beats working."

Flip it over and it says "Beats not working."

On either side of the paper, along the top, it says:

"TV writing."

I really do love TV.

AFTERWORD

I don't know what reading this book has done for you, but I can tell you what writing it has done for me. It's made me think about my life and my career. About my work and my dreams. About the art and the business of TV. Here are my conclusions. Maybe you'll like them. Maybe you won't. But I think you should know them.

Good writing sells. It sells itself and it sells the writer. Passionate writing is good writing. Passionate writing in which strong characters are involved in strong situations and express strong feelings that elicit strong responses from readers and viewers *sells*.

It doesn't matter if you're writing on the backs of envelopes in longhand and mailing it in from Peoria or if you're using the newest formatting program on the newest computer. If your work touches an emotional chord, it will be bought and you will be discovered—and the next thing you know you'll be in the middle of Hollywood, enveloped in all the trappings.

Television buys writers the way people buy houses. Because they create some grand feeling in them. Because they fill an otherwise empty cavity in life. Many times home buyers completely remodel their newly bought houses. And many times television, as an industry, completely reshapes the writers as well. But both processes are done out of an awesome combination of need and love.

Knowing story structure and being able to write dialogue that flies off the page are crucial in TV. Everything else—knowing where you should live and what you should wear and who in God's name you should be are bonuses, extras, lessons to be learned and applied in conjunction with writing that perfect script, the ultimate sample episode.

But if that sample episode is a work of genius, who the hell cares about the rest? You're in, and you deserve to be in. And if your spec script isn't a work of genius, then what the hell are you doing?

Does television as a medium need another mediocre writer to bring mediocrity to millions of viewers, who simply by being living, breathing, feeling human beings deserve more?

Do all the viewers who turn on their sets hoping for entertainment and enlightenment and an insight into the world around them need more mind-numbing pap?

Do you as a writer—and a human being—want to be just another purveyor of unaffecting nonsense content because, "Hey, I'm a pro?"

Write television. Please. But write *great* television. Reach into your soul and put what you find out there on the page for everyone else to see. Write the best you can write. Be the truest and most open you can be.

Don't settle for being a contender. Go for champ. Those who love you, those who are waiting to love you, those who need you, and those who are waiting to need you will all be much better served. *You'll* be much better served.

Listen to your muse. Check things out with your inner editor. Confirm them with your inner salesman. But listen to your muse.

Please.

appendix A:
sample scripts

Just as television writing demands that the action be shown whenever possible instead of merely told, so does a book about television writing demand that the reader be given concrete examples so the new TV writer can see exactly what goes on in a writer's work from step to step.

There's just one problem. If all the samples I've gathered were printed here in exactly the right format with precisely the correct font, layout, and design this book would be over twice as long as it is. It would be unaffordable to publish and outrageously expensive to buy.

So to avoid this problem and yet give you, the aspiring television writer, all you need and deserve, the folks at Applause and I have come up with a first. *Telvision Writing From The Inside Out: Your Channel To Success* is now a multi-media extravaganza, with draft after draft, version after version, of episodes of televised drama shows, sitcoms, animated shows, and even sitcoms available for your perusal at either of these URLS:

http://www.tvwriter.com/insideoutinsiders/
http://www.televisionwriting.com

A veritable font of further information awaits, clickable online Table of Contents and all. (And while you're at it, check out http://www.tvwriter.com—it's my favorite website, which probably doesn't come as a surprise.)

appendix B:
sample credits

Sooner or later, you're going to have to put together a list of your professional credits. Either you'll do it in order to attract the attention of an agent, or you'll do it at the behest of an agent so the agent can attract attention to you.

I don't know anyone else's career as well as I know my own. Here's my list so you can see the best format I know.

LARRY BRODY — WRITER / PRODUCER

Current Employment

CLOUD CREEK INSTITUTE FOR THE ARTS | 2002 –

NON PROFIT CORPORATION FOR THE ADVANCEMENT OF THE ARTS
President & Executive Director

Previous Employment

VEGAUNIVERSE, THE VIDEOGAME CHANNEL | 2001 – 2002
New Cable Channel Financed by Sega S.A.
President

Television Staff Positions

SPIDER-MAN UNLIMITED | 2000
Fox Kids
Executive Creative Consultant / Writer

DIABOLIK | 1998 - 2000
M6 Network (France)
Producer / Creative Consultant / Writer

THE SILVER SURFER | 1998 - 1999
Fox Kids
Creator / Creative Consultant / Writer

SPAWN | 1998
HBO
Executive Consultant / Writer

SUPER FORCE | 1990 - 1991
Syndicated
Supervising Producer / Developer / Writer

THE NEW ADVENTURES OF RIN TIN TIN | 1988 - 1990
Family Channel
Executive Producer / Writer

MICKEY SPILLANE'S NEW ADVENTURES OF MIKE HAMMER|1985–1987
CBS
Supervising Producer/Writer

PARTNERS IN CRIME | 1984
NBC
Supervising Producer/Writer

AUTOMAN | 1983
NBC
Executive Producer/Writer

THE FALL GUY | 1981–1983
ABC
Supervising Producer/Writer

POLICE STORY | 1976–1978
NBC
Producer/Executive Story Consultant/Writer

BARETTA | 1972–1973
ABC
Executive Story Consultant/Writer

GIBBSVILLE | 1975
NBC
Executive Story Consultant/Writer

MEDICAL STORY | 1974
NBC
Executive Story Consultant/Writer

THE STREETS OF SAN FRANCISCO | 1971
ABC
Executive Story Consultant/Writer

THE MAGICIAN | 1970
NBC
Executive Story Consultant/Writer

Motion Pictures for Television

THUNDER BEACH
Lifetime Movie of the Week
Supervising Producer/Writer

ROCK CITY
Showtime Pilot/Home Box Office Movie of the Week
Executive Producer/Writer

THE RETURN OF MIKE HAMMER
CBS Movie of the Week
Writer

FARRELL FOR THE PEOPLE
NBC Movie of the Week
Writer

THE NIGHT THE CITY SCREAMED
ABC Movie of the Week
Writer

Episodes

Writer of over 500 episodes of primetime TV series, including:

THE HUNTRESS
ACE LIGHTING (BBC)
DIAGNOSIS: MURDER
STAR TREK: VOYAGER
WALKER, TEXAS RANGER
HEAVEN HELP US
STAR TREK: THE NEXT GENERATION
SUPER FORCE
THE NEW ADVENTURES OF RIN TIN TIN
MIKE HAMMER
PARTNERS IN CRIME
AUTOMAN
THE FALL GUY
POLICE STORY
BARETTA
MEDICAL STORY
GIBBSVILLE
PETROCELLI
THE MAGICIAN

POLICEWOMAN
THE STREETS OF SAN FRANCISCO
MEDICAL CENTER
CANNON
BARNABY JONES
THE SIX-MILLION DOLLAR MAN
HAWAII FIVE-O
IRONSIDE
THE SIXTH SENSE
GENESIS II
THE BOLD ONES
THE NEW LAND
THE INTERNS
HERE COME THE BRIDES

TV Animation Episodes

Writer of over 100 episodes of various animated TV series, including:

MACE 2200 (FOX KIDS PILOT)
XENO'S INTERGALACTIC ZOO (FOX KIDS PILOT)
GHOST RIDER (UPN PILOT)
SPIDER-MAN UNLIMITED
DIABOLIK
THE SILVER SURFER
XYBER 9
SUPERMAN
SPIDER-MAN
STAR TREK: THE ANIMATED SERIES

Internet Series

AFTER THE FALL
Eruptor.com
Creator/Producer/Writer

TOGA TV
Syndicated Web Animation content
Co-Creator/Co-Producer/Co-Writer

Computer Games

SPIDER-MAN
Sony/Cingular
Writer

World Wide Website

TV WRITER.COM
http://tvwriter.com
Owner/operator of most awarded and visited television site on the Web

Awards

ENVIRONMENTAL MEDIA AWARD
Co-Writer, Best Dramatic Episode, *Star Trek: Voyager*

WOMEN IN TV & FILM AWARD
Writing Excellence, *Farrell for the People*

POPULATION INSTITUTE AWARD
Outstanding Writing Achievement, *Medical Story*

EMMY AWARD NOMINATION
Best Dramatic Writing, *Medical Story*

HUMANITAS CERTIFICATE
Outstanding Achievement, *Medical Story*

NOSOTROS AWARD
Best Portrayal of Hispanic Culture and Problems; Best Dramatic TV Episode, *Police Story*

WRITERS GUILD AWARD NOMINATION
Best Dramatic Writing, *Medical Story*

Books

Writer of nine novels, four books of poetry, one textbook, numerous online
e-book texts including:

TV *Writing From the Inside Out: Your Channel to Success (2003)*
TV *Writers Market 2002 (2001)*
The TV *Writer.com Book of* TV *Writing (1999)*
The Wind of God (1997)
A Song of the Spirit (1996)
The Return of the Navajo Dog (1995)
Kid Hollywood & The Navajo Dog (1994)

Articles

SCREENTALK MAGAZINE (current)
"From the Trenches"
Monthly education and opinion column about television and television
writing

SCRIPT MAGAZINE (2001)
"From the Trenches"
Monthly education and opinion column about television and television
writing(moved to ScreenTalk in 2001)

SANTA FE NEW MEXICAN (1991–1993)
OffCamera
Weekly opinion column about films and television

Academics

VISITING PROFESSOR—
The College of Santa Fe, Santa Fe, New Mexico (1991–1993)
   Visiting Professor: Screenwriting
   Visiting Professor: Documentary and Public Affairs Writing
   Visiting Professor: Television Production

Professional Affiliation

WRITERS GUILD OF AMERICA, West

Unlike corporate resumes, which demand brevity, TV *credit lists are better the longer they are. However, so you'll have a better idea of what yours may look like, here's what my agent wants my credit list to look like so I can be "discovered" by the newest generation of execs.*

LARRY BRODY — WRITER / PRODUCER (revised)

Television Staff Positions

SPIDER-MAN UNLIMITED
Fox Kids
Executive Creative Consultant / Writer

DIABOLIK
M6 Network (France)
Producer / Creative Consultant / Writer

THE SILVER SURFER
Fox Kids
Creator / Creative Consultant / Writer

SPAWN
HBO
Executive Consultant / Writer

SUPER FORCE
Syndicated
Supervising Producer / Developer / Writer

Episodes

THE HUNTRESS
ACE LIGHTING (BBC)
DIAGNOSIS: MURDER
STAR TREK: VOYAGER
WALKER, TEXAS RANGER

TV Animation Episodes

MACE 2200 (FOX KIDS PILOT)
XENO'S INTERGALACTIC ZOO (FOX KIDS PILOT)
GHOST RIDER (UPN PILOT)
SUPERMAN
SPIDER-MAN
THE SILVER SURFER

Internet Series

AFTER THE FALL
Eruptor.com
Creator/Producer/Writer

TOGA TV
Syndicated Web Animation content
Co-Creator/Co-Producer/Co-Writer

Computer Games

SPIDER-MAN
Sony/Cingular
Writer

Awards

ENVIRONMENTAL MEDIA AWARD
Co-Writer, Best Dramatic Episode, *Star Trek: Voyager*

INDEX

ABC, 5, 6
A.C. Nielsen
    Company, 289
Action
    dialogue v., 195–197
    format of stage
        direction and,
        168–169, 184
    not overwritten,
        197–199
    not underwritten,
        199–200
    series, 129
Actor(s), 48, 257
    in animated series,
        179, 295
    character input
        from, 73, 304
    control of, 73

dialogue's
    interpretation
    of, 215–216
important scenes for
    star, 149,
    292–293
inflection in
    animated series
    for, 179
problems with,
    277–278
scheduling of, 12
as showrunner,
    252–253
would-be, 238
Act(s)
    in animated series,
        108
    ending, 174, 185
    Four, 128
    heading, 166, 182

length of, 92
One, 92, 129
in one-hour series,
    92–93, 128
scenes between, 128
in sitcom, 93
Three, 128
title of, 166, 182
twists, 129
Two, 128, 129
Adaptation, 164
ADR, 170
*Adventures of Tom
    Sawyer*, 33
After the Fall, 62–65,
    66–67
Agent, 318
    actor/director,
        247–248
    contract, 246
    credibility of, 22–23